Choose Panama

. . . the Perfect Retirement Haven

by

William Hutchings

i

William Hutchings

Choose Panama ... the Perfect Retirement Haven

Although the author and publisher have researched all sources to ensure the accuracy of the information contained in this book, no responsibility is assumed for errors, inaccuracies, omissions, or other inconsistencies herein.

2nd Edition
Copyright © 2007   William G. Hutchings
All rights reserved

ISBN-13: 978-0-9794886-0-3
ISBN-10: 0-9794886-0-5

Library of Congress Control Number: 2004095317

Attention Corporations and professional Organizations: Quantity discounts are available on bulk purchases of this book.

Published by
Mission Bay Publishing
438 3r^d Avenue Ste #438
San Diego, CA 92101

Choose Panama . . .

For

Natalie Bogardus

Henry Bogardus

Hudson Perez

William Hutchings

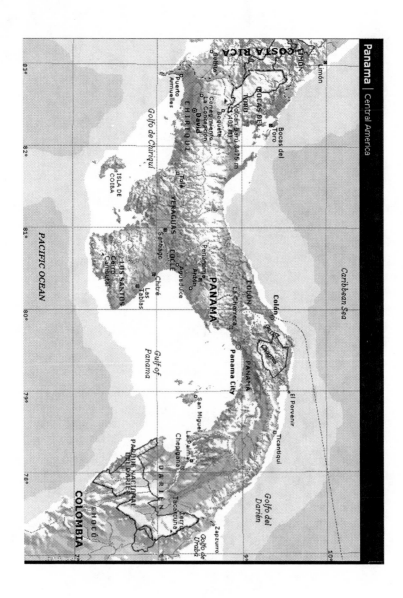

Table of Contents

William Hutchings

Choose Panama

the Perfect Retirement Haven

by

William Hutchings

When I first started the research on Panama, friends would say, "Panama? You're nuts. Panama's a jungle filled with crocodiles, snakes, and guerillas. The mosquitoes look like flying grizzly bears."

With those few words of encouragement, I packed up a few things, my trusty laptop, my digital camera, and called American Airlines. I left the pith helmet at home.

Two and a half hours out of Miami, I woke from a nice nap and was greeted by darkening skies punctuated with snowy white cumulus clouds. As the plane banked for its final approach to Tocumen International Airport, I saw a crystal blue bay bordered with miles of glistening skyscrapers. For a moment, I thought we'd returned to Miami, but the Flight Attendant announced, "Panama City." Wow!

Hutchings   Panama Skyline   Bay of Panama

This book was written as a result of the author's search for a retirement base. It had to be a place where the cost of housing and the overall cost of living could be accommodated on a fixed retirement income. Now, the Gobi desert might meet those financial considerations, but there are a host of other things to consider.

Panama was one of several potential choices. Its benefits and detractions were weighed against those of several countries: Mexico, Costa Rica, Nicaragua, Belize, Ecuador, and Argentina. Indeed, all of those countries have charm and advantages.

For many reasons, Panama rose to the top. However, each reader thinking of a second home or of becoming an expatriate retiree, should do their own research on the countries they are considering, and *then weigh their assets and liabilities against those of Panama.*

Choose **Panama. . . .** is <u>not</u> intended to be the ultimate Guide Book for vacationers. It is intended to be a reference manual to help you choose a retirement location or a second home. We assume that if you're serious about considering Panama as a choice for retirement or a second home, then you will visit before making your decision. To that end, we include many hotels, restaurants, and areas of interest as a convenience while you're looking the country over.

Examples of restaurants, places to stay, and other points of interest are listed here to meet a wide choice of budgets when you visit. The list is by no means complete, but it will give you some idea about the country, its accommodations, attractions, and prices.

Enough details on Panama are provided that will enable you to make a quality comparison with the other places you might be researching. Our main focus will be on the elements of day-to-day living costs, real estate, medical care, and the economic as well as political stability of the Republic of Panama. Perhaps most important, are the steps and paperwork you'll need to become a permanent resident with a Pensionado or other visa. We've provided the descriptions of these visas and how you can qualify.

Why *Choose* Panama?

Each of us, if we're lucky, will one day retire. Those with
only Social Security, military, or other government benefits
are going to be hard-pressed to survive and maintain a
reasonable standard of living – unless we can find a place
whose cost of living will not exceed our retirement benefits.
And, maybe a place where the days ahead can be exciting and
fulfilling – perhaps in an exotic setting.

Those with pensions, savings accounts, and home equity will
want to be able to preserve their savings and still live
comfortably in a community of their peers.

How would you like to retire?

- Where you can live comfortably on $1,200 a
  month?
- Where quality medical care and insurance is
  available?
- Where medical & dental costs are a fraction of
  U.S. costs?
- Where the paper currency is the U.S. dollar?
- Where you don't have to worry about currency
  devaluations?
- Where you can earn up to $76,000/year tax-free
  from Uncle Sam?
- Where there are a variety of climates – from
  temperate to tropical?
- Where you can choose beachfront, the
  mountains, or the city?
- Where you can buy an oceanfront lot for less

than $40,000?
- Where you can rent a nice small home for $350/$400 per month?
- Where you can grow your own coffee?
- Where you can grow your own oranges, bananas, and vegetables?
- Where you can hire a maid for $6-8/day?
- Where infrastructure is *First World?*
- Where you can safely drink water from the tap?
- Where the streets and roads are good ?
- Where you can fly home in 2-1/2 or 3 hours?
- Where your business can be tax-free?
- Where the internet is readily available?
- Where satellite TV brings in your favorite programs – in English?
- Where the government grants $$ incentives to foreign retirees?
- Where there's a variety of recreation – golf, tennis, birding?

These are great parameters . . . all apply to Panama!

Panama has been the best-kept secret for retirement and as a tax haven in the Western Hemisphere – perhaps the world.

Modern Maturity, the monthly magazine published by AARP, listed **Boquete, Panama** as one of the four best places in the world to retire!

Perhaps you're already retired, or thinking about your upcoming retirement. There's always a little worry, a little voice that keeps asking, *"Will I have enough retirement income to survive comfortably without eroding my savings and equity?"*

". . . And, will my medical insurance cover any costs associated with a possible devastating illness? Will I like the culture? What's the climate like?"

To be practical, we must be able to answer those questions.

Perhaps you want to find a place where you can buy a home, use it for vacations, and rent it out the balance of the year until you finally do retire. This is certainly an option. If this is part of your plan, your rental income is tax-free of Panamanian income taxes.

To be sure, the world's finest retirement haven will not be kept a secret forever. When considering the benefits and advantages that Panama offers, that 'secret' will become common knowledge - sooner rather than later.

And then you know what will happen? The same thing that happened in California, Arizona, Florida and other "retirement havens and communities." Prices will rise.

It is a fact that millions of "baby boomers" are fast approaching the age of retirement. Over seventy million will reach retirement age within the coming decade. And, there are enough 'younger' retirees who watch their savings dwindle every month and should be considering an alternate home.

The bright side of this is for those who own their own home, their equity might be substantial. This equity could be the very thing that will provide economic security for retiring.

According to *Time* magazine, "Many of the seventy six million American baby boomers are more likely than their parents to consider retiring to a foreign land. They have traveled more, have higher hopes for retirement, and tend to be more active and adventuresome."

It is a fact certain that many retiree's Social Security or other retirement benefits will not stretch to afford a comfortable standard of living in the U.S.

Each of us must ask the question, what kind of retirement can be anticipated where I currently live? With taxes, prices, medical care, insurance costs, and real estate escalating not only in the Western Hemisphere, but in Europe as well, it's going to be difficult to survive without some form of additional income.

As retirees, do we want to take part-time work at McDonalds or Wal-Mart to supplement our benefits? Not if we can retire to a paradise where a comfortable lifestyle is within the means of our benefits.

Of course there are a myriad of other questions besides the economics of Social Security or other retirement plans that must be answered.

Retirement Questions

- Medical care and insurance?

- What's the cost of living?

- How about transportation?

- Is the climate desirable?

- How about housing?

- What will housing cost?

- Are the appliances modern?

- Are there many expatriates?

- What about economic stability?

- What if I don't speak the language?

- Isn't Panama 'buggy' and hot?

- How about public safety?

Whether searching for a retirement haven, or seeking a place to vacation, Panama offers:

- Near-perfect weather in a variety of locations.

- A low cost of living.

- A stable political and economic climate.

Panama is easily accessible: 2-1/2 hours from Miami, 4 hours from New Orleans or Houston, and six hours from Los Angeles. The cost of the airfare is readily affordable. The national language is Spanish, but approximately 25% of the population speaks English. Language tutors are readily available.

The Republic of Panama welcomes retirees with financial incentives not found anywhere in the world.

Two major factors have contributed to Panama's becoming such a major bargain for investment and real estate.

- On December 31, 1999, the United States turned over the complete operations of the Panama Canal to the Government of Panama, and abrogated the lease held on Panamanian property since 1904. Over 50,000 Americans left the country. This left a huge hole in the Panamanian economy. It is estimated the lost payroll was more than $400 million. That's a major cash deficit to overcome, especially when the country's entire revenue was only $2.4 billion.

- Panama is a major producer of fine coffee. World coffee prices have decreased but are showing signs of a rebound. The reason for this price deflation is the introduction of cheap Asian beans, which have flooded the market. According to one report, there is so much excess coffee in Asia, the beans are being ground up for fertilizer. The deterioration of this market is having an economic impact on not only Panama, but all Central and South American countries who are primary coffee producers.

Of course, the 50,000 Americans who were called back to the United States also left a big hole in the real estate market. Especially, in Panama City. Houses, condominiums, and apartments are now selling and renting for bargain prices. The current opportunities for an investor or retiree are not better anywhere in the world.

Panama offers the retiree or investor a combination of economic advantages not available in other countries. Add these economic opportunities to a fine choice of climates, a country of near-zero inflation, a low cost of living, a stable political environment, and a country whose banking and asset protection laws offer privacy not even seen in Switzerland. And, there's a community of fellow expatriates in every city.

Panama's Infrastructure

Panama City has a *First World* infrastructure (you can drink the water from the tap). The telephone system works reliably. Fiber-optic cables have been laid around the country and to Panama from overseas, enhancing telephone and internet connectivity. Air travel is reliable and frequent, within the country and overseas. *Satellite TV is available throughout the country – from the U.S.*

The Republic of Panama offers a *Pensionado* Visa program that grants unparalleled discounts on travel, restaurants, medical care, utilities, and entertainment to retiree expatriates. And to top it off, affordable, first-class housing is available.

- Panama's cool mountain slopes burgeon with flowers, and the rich fragrance from hillside coffee plantations seem intoxicating. The white sandy beaches appear to be endless stretching along the coastline.
- Enjoy its roads – better than any country's in Central America,
- Enjoy its rain forests, and raft or fly-fish (for trout) the roaring rivers in the mountains.
- Fish Panama's Pacific or Caribbean waters for the finest sport fishing in the world.
- Play golf or tennis at a world-class country club or convenient resort.
- Enjoy the wonderful restaurants, luxurious hotels, and the safe environment.

Pinkerton's Global Security has recently named Panama as one of the four safest places in the modern world.

It's difficult to transcribe these advantages without sounding like they were penned by a tourist agency. In truth, the author was a skeptic about Panama and was nearly convinced to retire in Mexico, Puerto Rico, or Costa Rica. Then I visited Panama.

Panama is beautiful. Its people are beautiful. They're warm, friendly, and hard working. "Welcome" is written on their faces and reflected in their demeanor. Panama and the United States have been partners for many years, and *Norte Americanos* are welcomed.

Economic Stability

Panama's paper currency is the U.S. dollar.

Think of it: there are no concerns about currency devaluations as you might have in other Central or South American countries. Inflation is currently less than two percent. Panama is the exception to the high rate of inflation predominant in so many countries south of the U.S. border.

Panama has put its act together, but until now, has not benefited from the tourist or retirement attractions it deserves. Remember the stories we've all heard from Florida, Arizona, and California, 'You should have been here ten years ago?' That's where Panama is today.

Recent statistics released from the World Tourism Organization show that the country's annual visitor count was slightly more than 400,000. More than 100,000 of these came from the United States.

Compare that figure with Disneyland: the amusement park's average daily attendance exceeds 160,000. In three days, Disneyland attracts more total visitors than Panama does in a year, and more visitors from the U.S. in a single day than Panama attracts from the U.S. in an entire year.

As a destination, Panama's tourism statistics aren't even close to the numbers of tourists or retirees visiting Mexico or Costa Rica. At least not yet. And what is the significance of a low tourism rate? It means those who get to Panama sooner rather than later will enjoy lower prices and can look forward to the value of their investments escalating.

Entry Requirements

Every visitor needs a valid passport and an 'onward' or return ticket.

Those visitors who are Naturalized citizens will need their Certificates of Naturalization.

A Tourist Card is required of everyone, and is sold for $5 by your airline prior to departure. Tourist Cards can also be obtained from Panamanian authorities after your arrival at Tocumen International Airport. They used to be valid for only 30 days, but are now valid for 90 days, and with authorization, can be extended to six months.

An **Exit Permit** is required of all visitors – no exceptions. The fee for a one-time departure is $20. A multiple entry/exit permit is available for $75. If you were to fly in and out of Panama several times, this is obviously cost effective.

Minor Children

A word about traveling with minor children who accompany only one parent: a notarized letter of permission from the other parent is required.

The airlines will not issue a ticket without this letter. The purpose, of course, is to prevent one parent from leaving the country with children without authorization from the other parent, i.e., "parental kidnapping."

For those countries whose airlines may have overlooked this requirement, then immigration will stop you from entering Panama.

Currency

Panama's official currency is the *Balboa*. It is pegged to the U.S. Dollar and has been since 1903. Coins for Panama are minted in the U.S. Their size and value are identical to our penny, nickel, dime, quarter, half dollar, and silver dollar. There is **NO** Balboa paper currency.

When you come to Panama, do not bring denominations larger than $20.

Most stores simply will not accept $50 and $100 dollar bills. Some of the larger hotels might, as will the banks, but they'll put the bills under a magnifying glass to determine their authenticity. Large denomination bills have been a favorite target of counterfeiters from South America to North Korea.

If you're entering from a country other than the US, change your currency at the airport.

Most banks offer no currency exchange – other than U.S. dollars.

But why go through the hassle? There are ATM machines (called "Claves" - pronounced clah-vays) everywhere, and most credit cards (Visa, Master Card, and to a slightly lesser extent, American Express) are widely accepted.

When using the *Claves*, always ask for a printed receipt. The receipt will not show an account balance as they do in the U.S. At first, this is a bit disturbing, but you can reconcile the receipt when you actually check your balance. I used the internet phones ($0.20/minute for international calls) and called my bank's automated service every week or ten days to reconcile my ATM withdrawals.

Travelers Checks are also a hassle. Merchants – even hotels – don't like them. And personal checks? Forget it.

Your ATM Card will become your best friend in Panama.

How to Get a Visa

First of all, you must be in Panama to obtain any visa. You cannot accomplish this at a Panamanian Embassy or a Consulate in your country. Most visas take three to four months to be issued (except for the *Pensionado* Visa, which is typically issued in three to four weeks).

- For most visas, an interim card is issued until the formal application is approved.

- You need to physically be in Panama **when the visa is issued.**
- It is also preferable that you stay in Panama from the time of the application until the issuance of the visa.
- The minimum age limit for a Pensionado visa is 18. **You don't have to be a senior citizen to qualify.** Children under 18 will qualify for their own visas as dependents of the parents.
- All documents from the applicant's country must be notarized and/or authenticated by the consulate office nearest you.
- Canadian citizens should check with the Panamanian Embassy or the Consulate nearest home.
- Documents must be dated within two months of application.
- Spousal and juvenile dependents must have *original* marriage and birth certificates, respectively.
- Health certificates and AIDS certificates are required of all persons.

A visa is not a work permit. There are special rules for a work permit.

Permanent Visas

The Panamanian Government has developed a number of visa programs in order to attract investment in the country. Not only investors, but qualified immigrants who will help build Panama far beyond the developed state it enjoys today.

And rest assured, the government's compulsory educational programs and dedicated philosophy to propel Panama into the future as a model country is similar to the philosophy instituted by the United States at the beginning of the twentieth century.

The programs outlined below are just that. Brief outlines. Not only must an attorney be employed to file your papers, you should consult a Panamanian attorney before ever investing, before the consideration of an investment, or thinking of a visa. Carefully go over the details of the outlines presented in this book, and then consult a Panamanian attorney to see which visa might be suitable for you.

Turista Pensionado
(Visas for retirees)

Panamanian immigration laws authorize an alien to reside in Panama, provided they meet certain requirements. One of the most attractive residency programs anywhere is Panama's *Pensionado* program. It may well be the very best in the entire world.

A similar program was instituted in Costa Rica several years ago, and was very attractive. Thousands of expatriates immigrated to Costa Rica from all over the world. They signed up to be *Pensionados*, but the Costa Rican Government has retracted the program and none of the recipients were "grand fathered." They no longer enjoy the benefits that lured them to retire in Costa Rica.

Many of those people who went to Costa Rica have now immigrated to Panama where they not only benefit from the *Pensionado* program, but they now have a lower cost of living, a lower crime rate, and significantly lower real estate prices than in Costa Rica.

Panama's law specifically states that retirees who have qualified for the *Pensionado* program <u>cannot lose their benefits</u>. Period. So what are the qualification requirements?

- You must apply in Panama
- Your application must be processed by a Panamanian attorney
- You must be at least 18 years of age
- You must be of good health and free of HIV (A blood test costs $25 and a doctor's visit costs $1
- You must have a verifiable minimum monthly income of $500 per month from a government program or private corporation. This could be Social Security or any other government retirement fund, such as military, state, police pension, etc., or a program retirement from a private corporation.
- For your spouse or minor children, your minimum income must be increased by $100 per month per dependent.
- You must have a certified, clear police record for the past five years. This can be obtained at your local police station or sheriff's office.

All of the required documents must be notarized and authenticated at the Panamanian embassy or consulate office nearest your home. (see the glossary)

If you don't have a retirement program, does that mean you can't get a *Pensionado* visa? Not at all. There are financial requirements that may be substituted:

- A verified Certificate of Deposit in a Panamanian Bank that generates $750 per month for the retiree. The face value of the CD may vary because of interest rates offered by the National Bank of Panama. Currently, an approximate face value of the CD would be about $260,000. No additional amounts are required for dependents.

Pensionado Benefits

A *Pensionado* Visa entitles the visa holder to a 50% discount on the price of admission to recreational and entertainment activities. Movies, sporting events, theatre events, concerts, etc. (Discounts do not apply where proceeds are designated for the benefit of charities.)

Discounts on other services:

- 50% on hotels, motels, and pensions Monday through Thursday, and 30% on Fridays, Saturdays, and Sundays
- 50% discount on real estate closing costs and commissions for personal and commercial loan transactions in your name
- 30 % on inter-urban and city buses
- 30% on trains
- 30% on charges for small boats and ships
- 25% on air fares (Domestic)
- 25% discount on your electrical bills if the monthly bill is less than $50

- 25% discount on the fixed charge for personal telephone service (one phone only)
- 25% discount on domestic water bills provided they don't exceed $10 per month
- 25% discount in restaurants (except for fondas – the small food servers not requiring a commercial license)
- 20% discount on general, specialized, or surgical fees
- 20% discount on technical and professional services
- 15% discount in fast food restaurants – those belonging to national or international franchises
- 15% discount on medical and hospitalizations clinics unless you have medical insurance
- 15% discount on dental services
- 15% discount on optometry services
- 10% discount on prescriptions prescribed by a doctor
- 15% discount on interest rates charged by lenders on personal and commercial loans in your name
- A freeze on personal residential real estate taxes as long as the home is in your name
- Entitlement of a one-time exemption of duties on the importation of household goods (max of $10,000)
- An exemption of duties on the purchase of an automobile (every two years)

The *Pensionado Visa* will <u>not</u> qualify a recipient for a Panamanian passport or full citizenship, but it will grant residency for life with the above benefits. Most important, you do not have to leave the country every 90 days as you do with a *turista* card.

Other Visa Programs

Rentista Retirado (Private Income Retiree Visa)

For those retirees who are no longer working, but have no monthly pension - perhaps having received a lump retirement sum or inheritance.

This Visa requires money to be deposited in a five-year Certificate of Deposit with the National Bank of Panama. The amount to be deposited is to yield a minimum of $750 per month (at current interest rates, the face value of such a CD would be about $270,000.) The Visa is renewable every five years as long as the CD is renewed.

The *Rentista Retirado* Visa **includes such benefits as a Panamanian Passport**, but does not include citizenship. There is a one-year exemption of import duties on household goods ($10,000) and the exemption of duties for the importation of an automobile – every two years.

The following requirements must be satisfied in addition to the monetary requirements above:

- Application must be made through a Panamanian attorney

- You must have a valid passport with at least one year before expiration

- Six passport sized photos – gentlemen in suit & ties, ladies in long sleeve blouses

- A police record from your place of residence, properly authenticated, for the past five years

- Marriage Certificate, notarized (if spouse included)

Solvencia Economics Propia
(Person of Means Visa)

This visa is designed for those persons who wish to live in Panama, fully retired, without the need to work. The applicant must make a one-year Certificate of Deposit in a local bank of at least $100,000. Upon application for the first renewal (provisional) the CD must also be renewed for one year.

After renewal, the visa is granted permanently with the right to a *cedula* (a local Identity Card). Five years after obtaining the permanent Visa, holders will be eligible to apply for Panamanian nationality.

The following requirements must be met to apply:

- Valid passport (with at least one year remaining before expiration)
- Six passport photos (same as per Rentista Retirado)
- Police Record from your city of residence (Five years)
- Marriage Certificate (notarized) if your spouse is to be included
- Monetary requirements as above

Inversionista
(Investor Visa)

Designed for those who want to establish a business in Panama. Please note: all retail businesses and some professions are reserved for Panamanian citizens. Please check with your attorney.

There must be a minimum investment of $100,000 and at least three permanent Panamanian residents hired. This visa is granted provisionally for one year. After renewal, it is granted permanently, and a *cedula* (Panamanian I.D. card) can be issued. Five years after permanent status is granted, holders may apply for Panamanian citizenship.

The following requirements must be met upon application:

- Valid Passport with one year before expiration
- Six passport photos (as in above)
- Police record (authenticated) from your city of residence for past five years
- Marriage certificate (authenticated) if your spouse is to be included
- Monetary requirements as shown above

Inversionista de Pequena Empressa
(Small Business Investor Visa)

This visa is established for those people who wish to start a small business in Panama.

You must invest a minimum of $40,000 and hire three Panamanian permanent employees.

This visa is granted provisionally for one year. It must be renewed three times before it is granted permanently, whereupon a *cedula* may be issued. Five years after obtaining the permanent visa, holders will be eligible for Panamanian citizenship.

The following requirements are required for application:

- Valid passport with more than one year before expiration
- Six passport photos as in above requirements
- Police record, duly authenticated
- Marriage certificate (authenticated) if spouse is to be included
- The financial requirements listed above
- This visa will also require setting up a Panamanian corporation and appropriate bank accounts.

Inversionista Forestal
(Forestry Investor)

This visa is no longer available. However, the program is currently being reviewed and will probably be re-instated.

Further information is available at the Ministry of Agriculture, Panamanian Environmental Agency. Also, see the Business Opportunities section.

Business Opportunities

Not all retirees are satisfied to retire. They may want to remain active. Panama offers a unique opportunity to do both.

Panama enacted Law # 8 in 1994. This legislation enabled the promotion of tourism and foreign investment. And to date, it's the most comprehensive legislation to facilitate investment anywhere in Central or Latin America.

Hutchings   Punta Paitilla

Many of the world's largest hotel chains, including, Marriott, Radisson, Holiday Inn, Sheraton – with more to come – have launched new hotels in Panama. And, there's more than $500 million in projects being planned on Panama's coming of age as a tourist destination.

But the legislation is not just for the giants of the industry. Anyone willing to invest as little as $50,000 in a tourist related business can take advantage of the law, which grants large tax and financial incentives.

For instance, several people I know have bought property, built a home and a guest-house. They receive, (with a minimum investment of $50,000) the benefits outlined below. They rent the guest-house like a bed and breakfast, an apartment, or mini-hotel.

Others have started charter diving operations on Bocas del Toro, or a River Rafting business. Or, you might start a touring business for eco-tourists, bird watchers, etc.

The benefits are substantial for any tourist related business:

- A 20 year exemption of any import taxes due on materials, furniture, equipment, and vehicles
- A 20 year exemption on real estate taxes for all assets of the enterprise
- Exemption from any taxes levied for airports and piers
- Accelerated depreciation of real estate assets of 10% a year.

The investment of $50,000 does not include the cost of land, and the program is limited to projects in the interior, i.e., Boquete, Volcan, El Valle, etc. These specific regulations can change, so be sure to go over them carefully with your attorney.

Real Estate and Tourism are some of the more popular investments for individual investors. Forestation investors should have knowledge and expertise before investing in forestation projects.

Panama is one of the most technologically advanced countries in Central or South America. Communications are the backbone of any nation's future, and Panama has state of the art communications infrastructure with multiple high band-width fiber optics networks.

Panama's strategic location at the mid-point of the Americas has been, and will continue to be, a critical advantage for long-term development. As industry grows in Asia, transportation to the Eastern seaboard of the U.S. and Western Europe is most easily reached through the canal.

In real estate, there are properties available from the government that were part of the compounds originally built by the U.S. and then handed to the Republic of Panama with the abrogation of the Canal Treaty by Jimmy Carter and the U.S. Senate under his administration.

The port city of *Colon* is the second largest free port in the world, exceeded by only Hong Kong. Colon is on the Atlantic side of the Canal. Consequently, a huge amount of commerce, import and export, is being conducted. The opportunity to set up an import-export business in Panama is outstanding because of these facilities.

Real Estate

Many visitors coming to Panama are obviously interested in the real estate opportunities. As in any emerging market, opportunities are excellent.

Words of Caution

As stated earlier, it is important that you engage an attorney before making an offer on any property. This is true whether you have engaged a real estate agent or not. (This will not apply on property being developed and offered as new homes from established real estate developers.)

- Do not judge values based upon prices at home – whether you're from the Americas or Europe.
- Unfortunately, some real estate operators can be found who are guilty of blatant 'puffery,' e.g., "Buy now, because tomorrow it'll be double in price. There's very little left and the market is exploding!" Some of these "puffers" are 'gringos.'
- They may make claims and statements comparing Panama with California, Aspen, Florida, etc.

Insist on Sales Comparables

If the seller or person showing the property says, "Comparable sales records aren't available," then you'll have a pretty good idea the quoted price may be puffery. Comps are available, and your attorney can get reasonably accurate sales data from the National Registry, which records all real estate transactions. ***Caveat Emptor!***

Casco Viejo – Renovations

Casco Viejo was built after Henry Morgan sacked and destroyed the original Panama City. It was burned by the Spaniards to keep Morgan from occupying the city. It's located on a small peninsula near the western entrance to the Panama Canal, and in all of the Americas, it's the oldest city on the Pacific Coast.

William Hutchings

Marni   Casco Viejo Balconies

The buildings are French and Spanish Colonial in architecture. The streets are narrow and mostly cobblestone or brick. The grill-work on the balconies is fancy wrought iron.

The French moved in to build their canal, and built their colonial buildings in the late 19th century among the original Spanish colonials. In places, there is a 300-year difference in the age of buildings sitting side by side.

As the city modernized and grew, the narrow brick and cobblestone streets were not adequate for the traffic, so the city expanded away from Casco Viejo.

In 1977, UNESCO classified Casco Viejo as a World Heritage site. At that time, the government realized what a treasure it had in the community and initiated a plan for restoration.

Most of the buildings were in some stage of disrepair – even decay, but some structures have been fastidiously maintained. Many local families have stayed through the years in Casco Viejo. Among these are some of the nation's wealthiest.

Panamanian Law #9 was created to give incentives to property developers who renovate buildings in Casco Viejo. After renovation, all income derived from the sale or rental of the property is exempt from income taxes for a period of ten years. In addition, 100% of the cost of renovation is deductible from any other Panamanian Income tax you might owe.

Property taxes are exempt for a period of thirty years, and real estate transfer taxes are excused.

Hutchings   Casco Viejo Renovations

Parking in Casco Viejo is limited, so a parking garage is an excellent business opportunity. Income would be tax free for ten years.

Casco Viejo is a large area. It will take time to fully renovate, but progress is being made, and the results are spectacular. Be sure to visit *Parque Bolivar* to see an excellent example and architectural beauty of what can be done. Most of the buildings surrounding this beautiful small park have been renovated.

Renovation from the *Plaza de Independencia*, up to the Presidential Palace and along Panama Bay to the French Embassy is under-going a great deal of growth.

There's no denying the charm of this colonial heritage. It is a compliment to the foresight of the government for their wanting to see the treasure of *Casco Viejo* sustained, improved, and not allow it to fall into further decay.

Hutchings   Casco Viejo Apartments

If property development is in your area of investment expertise, don't miss the opportunity provided by the government in Casco Viejo.

Hutchings   Casco Viejo

The government is anxious to work with investors and developers who want to build or renovate in *Casco Viejo.* So far, their foresight has been rewarded.

Reforestation Investments

Much of the world's exotic hardwoods are grown in the tropics. Teak, Mahogany, Coco Bolo (Rosewood), and others are a few of the wonderful woods that are now in short supply. Teak in particular has been over-logged – especially in the far-east countries of Thailand and Myanmar (formerly Burma). Thailand's exports have been reduced to a trickle, and the National Geographic estimates that Myanmar will be out of production by 2010.

Panama has the soil, rainfall, humidity levels, and an ambient temperature conducive for teak production. In many instances, Panama's production and growth of their teak forests has reached optimum conditions not achieved anywhere in the world – including Myanmar. Not only is the re-forestation program doing well in the Darien, but other teak farming has started near David, in *Chiriqui* Province.

It is estimated that with a $40,000 dollar investment in a three plus acre teak farm, it's possible to return a reasonable multiple of that investment when the trees are ready for harvesting in 20 years. The investment is long term, but generally, a percentage of the investment can be recaptured from the three initial thinnings – between the sixth and eighth year. Of course, inflation and teak prices could increase significantly, yielding a multiple of these figures.

Teak forests are usually planted about 1,000 trees per hectare (2.47 acres). Initial cuttings (thinnings) may yield saleable wood, but shouldn't be counted on. One local arborist estimates that by the eighth year, the yield from the first thru third thinnings might return some of the original investment. By the eighth year, the trees have been thinned enough for them to achieve optimum growth and to reach maturity without further thinning. Final count per hectare is about 700 trees. At maturity (20-25 years), a teak tree will yield approximately 400-500 board feet of wood. The current value of teak is about $2.00 per board foot.

For more information, go to: www.panamadera.com

A local study, near David, is being conducted jointly by Yale University, and the Smithsonian Institute.

Since a Teak reforestation project is a long-term investment, *Panamadera* is looking at an interesting concept: a four-hectare (almost 10 acres) section planted in half teak and half pineapples. None of these investments will qualify for residency, as the government has withdrawn the program.

The coastal area of *Chiriqui* province has rich, volcanic soil. The pineapples are expected to yield a 100% return on the investment in five years (at today's pineapple prices). They will continue to be harvested during the entire growing term of the teak plantation. Mr. Barker's U.S. associate is Mr. Randolph Hancock, (617) 901-3511.

Again, the author has no interest in any of the projects detailed in the Business Opportunities Section or elsewhere in this book. Their accuracy is unverified and must be pursued with diligence. They are presented here simply as potential opportunities for the investor or retiree.

Where to Retire – City or Country?

Let's look at the country as a whole and give specifics on places you might like to consider.
For your convenience, while looking at several potential retirement locations, we'll list a few hotels, restaurants, and places to go, but certainly not all of them. It is important that when you come to visit Panama for the first time, you have a grasp of some of the hotel and restaurant options.

There are other excellent Guide Books, such as Lonely Planet's, "*Panama*," that are good accommodation sources.

We want to give you a broad perspective of what Panama can offer you as a potential retiree, and details on visas that are available. At the same time, a few facts on the country in general are in order – especially about places to stay, restaurants, and the real estate and investment market.

William Hutchings

Panama City

Hire an English-speaking guide if you don't speak Spanish! If
your first guide is not fluent in English, you could waste a lot
of time and money. You might also get misdirected.

The skyline of Panama City is spectacular. Modern
skyscrapers stretch upward, the sun reflecting from their glass
walls. Tall palm trees line the avenues skirting the ocean.

Hutchings   Skyline: from Amador Causeway

Panama (*Ciudad*) is a cosmopolitan city and ranks with
Buenos Aires as the best in all Latin America. No smog,
noxious fumes, or poor air quality to choke your breathing.
Best of all, there is decidedly less traffic congestion than in
Miami, Mazatlan, or Mexico City.

As you tour the city, there are other neighborhoods to consider
as residential options.

Hutchings   *Carmen Iglesia*

Marbella is generally a community of high-rise apartments and condominiums, bordered by *Balboa Avenue and Calle Cincuenta*. It affords wonderful views of Panama Bay. This is also an area of night clubs, restaurants and chic shops. It adjoins the financial district.

Punta Paitilla is an affluent area dominated by high-rise apartment and condominium buildings. The views are superb. Most residents are wealthy Panamanians or immigrants from other Latin American countries. There is a nearby waste disposal facility, so check any building in which you have an interest several times during a day for odor.

El Congrejo is a hilly area of high rises and single family residences. It is centrally located near Via Espana and the University. It also boasts of having many fine restaurants and apartment hotels.

La Cresta is a very affluent community of older, lovely homes and buildings. Many expatriates live here as well as the U.S.

and French Ambassadors. Most homes have beautiful Bay views.

Obarrio is adjacent to the central banking district. Many fine residences are in this upscale neighborhood, and it is also the home of most of the up-scale retail shops in Panama City.

There are other areas of the city that are appropriate for expatriates. Your guide or real estate agent can direct you.

Shopping

Panama City is a shopper's paradise. Prices are very reasonable, whether you're looking for furniture, electronics, clothing, food, or souvenirs. Every imaginable product, from the latest in electronics to designer clothing, is readily available. Bargains are the rule. Colon is a major free port, second in world size only to Hong Kong.

For comparison, a new car in Panama is roughly half the price of the same car's price in Costa Rica. For this reason, Panama is not only a bargain when it comes to automobiles, but every other imported electronic and major appliance.

In addition to the stores and bazaars concentrated on *Via España*, shops are located on *Avenida Central* and several large malls throughout the city. Price Smart (Costco affiliates) stores are in Colon as well as in the city of *David* (pronounced Da-veed) – on the Pacific coast – in Chiriqui province. PriceSmart honors the U.S. Costco membership card.

For some real bargains, take the train to Colon (about one hour on an elegant train). This is an interesting trip, and you can shop in the free port of Colon. The train does not return until

5:15 PM, but a taxi back is inexpensive. (Be watchful for pickpockets, and purse snatchers in Colon)

Villegas   Typical Shopping Mall

A U.S. quality supermarket chain, *Supermercado Rey*, is on *Via España* as well as in several other locations. It's open twenty-four hours, 365 days per year. *Supermercado Rey* stocks everything from alcohol to pharmaceuticals. And, clothing is inexpensive. Don't pack heavily, because you can buy everything you need in Panama.

Bars, restaurants, and discotheques are everywhere. Panamanians love to dance. The *Salsa, meringue*, and *reggae* are popular, and everyone seems to perform them expertly. Great fun to watch. And, great fun to mix in and learn. Hotels run the gamut from five-star to *pensións*.

Do We Have to Speak Spanish?

The simple answer is "no." English is a required subject in all Panamanian schools, and it's estimated that 25% of the population now speaks English. However, **if you're going to live in Panama, you should make every effort to learn Spanish.** The people will appreciate you all the more if you try to speak their language, even if you struggle and you're anything but fluent. People will help you and respect you for trying to learn.

Is Spanish difficult to learn?

If you're of retirement age, it's more difficult than if you were a child. But people do it every day. Consider studying Spanish as a project and make it fun. As a matter of fact, it's a great way to become acquainted with other expatriates.

Won't just being around the people day in and day out make it easy to learn?

Not a bit. Your chances of picking up conversable Spanish this way are close to zero. There are better ways:

- CD's that teach basic Spanish are available in most book stores. Also, if you have a computer, there are programs that are quite good. These cost between $20 and $35. Before you leave for Panama, get a head start. Buy one of these programs and practice.

- CentroPan USA (232-6718) offers a four week course, two hours/day, four days/week for $205 in Panama City. U.S. Foreign Service personnel use this school. It's very good, but the intensity level of instruction is less than in a 'total immersion' course.

- Hire a private tutor. The tutor will come to your hotel room for $10/hour, or give six lessons for $50. (One popular teacher is Sr. Abdiel Marin, 507-268-1835)

- <u>Berlitz</u> is world-renowned for their language courses. You could start one at home, buy a Berlitz Home-study course, or take their course in Panama City. Berlitz recommends studying the Berlitz CD at home, then taking their 3-hour a day immersion course when you get to Panama.

- <u>Language & International Relations Institute</u> (LERI) Tel: (260-4424) Four hours of daily instruction, five days/week. Class is limited to four students. The price of $350 for the first week includes lodging, two meals/day, laundry, etc. Rates decrease each succeeding week. They have a U.S. Agent (Dana Garrison) 1-800-765-0025, who is very helpful. You can view the website at: <u>www.isls.com</u>

This is 'immersion' learning. You lodge with an upper-middle class family, and continue to learn with them after your four hours of schooling. This is an outstanding, fast way to become conversant in Spanish. And it's fun. They also teach you to Salsa and take you out to clubs for even more fun.

<u>Author's Note</u>: The author had serious doubts about immigrating to a country where he didn't speak a little of the language, although he knew it wasn't an absolute necessity. The author's aunt had retired to a foreign country, lived there 10 years, and knew little beyond 'yes,' 'no,' 'please,' and 'thank you.'

Even though a good percentage of Panamanians speak some English, I was uncomfortable not being able to speak their language, so I decided to take the ILERI course. I learned enough Spanish in a week to get along quite well as I traveled throughout Panama. Every day, I became more comfortable speaking with the people. And every day as I stumbled along, I received smiles, warmth, and lots of help.

The course was great, but very intensive. Some in the class were a little slower to learn, so the school quickly separated them so that each group was at the same per level. The instructors were wonderful.

The 'family' I stayed with was friendly, hospitable, and the time spent with them was terrific. The food was better than good. I believe I can count my hosts as being my first new friends in a new country, and I would not trade this experience for anything. Home-stay house below.

Hutchings   Home-Stay House

Social Customs – Do's & Don'ts

Panama is more formal than you might expect. This definitely applies to dress. Just because the country is in the tropics, sandals, torn jeans, and cut-off shorts are not acceptable attire in banks, business establishments, or government offices. (They're fine in *Bocas del Toro)*

In the evening, whether it's a restaurant, club, or disco, men and women "dress." For the men, the very least should be slacks and a shirt with collar. The loose fitting 'Guayaberra' shirt (available everywhere in Central America) seems to be universally accepted. Incidentally, when in the tropics, cotton is the fiber of choice. The synthetics don't 'breathe' as well They're 'hotter,' and not nearly as comfortable as cotton. When buying clothes, look on the label for – Algondon – it means cotton.

Drugs are not tolerated in Panama. If you are even in the proximity of someone using marijuana or cocaine, move away. Police might assume you have some connection if you're just nearby. And in Panama, you're considered guilty until proven innocent. Accusation of a serious crime (drugs are considered a serious crime) generally results in jail time. It can be months before a trial date is set, and your embassy cannot help you.

Always carry your passport, your tourist card, or a Xerox copy with you at all times. You must have a photo ID on your person. It's the law.

Always say, "*gracias*" (grá-ceeas) when thanking someone. Always say, "*por favor*" (poor-fa-vōr) as please. The standard greeting is "*Hola*" (Ōla) for hello, "*Buenos Dias*" (Bwaynōs Dee-az) for Good Morning, and "*Buenas Noches*" (Bway-nahs Nōchazs) for Good night. The Panamanians are very polite, and that politeness should be reciprocated.

Places to Stay – Panama City

There are many luxury hotels in Panama City. There are also many hotels offering good accommodations at lesser prices.

We will try to name a few in a broad range of price and amenities.

One thing to bear in mind: *Always ask for a commercial rate – whether you're on business or vacation.* Many times the desk clerk will give you a lower price.

As for hotels in the $7-$15 range, they do exist. Especially, in the Casco Viejo district. For the purpose of this book, we will not do a hotel-by-hotel listing of these facilities, but there are several available. Most of the rooms at the lower prices are not air-conditioned, baths are shared, and most do not have hot water. But some of them fill a need and do it nicely.

One of the newer "residencia" establishments is the *"Cibeles"* Hotel on *Calle Equador*. An associate of mine stayed there for $20/night (single) and reported it to be very clean, comfortable, air-conditioned, and with private bath.

Mid-Range Hotels

* Prices shown are for 'single/double'

Hotel Marparaiso – $25/$35 Tel:227-6767. Calle 34 Este between Avenidas 2 & 3. Built 1999, 72 large rooms, well-appointed. A/C, cable TV, telephones, secure parking.

Hotel California - $25/$35 Tel: 263-7736   Avenida Central Espana near Calle 43.   58 nice clean rooms, color TV, phones, restaurant & coffee bar in lobby.

Hotel Internacional - $30/$40 Tel:262-7806 Opened in '90's, so it's relatively new. Faces Plaza Cinco de Mayo. 80 rooms, A/C, cable TV, Restaurant & casino. (hint@latin1.net)

Hotel Lisboa - $25/$35 – Tel: 227-5916   On Avenida Cuba between Calles 30 Este and 31 Este. Spacious, attractive rooms, A/C, TV & phones. Good value.

Hotel Caribe - $30/$40 Tel: 225-0404 Calle 28 Este at Avenida Peru. Spacious, A/C Rooms, phone, cable TV, refrigerators, ice machines, pool on the roof. Another good value. (caribehotel@hotmail.com)

Las Vegas Suites Hotel - $40/$50 Tel: 269-0722 Calle 49B Oeste & Avenida 2A Norte. All rooms have kitchenettes, A/C, cable TV & phones. Café Pomodoro & The Wine Bar. Very popular. (hotel@lasvegaspanama.com)

Gran Hotel Soloy - $45/$50 Tel: 227-1133 Avenida Peru at Calle 30 Este   Nice rooms, A/C, Cable TV. Casino on ground floor and bar & dance club on 12th floor. (hgsoloy@pan.gbm.net)

Hotel Costa Inn - $44/$50 Tel: 227-1522   Avenida Peru near Calle 39 Este. 130 rooms, A/C, Satellite TV, Internet, Gym, Pool, good restaurant, secure parking, airport shuttle, & tours available. This hotel gets high marks. (costainn@panama.c-com.net)

Luxury Hotels

There are many 'luxury' hotels in Panama City. So many, we can't list them all. Prices shown are standard, 'walk-in off the street, rack rates.' One hotel where I stayed is listed at a rate of $100+. The author made a reservation over the internet for $60 during the height of the holiday season. (They were <u>not</u> informed I was a travel writer.)

*Hotel Costa del Sol (*do not confuse with Hotel Costa Inn)
$60/$70 Tel: 206-3333 Avenida 3 Sur at Avenida Federic
Boyd. Each A/C room has a kitchenette. Swimming pool,
restaurant, and bar on the roof. Also, tennis court and Spa.
Wonderful views. (www.costadelsol-pma.com)

Coral Suites Aparthotel - $60+ Tel: 269-3898 Via Italia
(Calle "D") & near Calle 49B Very comfortable with gym,
rooftop pool, laundry, internet connections, satellite TV, etc.
Breakfast is included. Larger suites are available for families.
The gym includes free weights, exer-cycles, treadmills, and
weight machines. Pool and laundry facilities are outstanding.
It would have been a $250 suite in metropolitan cities in the
states. (***coralsuites@coralsuites.net***

Hutchings   Coral Suites, Roof-top Pool

Crystal Suites Hotel - $70/$80. Tel: 263-2644   Avenida 2
Sur and Via Brasil. Newer hotel. Attractive executive suites
with kitchen and dining area. Internet service, airport shuttle.
Lovely hotel, even if a little isolated.
(atencion@crystalsuites.com)

Sevilla Suites - $70-$95 Tel: 213-0016 Avenida 2A Norte
This is an all suites hotel (opened in 2000). All suites have a
sofa bed, cable TV, VCR's, & kitchenettes. Facilities include
a roof-top pool, coin laundry, gym, breakfast included. This
hotel is family owned and operated. It is a superior place to
stay. Under the same ownership is the Hotel Marbella. It is
modern, clean, and well appointed, but no suites.
(sevillasuites@sevillasuites.com)

Hotel Plaza Paitilla Inn - $85+ Tel: 269-1122 Via Italia at
Avenida Churchill. A former Holiday Inn. Hotel is on the
water & all rooms have balconies. Lovely pool, and the hotel
has a very popular bar. (www.plazapaitillainn.com)

Panama Marriott Hotel $100+ Tel: 210-9100 Avenida 3 Sur
296 Rooms, restaurant & bar, offers concierge, childcare, etc.
Fine business hotel. Includes buffet desayuno (breakfast).
(www.mariotthotels.com)

Radisson Royal Panama Hotel - $110+ (Special discounts for
seniors) Tel: 265-3636 Calle 53 Este at Avenida 5B Sur.
Elegant hotel, tasteful rooms, pool, coffee shop, restaurant,
piano bar, tennis court, gym. (www.radisson.com)

Holiday Inn (new) - $105+ Tel: 206-5556 Avenida Manuel E
Batista & Avenida 2A Norte. 112 deluxe rooms, 38 suites, all
have many amenities. Restaurant, pool, gym, arcade, sports
bar. (holidayinn@holidayinnpanama.com)

Miramar Inter-Continental - $105/$185 Tel: 214-1000
Avenida Balboa near Avenida Federico Boyd 25 Story, 206
rooms. Gorgeous guest rooms, wonderful views. Informal
seaside restaurant and a fine dining restaurant on 5th floor.
Other features include a piano lounge, a bar and dance club,

pool, spa & gym, tennis courts etc. Celebrities are frequent guests. (www.interconti.com)

Suites Ambassador – Under $110. Tel: 263-7274 Calle D near Eusebio A Morales Very large rooms w/sitting area & Kitchenette. Rooftop pool. 1st class service. (ambassad@sinfo.net)

The Executive Hotel - $110/$125 Tel: 264-3333 Avenida 3 Sur & Calle Aquilino de la Guardia Modern hotel with large, well furnished rooms, a complimentary breakfast and nightly open bar for guests, (pool, restaurant, and business center. Popular hotel among business crowd. (hotelger@pty.com)

Hotel El Panama - $115/$130 Tel: 269-5000 Calle 49 B Oeste near Via Espana. An older landmark, yet fine hotel, with spacious poolside rooms. Wonderful bar, music, etc. for the true flavor of Panama.

Hutchings   El Panama

Hotel Granada - $110/$130 Tel: 264-4900 Calle Eusubio A Morales, near Via Espana. Comfortable hotel. Every room has A/C. Pool, casino, restaurant & bar. I stayed at this hotel. Rooms were clean, etc. (granada@hotelesriande.com)

Hotel Caesar Park - $99 (lowest promotional rate) to $800. Posted rate is $145+ Tel: 270-0477; (U.S.) 800-228-3000 Across from Centro Atlapa on Calle 77 Este near Via Israel. The *Caesar Park is* part of Westin chain. Frequented by celebrities and heads of state. Facilities include casino, sports bar, shops, athletic club & spa, 3 tennis courts, club, business center, and more. Dining is elegant and views magnificent from 15th floor dining room. (www.caesarpark.com)

The Bristol - $150+ Tel: 265-7844 Calle Aquilino de la Guardia near Calle 50. Part of the Rosewood Hotels & Resorts. Very elegant. Marble & mahogany everywhere. All guests are provided with personal butler and printed business cards. Dining is superb. Service is extraordinary. Each room has fax machine and internet. Tour their website: www.thebristol.com ejventas@psi.net.pa

For each of these hotels, from the more modest to the elegant, ask for their commercial rate and any "specials" or promotions they might be having on your expected arrival date. You'll save some money.

If you qualified for, and received your *Pensionado* visa, prices can be reduced by as much as 50% during the week and 30% on the weekends!

Restaurants – Panama City

Just a few of the hundreds of restaurant choices are listed below. Rather than categorize these by price, we've listed them by the type of food served.

In addition to these, most of the fast-food restaurants are here: McDonalds, Burger King, KFC, Pizza Hut, etc.

In most restaurants the servers understand English. If you should find one where communication is difficult, just ask for help at an adjoining table. People are friendly and helpful.

Panamanian Food

Restaurante-Bar Tinajas Calle 51, Bella Vista, 22 (206-7890) Very large restaurant. Décor is Panamanian. Long menu. Dinner prices average $7.50-$9.50. Panamanian entertainment and folk dancing on Fridays & Saturdays. Closed Sundays.

Café de Asis – Faces Parque Bolivar in Casco Viejo. Charm isn't descriptive enough. A wonderfully restored colonial building. It's an atmosphere where Graham Greene, John Le Carre, and Hemingway might meet at the next table. Don't miss this one. People-watching is one of the best things at Café de Asis – even if it's not on the menu!

Café Coca Cola – near Parque Santa Ana. 7:30 AM to 11:30 PM. Very popular. No breakfast items are more than $2.50. There's an extensive lunch & dinner menu of chicken, beef, and fish. Most under $4.50. Specialty: jumbo prawns @$6.00.

Restaurante Costa Azul – Calle Ricardo Arias near Via Espana. Very popular, open 24 hours. Sandwiches $1.50-$4.00. Dinner (variety of pasta, chicken, & beef) $5.50-$9.00

Jap-Jap – Calle F, El Cangrejo (This is a Panamanian restaurant – not Japanese – in spite of its politically incorrect name) Grilled chicken, chorizo hot dogs, tamales, & much, much more. Really low prices. Two people can eat for less than $8.00 – a great food bargain and fun!

Café Barko – Isla Flamenco Calzada de Amador is at the end of the causeway with a great view of the city. Specialty: Ceviche. Fun nightlife and very popular with locals. Almost a must!

Mi Ranchito – Amador, L-01 On the Amador causeway. Dining *al fresco* under a *palapa* (thatched roof hut). Excellent food, always crowded.

Restaurante Mercado del Marisco – Avenida Balboa, Calle 15. On the second floor of the local seafood market. Really fresh seafood, reasonably priced. Very casual and very good. Modest prices.

Spanish

Café La Plaza – Casco Viejo, next to the Cathedral. Open from 6 PM until early morning. Mostly a place to drink and party. Several varieties of Sangria. Excellent Spanish *topas.*

Steaks

Martin Fierro – Calle Eusebio A Morales. Imported, aged beef. New York strips $16. Local beef, (*bife chorizo*) not quite as tender, but very tasty $9.50. All their beef is outstanding. Prices include salad and potato. Open noon to 3PM and 6PM to 11PM. Walking distance to Granada, Coral Suites, and Sevilla Suites.

Gauchos Steak House – Calle Uruguay and Avenida 5 A Sur.
Excellent steak house. Dinner for two with wine about $60.

Argentinean

Restaurante Los Años Locos – Grilled Argentinean food.
Well prepared. Dinner for two about $25. Upscale and
intimate restaurant. Excellent food. Near Hotel Caesar Park
on Calle 76 Este.

Chinese

Madame Chang Restaurante Bar – Calles 48, Bella Vista and
Aquillano de La Guardia. Outstanding Chinese food.
Elegant, dressy, and really good. Excellent wine list & décor.
Dinner for two with wine about $50.

Palacio Ling Fung – On Calle 62 Oeste   Very large
restaurant with outstanding Chinese cuisine. Well-priced from
$9.50. Dim sung served daily until 11 AM. Good food, nicely
served. A bargain.

French

Restaurante Casco Viejo – Calle 53 Este at Calle 50.
Excellent French cuisine. Open Monday through Friday,
lunch and dinner. Saturday, dinner only. About $40 – dinner
for two.

La Cocotte – 138 Calle Uruguay.   Lovely nouvelle cuisine.
Excellent service. Closed Sundays. $30-$40 for two.

Crepes y Waffles – on Avenida 5B Sur west of Calle Aquilino de la Guardia. Very popular because it's very good. Fine selection of crepes, sandwiches, and desserts. Modest prices from $3.75 to $5.75. Open daily noon to 11 PM.

Italian

Restaurante de las Americas – Calle 57 Este near Avenida 1 Sur. Award winning food. Dressy and moderately expensive, but deserving of its awards. Entrees from $9-$15. They have a 'take-out' place around the corner where prices are substantially less.

The Wine Bar – on the ground floor of Las Vegas Suites Hotel. Open 5 PM – 1 AM. Extremely popular. Extensive menu of appetizers, and entrees. Daily pasta specials about $9.00. Individual pizzas about $4.00. Live jazz in the evenings.

Pizzaria Solemio On Calle Uruguay. Closed Monday. Open 11-3 and 6 Pm to 11 PM. Very good thin crust pizza from a wood-fired oven. Also, good selection of pasta and fish. About $7.00 for a medium pizza.

Cafeteria Manolo. Calle D and Calle 49 B Oeste. Good Italian food. Reasonably priced, copious dinners about $8, full bar with indoor and outdoor seating. Pleasant and fun people-watching.

If a restaurant is not listed, it doesn't mean it is of lesser quality. These are simply a representation of a few of the many outstanding eateries around the city.

And don't forget, if you have a **Pensionado Visa**, these prices may be reduced by 25%.

Tipping: The usual percentage is 10-15%.

Nightlife

Panama's sunsets are spectacular. Their beauty marks the end of beautiful days and the beginning of fun-filled evenings. There is a broad spectrum of things to enjoy in Panama after dark: movies, concerts, casinos, dancing, and the bar-discotheques.

Movies are first-run from Hollywood and generally viewed in the original soundtrack with Spanish sub-titles. Adult tickets are $3.75, and if you have the **Pensionado** Visa, that price is reduced to $1.75. It's also reduced on Wednesdays, whether you're a **Pensionado** or not, to $1.75

Panama City has always been noted for its varied night-life. Bars, discotheques, and restaurants are everywhere. "Happy Hours" are a tradition and generally start at 6 PM and last until 8 PM – sometimes longer. Another tradition is "Ladies Night." Usually on Thursdays.

Dancing is almost a national pastime, with the salsa being most popular, followed closely by merengue, 'rock'n'roll,' and reggae.

A word about dress attire: you won't be allowed in most clubs if you're not properly dressed. As a minimum, slacks and a shirt with collar to be safe. Many places require a suit or sport coat with ties.

Villegas   *Bucaneros* Night Club

Panamanians are less casual than other warm climes in the world – certainly than the dress common in Florida or California. No jeans, short-shorts, or sandals in the evenings at the nicer places.

Most ladies wear a dress with pumps in the evening. It's part of the Panamanian's lives to be a little more formal, and it may go a little deeper into the national psyche. Panama is a tropical country, and it would be very easy to start being casual about everything, starting with the dress code. But they haven't. It's refreshing. Almost like the '50's in the U.S. And it's great to watch people having so much fun.

A tip: if you're going to go clubbing, dancing, and drinking, **take a taxi!**

Salsa & Merengue

Restaurante Casco Viejo   Calle 53 Este and Calle 50. This elegant French restaurant and popular bar features live music – usually *salsa or merengue* every Friday night. Cover charge or $10.

Hotel Plaza Paitilla Inn   Via Italia at Avenida Churchill
Tuesday and Saturday Nights, a group of talented Cuban
musicians and dancers put on a great show, starting at 10 PM.
Cover charge of $10.

Many hotel bars have live salsa groups. *Caesar Park, El
Panama, and Hotel Paitilla Inn* are just three of several. Ask
a taxi driver for the most current popular clubs.

Rock

Señor Frog's Avenida 5A Sur   Live music Wednesday,
Thursday & Saturday nights. Similar to all Señor Frogs from
Mazatlan to San Jose. Loud, raucous, with the standard
Mexican-American décor. Cover $7. Wildly popular.

Skap   Down the street from Señor Frogs. Loud and popular.
Live music weekends. Cover $10.

Café Dali   Calle 5B Sur   Large dance floor, long wooden
bar. This is an upscale club. Could be in LA or New York.
Live music Fridays only. Very upscale club. Cover of $10
includes two drinks.

Mango's On Calle Uruguay Great restaurant by day, with
live bands Thursday, Friday, & Saturday evenings. Cover
charge: $8.

Jazz

Restaurante Las Bovedos   Plaza de Francia in Casco Viejo
A former dungeon, great jazz. Tables arranged intimately in

alcoves. Atmosphere is terrific. Music on Friday and
Saturday nights only.

Mi Rincon Lobby floor of Caesar Park Hotel. Calle 77 Este,
one block from the bay. Jazz only on Wednesday nights.
Very intimate and posh. No cover.

Casinos

The following hotels have Casinos. They're not as posh as
Las Vegas, Atlantic City, or even San Juan, Puerto Rico, but
they all play the same games of chance and can be fun.

- Hotel Caesar Park

- Hotel Granada

- Miramar-Intercontinental

- Hotel El Panama

- Gran Hotel Soloy

- Hotel Plaza Paitilla Inn

Sight Seeing - Panama City

The Canal. Once considered the eighth "wonder of the
modern world," the final construction was completed in 1914.
From that date until 1999, the Canal was operated by the
United States under a treaty with The Republic of Panama.

The Republic of Panama has taken over the complete
operation of the Canal and all its properties after President
Jimmy Carter negotiated and signed the Treaty.

Hutchings   Container Ship   *Miraflores* Locks

The Canal served both countries' national interests until the end of the twentieth century, and still offers transit to a huge number of ships passing from the Atlantic to the Pacific. The government has approved funding to widen the canal to accommodate larger ships. The largest aircraft carriers and tankers are too wide to negotiate the present canal dimensions.

Tours are available and you should not miss one – even if your stay in Panama is short. Visitors can go to the Miraflores Locks on the Pacific side 9 AM to 5 PM. A pavilion provides a good vantage point to watch and photograph the ships as they make their transit.

The Canal Train Trip

This is a great trip. It travels a route that parallels the waterway. Some of the tracks are laid along the trail used by the Spanish in the 16th century to carry gold plundered in Peru. The isthmus was the shortest route from the Pacific to the Atlantic.

The railroad was the predecessor of the Canal, and was completed in 1855. When gold was discovered in California in 1849, the trip around Cape Horn was long and treacherous. The railroad provided the link from the Atlantic to the Pacific and reduced the dangers and the time of the treacherous voyage – in both directions.

Operated by the U.S. government, it served to transport people, goods, and gold across the Isthmus until 1979. The Panamanian government succeeded the U.S. and operated it until 1998, when service was terminated, and the government sought bids for a private concession. The contract was awarded to a consortium from Chicago who proceeded to spend more than $60-million on a renovation.

The passenger cars are ex-Amtrak units completely rebuilt and refurbished. Coach walls are wood-paneled, carpeting is plush, and the seats very comfortable. (Reminiscent of the Orient Express).

The round-trip fare is about $30, and the trip takes one hour each way. Obviously, there has to be a better economic reason to spend $60 million than to collect $30-dollar fares. The containerization of ocean shipping is the answer. Containers are off-loaded on one side of the Canal, placed on the railroad, and transported to the other side of the Isthmus in one hour. The Canal transit time is twelve hours, and the fees are substantially more than the rail fee. We're coming full-circle to 1855 when the railroad was first constructed – an economical transit of the Isthmus.

Fees for ships transiting the canal vary by the size and tonnage of the vessel, but they are substantial. Ships pay according to their tonnage. The average cargo vessel pays approximately

$30,000 per transit. The very large cruise ships will pay an average of $150,000 to make the transit – one way.

Casco Viejo

The wonderful colonial architecture of the old city is preserved, although much of it has fallen into a state of disrepair.

The colonial charm of the area is most beguiling. When the French were dominant in Panama, they built their colonial structures adjacent and intermingled with 300 year old Spanish buildings.

Hutchings   Casco Viejo

Recognizing its visual and historic appeal, the government is offering some excellent incentives to attract investors to recoup this beautiful and romantic area. (see Business Opportunities)

Stroll the cobblestone streets, have an alfresco lunch at one of

the many delightful restaurants, and watch the world go past.

The charm of a renovated Casco Viejo is almost irresistible. It will be a few years before the rebuilding can match that of Cartagena, Colombia, but the wait will be worth it.

Hutchings   *Casco Viejo*   French Embassy

William Hutchings

Historic Panama

Panama City was founded in 1519 (on the Pacific side of the isthmus) by a cruel Spanish tyrant, Pedro Arias de Avila. The ruins of this initial settlement can be seen today, known as Panama *La Vieja* – pronounced "La Veeahaa" (Old Panama). The city became the focus for Peruvian gold brought by ship to Panama. It was then off-loaded and transported by mule *conductas* across the Camino Real (King's Highway) from Panama City to Portobello on the Atlantic side. The treasures were held at the counting house in Portobello luring Spanish galleons with European goods for trade.

The concentration of this treasure led to it being targeted by English, French, and Dutch pirates and buccaneers. The Spanish fortified Portobello, but in 1671, Henry Morgan, an English pirate, overpowered the Spanish fortifications and marched his small army of pirates across the isthmus. He sacked and burned Panama City. Some ruins are still standing.

Marni   Historic Panama Ruins

68

Morgan loaded 200 mules with the stolen treasure and returned across the isthmus to his ships on the Caribbean side. Morgan was knighted by King Charles II for his murderous efforts.

In 1739, the British destroyed Portobello, which forced Spain to abandon the Isthmus crossing and sail its ships from Spain across the Atlantic and around Cape Horn to reach the western coast of South America. Panama became less important to Spain, and eventually came under the control of what is now Colombia.

Present Day Panama

Casco Viejo is still an important part of present day Panama City. The beautiful colonial buildings, cathedrals, government offices, and *parques* still stand, but in various stages of disrepair. The government is offering substantial incentives for investors to purchase and modernize these wonderful structures. More on that in the Business Opportunities section.

Museums, Galleries & Cathedrals

If Panama has a weak point, it's in their museums. All descriptions are in Spanish, but English-speaking guides are available. Tip $3 or $5 dollars to the guide. It's worth it.

The best overview of Panamanian culture is found in the *Museum of the Panamanian*, in downtown Panama City. Its collection documents the evolution of human life on the isthmus from the earliest native settlements to the present.

Other cultural institutions (all in Panama City) include the Museum of Panamanian History, the Museum of Natural Sciences, the Museum of Religious Colonial Art, the Museum of Contemporary Art, the Museum of the Interoceanic Canal, and the national institutes of culture and music.

Hutchings   Simon Bolivar Statue

Museo Antropológicol – Reina de Arauz
(Anthtopological Museum) Named after the country's most distinguished anthhtopologist. This museum is in the old railway station on Avenida Central near Plaza Cinco de Mayo. Open Tuesday through Sunday, 9:30 am-4 pm. This is a <u>must-see</u> museum. Represented are many pre-Columbian artifacts and a well documented history of the Panamanian people.

Museo of Ciencias Naturales (Museum of Natural Sciences)
– Open 9am to 4pm Tuesday through Saturday. This Museum has very interesting sections on geology, paleontology, entomology, and marine biology. Wonderful taxidermy of many of the isthmus' wild, exotic creatures.

Museo del Canal Interoceánico (Museum of the Interoceanic Canal)

This is a terrific exhibition housed in a beautiful French Colonial Building. Opened in 1997 with varied display of Spanish armor, artifacts from the gold rush days, paintings, photos, and many canal railroad and canal construction exhibits. English speaking guides if you call ahead. (211-1650) @ Plaza de la Indepencia in Casco Viejo. $2 fee.

There are several other museums you'll find listed in guide books, but these three are by far the most interesting and well-displayed.

The Parks

Parque Natural Metropolitano

This wonderful 265 hectare (about 540 acres) park is located north of downtown and comprises a wild, tropical rain forest within the city limits. There are two walking trails: The Nature Trail and the Titi Monkey Trail. They combine to form a loop which leads to a *mirador* (lookout point) overlooking the city, the canal, and the bay.

Mammals residing here include anteaters, white-tail deer, sloths, and marmosets. There are more than 250 species of birds in the park.

The park is also home to the Smithsonian Tropical Research Institute. There's a nice visitor center, and Park rangers offer a one hour tour and slide show for a fee of $5 to groups of five or more.

The Panama Audubon Society holds a monthly meeting at the Visitor Center on the second Thursday of every month from 7:30pm to 9:30pm and these meetings are open to the public.

Sobernia National Park

This National Park is a very large natural rainforest and jungle. Please use professional guides when visiting Sobernia. This is a jungle, and one could easily get lost. It is populated by wild animals, and poisonous snakes are not uncommon.

Birders from the all over the world visit the area known as "pipeline road." This trail is legendary. More than 500 species of birds are known to use this habitat.

One of the nicest, though 'pricey,' ways to see this fabulous area is to stay at the $30-million Gamboa Rainforest Resort. This is a fantastic adventure, with 110 guestrooms, nicely appointed.

A tour-inclusive packages is $675 for four nights (double occupancy). It includes breakfast, a sunrise birding tour on Pipeline Road, a morning boat tour of Lago Gatun, a ride on the aerial tram through the rain forest canopy, unlimited use of kayaks and paddle boats, bicycles, gym, tennis courts, and unlimited access to all of the exhibits – including the butterfly and snake farm.

Getting Around

Rental Cars are available at the airports and in several locations in Panama City. A valid driver's license is all that is required. In Panama City, one other thing is a necessity. *Courage.* For the uninitiated, driving in the city can be an adventure, at the very least.

There is a lack of traffic lights, street signs, and traffic police. There is an abundance of really poor local drivers – who also are fearless. Driving here is much like driving in Mexico City, except there isn't the mind-bending congestion or smog.

Buses, taxis, motor scooters, and cars make up the vehicular population. Some of which are driven like *Via Espana* was on the NASCAR circuit. To get around the city, please take a cab or a bus.

This emphasizes a point. Americans are car-crazy and car-dependent. Do you really need to own a car in Panama? Whether you live in the city, the beach, or in the mountains, taxis are cheap. Really cheap. Buses even cheaper. Buses are frequent and can take you anywhere in the city or the country.

Hutchings   Panama City Bus

Intercity buses are ultra-modern and luxurious. And, they're inexpensive. For instance, bus fare to David, a city on the Pacific coast 250 miles northwest of Panama City, is $15. The vehicle is an air-conditioned luxury bus that shows movies, has toilet facilities, reserved seating, and an attendant who serves refreshments. (No chickens or goats!) Of course, if you're in a hurry to get to David, you can fly for $57. – about one hour. (Subject to the *Pensionado Visa discount.)*

If you are vacationing, why not relax and enjoy the trip. If you're going to retire here, you may not wish to bother with the expense of a car. Perhaps, the purchase price of a car is better spent buying or renting a nicer home. And, you'll not have the expense of maintaining and operating the vehicle. No car insurance, no title or registration fees, and none of the associated repairs.

You can take a taxi to the store for a dollar. You can take the bus to the store for fifteen cents. And, on the bus, you'll begin to know and appreciate the people – and vice versa.

How to Get There

The following Airlines serve Panama from the United States. U.S. cities served are: Los Angeles, Miami, Orlando, Houston, New York, Newark, NJ, Washington, DC, and Dallas. Some flights are non-stop. Others may make stops in Mexico City, Managua, Guatemala City, or San Jose, Costa Rica.

Airlines Serving Panama from the U.S.

American Airlines	800-433-7300
Continental Airlines	800-231-0856
COPA	800-25-2272
Delta Airlines	800-221-4141
EVA	800-695-1188
Lacsa	800-225-2272
Mexicana	800-531-7921
TACA	800-225-2272
United Airlines	800-241-6522

Typical coach fares* (Round Trip) and flight times

City	Non-StopFare	1-stop Fare
Los Angeles, CA	$897 – 6 hrs	$742 – 9 hrs
Houston, TX	$916 – 4 hrs	$ 975 – 8-1/2hrs
Washington, DC	$ n/a	$960 – 9-1/2 hrs
Newark, NJ	$883 - 5-1/2 hrs	$633. – 11 hrs
New York, NY	$1150 – 5 hrs	$885 – 9 hrs
Miami, FL	$707 - 5-1/2 hrs	$800 – 9-3/4 hrs

* Obviously, fares are subject to change. A premium is usually charged for non-stop flights.

Tocumen International Airport is about 20 miles from Panama City.   Taxis to the heart of the city are officially $25, but there are alternatives. You could share a cab with a fellow passenger. Some hotels have shuttles - free. And, there are regular buses to the downtown and business districts.

Entertainment & Recreation

Golf and Tennis

Panama welcomes visitors with several golf courses – and more are being built each year.

The **Summit Golf and Resort** is a world-class golf and country club located on the east bank of the Panama Canal. It was originally opened during World War II for American employees of the Canal and military officers. The club is less than thirty minutes from the city. The course is of championship caliber – 6,626 yards – touted by World Golf as the best course in Central America.

Facilities include a bar, dining room, pool, tennis, and squash. Memberships are less than $5,000. There are no greens fees for members, and monthly dues are $135. This is a private club, but is open to the public. Green fees, including a cart are $90 for tourists and $40 for residents. (507) 232-4653

Coronado Hotel and Resort

52 miles west of Panama City. It has a 7,000 yard course designed by George Fazio. This is a complete resort with an Equestrian Club, Spa, Tennis, Bar, & Restaurants. The resort has 75 suites and is located on a lovely Pacific beach. Call (507) 264-2863 for fees and tee reservations. **www.coronadoresort.com**

Tucán Country Club & Resort

This is a spectacular new development just fifteen minutes from the capital. The golf course (and property) is bordered by the Panama Canal on one side and a tropical forest on the other. Condominiums (1,060 sq ft) are luxurious. Prices start at $198,000 and range to slightly over a million for a 5,000 square foot villa. Call (800) 456-6016. Golf privileges are included in property prices. A video can be seen on their website.
www.tucancountryclub.com

Vista Mar Golf and Resort

Only 56 miles from Panama (on the Pacific side), this project is nearing completion. Ocean view villas and condominiums with many amenities, including a new 18-hole course designed by Michael Poellet, beach club, five lakes, and spectacular ocean and mountain views. The course will officially open in April, 2007. (507) 215-1111.
www.vistamarresort.com

Red Frog Beach and Golf Club

This is a new development on the Caribbean side in Bocas del Toro. An Arnold Palmer course and luxurious villas starting at $220,000 with a multitude of amenities. The golf course has not been completed, but is scheduled for late 2007 or early 2008. Call(800) 868-9906 or visit their website at: ***www.redfrogbeach.com***

Panama Golf Club

This is an 18-hole par 72 course (6,818 yards) located in Panama City and a private club. (507) 266-7068

Quebrado Golf and Country Club - Boquete.

This beautiful course is located at *Valle Escondido* only ¾ mile from the center of town. The course winds through an active coffee plantation, has bent grass greens, and is quite beautiful. The homes and condominiums are elegant. The *Valle Escondido* development is one of the premier projects in all of Panama.

Cielo Paraiso - Boquete

This is another project designed by J. Michael Poellet. The 18-hole course is scheduled to open near Boquete in September, 2007. It is an ambitious project and features many beautiful home sites bordering the golf course. The development has incorporated its own water supply (underground springs), and millions were spent on its infrastructure. Views are spectacular.

All utilities are underground. High speed internet, and modern electrical supply has been put in place. Several custom homes are currently being built. The course is on schedule for completion in September 2007.

The development of Cielo Paraiso is the dream of Raideep and Colleen Lal, who arrived in Boquete from Canada. They maintain offices in Boquete and Panama City.
www.cieloparaiso.com. *(507) 720.2431*

Fishing

The indigenous meaning of Panama is "abundant fish." It is a fact that more world records are held for fish caught in Panamanian waters than anywhere else in the world. Black Marlin, Blue Marlin, Blackfin Tuna, Roosterfish, Wahoo, Sailfish, Dorado, Pompano – and the list goes on.

One of the more popular charter fishing companies is *Pesca Panama.* Check out their website at www.pescapanama.com They are located out of David and offer great fishing near Coiba Island.

World famous for more than 200 world class records is *Tropic Star Lodge in Pinas* Bay. Fish the incomparable Zane Grey reef for the ultimate deep sea experience. www.tropicstar.com

Panama Yacht Tours specialize in trips to the Pearl Islands and Isla Coiba for sport fishing, snorkeling, diving, and Panama Canal Transits. www.panamatours.com

In addition, there is wonderful fly fishing for rainbow trout in the mountain streams of *Chiriqui* province on the *Rio Caldera* and *Rio Chiriqui.* So if you enjoy fishing, either fresh or saltwater, Panama holds a lot of adventure in store for you.

Birding

Panama is home to approximately 950 species of birds – more than the total of species found in all the rest of North America.

Birders are more likely to see the rare and beautiful *Quetzal* here than anywhere in the world. Although this resplendent creature is the national bird of Costa Rica, it is far more abundant in Panama, and is seen regularly here rather than the rare sighting in Costa Rica.

The top birding spots are easily accessible. The world famous "Pipeline Road" in the old canal zone is only 45 minutes from Panama City, as is the Canopy Tower. Other prime locations are Boquete, Bambito, Cerro Punta, and Volcan in the Chiriqui Highlands of West Panama. Eco and Birding guides are readily available in all of these locations. Except for Boquete and Volcan, the other villages are primarily inhabited by the colorful and friendly natives of the Ngobe-Buglé tribe.

Many people choose to combine the gourmet coffee farm tours with their bird watching and hiking. (See the section on 'Western Highlands) Mt. Baru, an extinct volcano, is Panama's highest peak at over 11,400 feet. If you're up to the hike, both Atlantic and Pacific oceans can be seen from the top of Mt. Baru. The hike will also reward you with wild orchids, waterfalls, and of course, many, many bird sightings. A good starting point for one of these expeditions is the charming village of Boquete.

Hiking

The rain forests of Panama offer an unparalleled opportunity for eco-hikes. Even the parks and forests near and in Panama City are abundant in flora and fauna.

A word of caution: taking off into these rain forests should not be attempted without hiring a qualified guide.

These are wild, primitive areas of forest and jungle. Besides the monkeys, birds, orchids, etc., there are jaguars, pumas, and snakes – not to mention the possibility of twisting an ankle, falling, or incurring some other injury.

Sailing, Diving, and Surfing

There is a fine yacht club near the end of the Amador Causeway. Panama is a great sailing area and is a frequent destination of both Caribbean and Pacific sailors. Panama Bay offers wonderful day sailing. The entrance to the Canal, and views of the City's exciting skyline are dramatic sights.

Hutchings   Yacht Club

The Pearl Islands (where many of the 'Survivor' TV series were shot), as well as *Tobaga* and *Contadero* Islands are also great sailing destinations.

On the Caribbean side, you can visit the **San Blas Islands** with sail tours of 2-14 days. There are more than 350 islands, with wonderful coral reefs to dive and snorkel, and the unique culture of the Kuna Indians who inhabit this archipelago.

As beautiful and interesting as the San Blas Archipelago might be, remember, it is not a choice for retirement. It is mentioned here so that whether retiring to Panama or just visiting, it is a trip highlight you should not miss.

There are more than 1,000 islands to explore off the Panama coasts. And, the waters are pleasantly warm in both the Caribbean and Pacific.

J. Miller   San Blas Beach

Surfing

While surfing is generally reserved for the younger set, some seniors still enjoy the sport.

Panama has surfing beaches on both the Atlantic and Pacific sides of the Isthmus. On the Atlantic side, *Bocas del Toro* is a favorite. The best time to surf *Bocas* is between December and March. Check with the local surf shops for location and current breaks.

Probably the best surfing conditions are on the Pacific side. Several beaches in *Panama Province* are excellent. *Los*

Santos Province is probably the best surf in the country although some addicts feel that *Veraguas Province* has the best surf in Central America.

Chiriqui Province has good surf, but the best areas are out among the remote off-shore islands. Again, consult with a tour operator.

Photography

Obviously, a country so rich in natural beauty and history grants the photographer a wealth of opportunity.

Certainly, the canal, the rail trip, and the many plazas are places to memorialize with your camera. And, the beaches of *Bocas del Toro*, the Pearl Islands, and *Contadora Island* all have the palms and sandy beaches we love.

The *San Blas* Islands and area offer wonderful photo opportunities not only of pristine beaches and azure waters, but the very interesting lifestyle of the Kuna Indians.

The skies over Panama can be truly spectacular. Cloud formations seem to billow forever, highlighted by morning or the setting sun. One can almost imagine Sir Henry Morgan or Sir Francis Drake sailing in from the horizon to their favorite uninhabited places of refuge within the Pearl Islands

J. Miller   *San Blas* Island

The electronic and camera shops in Panama City stock almost every piece of camera equipment made – at bargain prices – so if you don't have the latest in digital or film technology, don't despair. It's here.

The camera shops of Panama evoke fond memories. Many years ago, I purchased my first, really fine camera, a Nikon (f2) at a bargain price while I was transiting the Panama Canal for the first time.

Rafting & Kayaking

In the province of *Chiriqui,* there is rafting galore with rapids ranging from Class 2 to Class 5, depending on the time of year. They extend to Class VI but the local operators will refuse to run them when they are that dangerous.

Rivers flow from the mountainsides of *Volcan Baru* and are generally bordered by heavy forest and jungle. There are two rafting and kayak companies located in downtown Boquete.

Chiriqui River Rafting and **Panama Rafters** both offer trips ranging from family floats to the wild runs of Class IV and Class V rapids.

Panama is generally regarded as one of the top rafting locations in the world – certainly on a par, if not better than the Tuolumne River or the Middle Fork of the American River in California.

The operators of both companies, Hector Sanchez of **Chiriqui River Rafting** and Kevin Mellinger of **Panama Rafters** are highly regarded professionals.

The river environments of Chiriqui province are wild, wonderful areas. Wildlife is abundant. Monkeys and parrots screech as you invade their territory. Exotic birds, and once in a while a big cat – Jaguar or Puma – can be seen in the jungles as you roar down the rapids.

You can visit www.panama-rafting.com (Chiriqui River Rafting) or www.panamarafters.com for more information.

Kayaking has become very popular. The *Rio Chiriqui* is accessible by two-wheel drive for most kayak adventurers. The run that drains from *Volcan Baru* toward Costa Rica is the premier of Panama's white water runs. As you transit the river, one gets the feeling of being miles and miles from civilization. You'll pass through gorges surrounded by forest and waterfalls with areas of Class II to Class V water. During your run you'll hear the endless chatter of the "howler monkeys," zillions of birds, and toward sunset, it is not uncommon to hear the unmistakable voice of the jaguar.

William Hutchings

People of Panama

Panama's diverse population is approaching 3,000,000. A high percentage of this population is concentrated along the Panama Canal.

Almost 70% of Panama City's 700,000 residents are either Mestizo (mixed Native American and European background) or Mulatto (mixed European and African heritage). Others are descended from European and Caribbean immigrants who arrived in the 19th and 20th centuries as labor for construction of the Panama Canal.

Approximately ten percent of the population is of European and/or North American descent, while Native Americans account for six percent.
Panama has long served as a crossroads between oceans and continents, and thus has attracted immigrants from all over the world. This diverse population is concentrated in the capital, as well as in other cities such as David (population 130,000) and Santiago (35,000). People from the West Indies, the Middle East, Asia, and North America are now represented in Panama City. Most of the city's residents are Roman Catholic, but Jewish and other religious communities are also present.

Away from the major urban areas, residents are mestizo and Native American. Many of the agricultural workers are Native American. This is especially true in *Chiriqui* province where they labor in the coffee plantations on the slopes of *Mt. Baru.*

J. Miller   Kuna Woman

The principal Native Americans are the *Ngobe-Buglé* (the largest group) who inhabit the mountains of *Chiriqui* and the *Bocas del Toro* region. The *Chocó* people inhabit the Darién jungle on the Panama and Colombian border, and the *Kuna* people live in the *San Blas* Archipelago on the Caribbean coast, east of Colón, in an area known as the *Comarca of San Blas*.

Most of the indigenous people live apart from the majority of Panamanians. The *Kuna* interact more than the others, but still maintain and preserve their culture.

Government

Politically, the government of Panama is a democratic republic. The country's official name is: *Republicá de*

Panamá. It has well-established democratic traditions since its declaration of independence from Spain in 1821.

The president is the most powerful political figure. The president runs the executive branch and wields a good deal of influence over the legislative and judicial branches of the government. The presidential term is five years, and the president cannot succeed himself. Two elected vice-presidents assist the president.

The Presidential Palace and the legislative buildings are located in Casco Viejo. The legislature is composed of 72 members, who are also elected for a term of five years. Like the president, they cannot succeed themselves.

There are nine provinces, each administered by a presidential appointed governor. Local government is divided into sixty-five districts and 505 sub-districts. Mayors are elected by the local population, and do have significant power.

Marni   Presidential Residence *(Las Garzas*

The voting age is 18, and <u>voting is compulsory</u>.

The Native American groups negotiate directly with the national government, and the Kuna enjoy special rights to conduct and administer their own affairs that pertain to their reservation, the *Comarca of San Blas*.

There is no standing army, and the closest thing to a military organization is the police.

Why no standing army?

First of all, there is a mutual defense pact with the United States. The U.S. is obligated to protect the Republic. Secondly, most standing armies of small countries are not there to protect themselves against invasion. They have been formed to protect the rulers – most generally dictators. *Witness the regime of Manuel Noriega.*

Language and Religion

Panama's official language is Spanish. About 25% of the population speaks English. Some of the Native Americans (Kuna, Chocó, Ngobe-Buglé) prefer to speak their own dialects instead of Spanish.

About 80% of Panamanians are Catholic, although the percentage of those who practice Catholicism is somewhat smaller. Protestant denominations account for about 15% of the population.

The constitution of Panama does not specifically separate church and state, but the constitution does guarantee freedom of worship.

There have been no incidents of religious conflict, civil violations, or religious discrimination recorded.

Education

Education of all citizens is provided free through four-year university level. The government budget for schooling is 18% of its expenditures. There are several private schools and a Roman Catholic University. Many of the wealthier students receive their university education in the United States.

Some private schools and trade schools have started up in recent years. With the government's budget for education and their efforts to educate the youth of the country, Panama's literacy rate has reached 97%.

Climate

Panama is in the tropical zone, but cooler temperatures prevail at higher elevations. If it's too warm at sea level, pick the climate of your choice by going higher in elevation for your place to live.

Temperatures in the coastal area range from 85-degrees to 95-degrees, year round. On the mountain slopes, daytime temperatures will average 72-degrees year round, and they cool down substantially at night. In the regions of Boquete or Volcan, a sweater or light jacket will be needed in the evenings. And, you'll sleep under a light blanket.

Because of its proximity to the equator, Panama does not have temperature-defined seasons as we do in temperate zones north of the Tropic of Capricorn, or in South America, south of the Tropic of Cancer. Seasons in Panama are defined as "wet" and "dry."

The "dry" season is December until May. The "wet" season is May through November, with October and November experiencing the heaviest rain. During the "wet" season, the mornings are usually sunny, and by noon, it can begin to get cloudy. One or two afternoon showers are normal. These are usually brief in duration, but can be quite heavy. The rains tend to get heavier toward the end of the wet season, particularly in November and early December. It also rains during the "dry" season, but the rain is less intense and of shorter duration. The closest thing to Panama's climate in the States would be Miami – although that is not similar in the highlands where it is a perpetual springtime.

The Caribbean (northern) coast receives much more rain than the Pacific (southern) coast or the Western Highlands. The average rainfall on the northern coast around Bocas del Toro is about 115-inches per year – most of which falls during the "wet" season.

The Pacific winds hitting the southern coast are drier and consequently, rainfall is substantially less – about 65-inches per year. Again, the bulk of this moisture occurs in the "wet" season. Panama City is on the Pacific coast.

Panama is located far outside the paths of Caribbean and Pacific hurricanes that track several hundred miles to the north. There are no active volcanoes in the country. *Volcan Baru* has been quiet for hundreds of years.

However, Panama is on the western edge of the American Continents. Earthquakes do occur along the Americas from *Tierra del Fuego* in the south to the Aleutian Islands in the north. Anyone living in the U.S. from California to Alaska can attest to tremors and occasional earthquakes.

It is important to note that one of the primary reasons for choosing the isthmus as the site of the Canal over Nicaragua (the second choice), was the decidedly lower incidence of earthquakes in the isthmus region.

Staying Healthy

No inoculations are required to visit Panama, but it is recommended that all travelers get the series of Hepatitis A and B, Tetanus, and Typhoid before traveling anywhere. This is probably more important in the rest of Central America than in Panama.

The Hepatitis series is taken in a series of three inoculations, which are spaced 30, and 150 days apart. Therefore, try to plan ahead. This is excellent advice for any Caribbean, Central or South American country. The most economical place to receive inoculations is from the County Health Department near your home.

Medical facilities in major cities (Panama City, Santiago, and David) are excellent. Many doctors on the medical staffs have received their training in the U.S. Hospitals are very modern and are equipped with the latest innovations in medical technology. One person has described entering the *Paitilla Hospital* in Panama City similar to "walking into the Marriott."

Most communities have a medical clinic with a staff of
doctors and nurses. If a serious illness should occur, and the
patient or family would like to go back to the states, Miami is
only a 2-1/2 hour flight from Panama City.

While visiting Boquete, the author suffered a badly broken
leg, and was rushed to the Chiriqui hospital in David, twenty-
two miles away. (I slipped on a wet tile floor) The hospital
care was excellent, and the orthopedic surgeon was terrific. I
had suffered a severe helical fracture, and the surgery was
complex. The total bill for hospital and surgical care was less
than $5,000. After returning to California, I was told the same
operation in the States would have probably been at least ten
times that amount.

The nursing staff at *Chiriqui* was attentive and always
responded immediately to my needs. At every shift change,
day or night, the nurses would check temperature, blood
pressure, and pulse, ask if I was in pain, etc. The staff was
wonderful, but the food was like hospital food everywhere.

I suspect that hospital and airline chefs have all attended the
same school where they learn how to change the color of meat
from red to gray. (It's their form of alchemy) I lived for
breakfast with ham and eggs. Two friends kept me from
wasting away to nothing by sneaking in BLT sandwiches.

Your Medical Insurance

Before visiting any foreign country, check your medical
insurance to see if you're covered for emergencies while away
from home. It's not uncommon to turn an ankle on a
cobblestone street or slip on a glazed tile floor.

While Medicare does not usually provide coverage out of the country, some HMO supplements and PPO's do. Also, check with your travel agent. There are plans available designed for your trip that will give you that extra protection, and they are not terribly expensive.

Medical insurance in Panama

Insurance is available, and it's reasonable. The average Panamanian earns a little over $300 per month. And, the doctors and hospitals do not have to pay the outlandish cost of malpractice insurance so pervasive in the U.S. These factors tend to keep the premiums of medical insurance significantly lower.

Several private insurance plans are available. Many have one thing in common: enrollment must be made by age 59. Once you're enrolled, you can still be covered as long as you pay your premium. However, the premium will rise with age.

One company, Capital de Seguras, S.A., (507-223-1511) allows enrollment up to age 64. Most companies require that you be a resident of Panama for 3 to 5 months. A popular plan for expatriates is offered by *British American Tu Seguro Principal* (507-269-0515). For age 59 their premium is $59 month for an individual, and $104. for the family.

Two hospitals, San Fernando in Panama City and *Chiriqui* Hospital in David have their own plans. Joining these plans is not limited by age at the time of enrollment, and I believe you can enroll up to the age of 80. These plans cover the cost of hospitalization and surgery with a 30% co-pay and a $10,000 maximum annual coverage limitation.

There are some exclusions or waiting periods for pre-existing conditions, as in most insurance plans. Cost rises with age, but a 65 year old is looking at a monthly premium of about $50 at *Chiriqui*, or $70 for husband and wife.

The important thing is that coverage is available. Medical care is excellent, and if you prefer to be seen in the states, remember, it is only a 2-1/2 hour flight from Panama City to Miami.

Personal Safety

Pinkerton Global Intelligence Agency, the world-renowned security firm, has given Panama its highest rating for tourist security. Panama has a low rate of violent crime and is one of the four safest places to reside in the world. It is considered to be much safer than Mexico or Costa Rica.

Since turning the Canal over to Panama, relations with the U.S. and Panama have improved dramatically. Citizens of the U.S. are welcomed by the government and by the people of Panama.

Places to Avoid

Although Panama is generally quite safe, and the incidence of violent crime is very low, there are places to take caution, just as you would in Miami, Chicago, Los Angeles, or New York.

I had a friend mugged by two women in New York just outside the Hilton Hotel on Avenue of the Americas. Flamboyant displays of jewelry, fat wallets, flashing of cash, etc., should be avoided wherever you travel in the entire world. Use common sense.

After dark, always take a cab – especially if you're club-hopping in Casco Viejo. It's not like going to South Central in LA, the Bedford-Stuyvesant in New York, or certain areas in Miami, but caution is always best.

The usual concerns about petty theft should always be observed. Pickpockets and purse-snatchers have been around since pockets and purses were invented. Colon, on the Atlantic side, is much more of a concern than Panama City.

Truly dangerous is the area known as the Darien Gap. This is the dense jungle along the Panamanian-Columbian border. There are simply too many great places to go in Panama other than the Darien Gap. Even the Pan-American highway stops here. The area is infested with thugs and bandits. Several backpackers have been missing after attempting to penetrate this jungle. It's best to avoid it.

Banking

The skyscrapers, palm-lined boulevards, and the modernity of Panama City are truly eye openers. Almost one hundred banks populate the financial district. Tall, solid looking structures of glass and steel are everywhere. Not the brass plaque "banks" you find in front of a lawyer's office on Caribbean islands. These are real banks with vaults, tellers, safety deposit boxes, wire services, etc.

It is not easy to open a Panamanian bank account unless you have obtained a permanent visa. Since Noriega's capture, the banking system has been revised. The country is particularly sensitive to elements that may have some connection with drugs or organized crime.

Panama has made a concerted effort to become one of the most modern banking centers in the world. Their laws encourage privacy and restrict the invasive access by governments of all nations. They do have numbered accounts, and bearer bonds are legal. But the banks are terribly conscious of attempted illegal "laundering" of monies and deposits by criminal elements. In many respects, Panama has "out-swissed" the Swiss.

To open a bank account, you will need reference letter(s) from your current bank(s).

Hutchings   Financial Area – Panama City

Real Estate

Foreigners are permitted to own property anywhere in Panama except within 3.7 miles of a national border. Foreigners have the same property rights as citizens.

Real Estate Taxes

Real Estate is appraised by an Agency of the Ministry of Economy and Finances. The taxable base is determined by the total value of the land and all improvements.

1. All land and improvements thereon located in Panama are subject to Real Estate tax. Real Estate transactions at prices above the appraisal automatically increase the value of such properties for tax purposes
2. Certain properties or improvements are exempt or can be qualified for exemption according to special incentive tax laws. (see visa incentives)
3. Real estate properties with assessed value of less than $20,000 are exempt from taxes. Real Estate taxes have priority over any other encumbrances
4. Taxes can be paid in three installments: April 30, Aug 31, and Dec 31.
5. A Tax Clearance Certificate must be obtained before any Real Estate transaction can be completed.

It is highly recommended you hire an attorney for any real estate transaction. Property in most areas can be purchased legally and safely. (In Bocas del Toro there are some special circumstances. Be very careful in Bocas)

Once you've found a property and you want to make an offer to buy, (and the Seller wants to sell) the owner must give you three vital documents that your attorney will need:

1. The *Escritura* (The Title & Public Deed):

2. *The Certificado de Registro Publico* (Ownership and Encumbrances Certificate) These documents are available from the Public Registry.

3. The *finca* number (*Finca* is a small farm), but this even applies to property in urban areas.

With these documents and their information, your attorney can perform a title search. (Very similar to a Title and Abstract search in the United States)

- These documents must be originals and bear the stamps, signatures, and seals of the Registration Office. The seller must provide the survey plans of the property with a description of all buildings, their size, and location on the property. (Very similar to a plot map in the U.S.)

- Enter into a purchase contract with the Seller. Your attorney will draft this. Upon signing, a down payment is required. Normally the agreement provides for liquidated damages should either party default, and a closing date is established for the transfer of title.

- The attorney should make a complete search at this point for any liens or encumbrances on the property. The seller normally pays the transfer taxes and obtains the clearance certificates required for title transfer.

- The buyer arranges payment (cash or financing) and at the stated closing date, Buyer and Seller sign the final contract.

- The attorney will formalize the final contract and draw up a public deed. The attorney(s), Buyer and Seller take the documents to a Notary Public for signing and authentication. Notary Publics in Panama (actually, in all Napoleonic Code countries) are significantly important. They are more important to the transaction than in Common Law countries and are considered high ranking officials. Like escrow officers, they are strictly neutral and represent neither Buyer nor Seller.

- The attorney will assist in transferring final payment. One of the safest ways to transfer the funds is through an irrevocable letter of payment from your bank. This letter will promise to pay the seller the final amount due upon the recording of the new title. In this way, the Buyer avoids the risk of payment if for whatever reason title is not properly recorded.

- It is highly recommended you have your attorney follow through with the recording at the main office of Public Registry in Panama City. The normal time for final recording is a few weeks. However, for costs of about $250 this time can be cut to ten days. <u>Consult with your attorney.</u>

There are certain areas in the country where titles can be a gray area where there is a definite risk. Never try to buy property in the *San Blas* region. The *Kuna Indians* have been granted sovereignty in this area. The *Kunas* are dedicated to maintaining their present way of life, and would unequivocally refuse to sell one grain of sand or one coconut tree to any one.

Around *Bocas del Toro*, most of the land is owned by the Panamanian government, so it is not legal for a foreigner to buy – at least not until it has been first owned by a Panamanian. (This restriction only applies to land not previously owned and titled by a Panamanian citizen)

There are also problems with possessory rights in *Bocas*, as well as squatter's rights in this area. You might buy a property, think all is well, and wake up some morning to find a native sitting in your back yard claiming it's his home. Another nightmare.

Panamanian Labor Laws

One of the joys of moving to Panama is the abundance and quality of good labor. Generally, the people are kind and of good humor. There are exceptions as in any generalization, but I don't believe I've ever encountered people of such grace and strong work ethic. They are scrupulously clean and detailed in their assignments. The Panamanians are lovely people, diligent, and very hardworking.

However, Panamanian labor laws apply to all of them. It is important that you understand the law and the government's paternalistic attitude. The government will not allow their people to be taken advantage of – in any way. The doctrine is best expressed in Latin:

"In Dubio Pro Operario"

Simply stated, if there be a labor dispute, the burden of proof lies with the employer. The **employee** is always right unless the **employer** can prove otherwise. So, what can we learn from this?

- Never hire anyone - whether maid, part-time maid, gardener, or a handyman without recording a signed agreement in writing – in Spanish and English.

- The operative word here is **"NEVER."**

- Understand and recognize the different types of contracts according to Panamanian law:

  1. A specific period of time contract
  2. A non-specific period of time contract
  3. A specific work contract (plumber, builder, etc.)

The labor rates are very affordable. Never, ever, try to take advantage of the workers.

This can be a confusing subject for newcomers. To give an example of possible liabilities unless you protect yourself:

- You hire a maid to work for **three hours a day, three days a week**. She is the best maid you could possibly imagine. Three months into her employment, she becomes pregnant.

- *You might be liable for her medical care, her child's medical care, the child's up-bringing and schooling, etc., etc.*

What can you do to prevent this calamity? As in Real Estate, consult a good Panamanian attorney before hiring. We talked with Lea del Adames Franceschi in David. (507) 774-4426 of **Burbano y Adames,** Abogadas (Attorneys).

Sra. Franceschi is fluent in English and very conversant in Real Estate and Labor law. A short consultation with her on domestic labor law will cost about $50. Tell her what you want, and she will draft a contract to cover your needs. Save yourself a lot of potential headache. (An attorney is an absolute **MUST** on real estate transactions where 'possessory rights' are involved.)

The laws are different in Panama. Don't think of the norm in your home country and believe that it might apply here. It probably doesn't.

Real Estate: Panama City

When 50,000 Americans left Panama in December 2000, it left a deep hole in the real estate market in and around Panama City. The Panamanian government took over all of the military bases and buildings including the military housing. Officer's quarters, enlisted barracks, and of course, everything the United States had established in the "zone," including some very impressive housing.

It's important to reiterate that in Panama, foreigners have the same rights as citizens to own property.

It's also important to understand the author is not in the real estate business and has no interest whatsoever in any properties mentioned in this book. For you to determine whether or not Panama is within your budget, examples are simply given so that you will have an idea on what to expect. Or at least, what prices and availability were in early 2004. The Panamanian government has been auctioning or selling much of the real estate formerly held by the United States in the Canal Zone and on military bases to private citizens and investors. Although quite a bit has been sold, there's a significant amount still available.

For example, there are four-plexes, containing 1,200 square feet in each unit, which are currently being sold for less than $140,000. That's approximately $30 per square foot. These were all built to U.S. standards for the U.S. government. Some buildings need work since they've been empty for four years, but those representative prices warrant investigation as a potential for rental income units.

There are new condominiums in the city that are also bargains. A new 2 bedroom, 2 bath condo containing approximately 900 square feet was recently purchased for $65,000. This apartment has a balcony and beautiful view. It is air-conditioned, and in a full-service high-rise building in an up-scale neighborhood of Panama City.

If you have a significant budget, there are 3,000 square foot high-luxury apartments available that may cost as much as $250,000 to $300,000. Obviously, there is a lot of available real estate between $50,000 and $300,000. If urban living is your choice, there are excellent values available.

Listed below are a few representative apartment and single-family residence prices in Panama City. Most have separate maid quarters.

Apartments – Panama City

Newer apartments in Panama are as modern as any in the rest of the world, employing breathtaking architecture and the latest in appliances and amenities. Prices are reflective of the values which are current in Panama. Apartments of similar size and quality would cost many times more in the States.

Most apartments also have separate maid quarters, as this is a way of life among the middle class of Panama – not just the wealthy.

Fiber-optics, internal computer wiring, cable, and satellite TV are generally standard. Luxury apartments can range from $50,000 to $400,000 and from 900 square feet to 3,500.

It is customary that apartments can be purchased as well as rented. Obviously, prices are subject to the same valuation swings we see in any growing country.

Single Family Residences

Panama is undergoing a mini-building boom. Properties in and around Panama City are exceptionally well designed with underground utilities, pools, etc. Architecture seems to be a blend of Florida-California-Caribbean, and very practical with lots of tile, marble, patios, and areas for outdoor living. It is refreshing to visit a new development where power and telephone lines are underground. The resale market offers a wide choice.

Island Living

There are nearly 1,000 islands off both coasts of Panama. Several of these offer a wonderful opportunity to enjoy one's dream. The Caribbean coast differs greatly from the Pacific coast, so we'll look at the pros and cons of each area.

Remember, our perspective is to view these options as destinations for potential retirement – not as vacation destinations . They might be an excellent investment, and/or great vacation spots once you've moved here, but not necessarily the place you'd choose.

Bocas del Toro – Caribbean Side

Interpreted literally, *Bocas del Toro* means Mouth of the Bull. If you check the maps of the region, it is easy see how well the name fits.

Marni   Bocas Beach

For years, this area was the principal headquarters and export area for the famous *Chiquita* bananas of the United Fruit Company. In the late thirties, a local banana blight radically reduced the operations in the area. Because of its beauty and tranquility, Bocas developed as a prime tourist attraction.

Bocas (The Town) is about 10 hours driving time from Panama City via David, and about a 55 minute flight from the

Albrook airport. It's only a half hour flight from David, and is one of Panama's top tourist attractions.

The town of Bocas is 'quaint,' with a permanent population of approximately 4,000.

Marni   Bocas Bar

The Jamaican descendents usually speak some form of English. The Latins speak mostly Spanish. Accommodations in town (Bocas Town) are increasing. The atmosphere is one of "early" Caribbean.

The town is located on the island of Colon, the largest island in the group, and is the seat of government for the province. (Don't confuse this with the city of Colon at the Atlantic entrance to the Canal.)

107

There are few autos on the island and not many full-time gringos. Its nightlife can be hectic at times with the many young people who love to come here. Salsa and Carib-Afro music dominate the dancing.

Hospedaje Heike on Calle 3 near the center of town was rebuilt in 2001. It has seven rooms with ceiling fans, mosquito nets and two shared bathrooms (with hot water) ranging from $5 - $15 per night. This is a good value.

Marni   Bocas Town

Several other small, quaint hotels offer similar facilities in town: *Hospedaje Emmanuel, Hospedaje EYL, Hotel Las Brisas, Hotel Casa Max, Hotel Angela.* These are all small hotels of six to eight rooms. Others, more mid-range are: *Hotel Dos Palmas,*

Hotel La Veranda, and the older, stately hotel built by United Fruit in 1905, *Hotel Bahia – at $40-50 per night.* All rooms are air conditioned, with private hot-water baths. Some have balconies and ocean views. (507) 676-4669

Upscale facilities include: *The Bocas Inn,* (507-269-9414) 12 lovely air-conditioned rooms, including breakfast, ranging

from $50-70. There is a restaurant and bar.
www.anconexpeditions.com

Cocomo on the Sea, small but attractive seaside inn (4
rooms). Nicely decorated. No pets or children under eight.
Rates are $55 including breakfast. On *Calle H.*
www.panamainfo.com/cocomo

Another nice resort is ***Punta Caracol*** (507-676-7186) whose
2-story Cabins are on stilts, built over a coral reef, so diving is
easy. And great. About 20 minutes from town, and far
enough away from the mangrove swamps to minimize the no-
see-ums and mosquitoes. Price is $110/couple including
breakfast. The beautiful restaurant is excellent.
www.puntacaracol.com

Bocas is typical Caribbean beauty, charm, and quaintness.
Most of the beaches are beautiful.
There are also the mangrove swamps that harbor lots of 'no-
see-ums' and mosquitoes.
It's a place not too different from what you'll find on many of
the islands of the Caribbean. Stunning beaches, palm trees,
and warm azure waters teeming with the color of tropical fish.

Homes in Bocas vary from older dilapidated places you wouldn't choose to own, to modern residences you'd love to own. (Note the sleeping pig in the photo below)

Marni   Dilapidated Water Front

Prices of *Bocas* waterfront property can be almost beyond belief when compared with the rest of Panama. Even for rundown shacks. However, when compared with the more popular Caribbean resorts, they seem to be a bargain.

Modern Home   Bocas

Bocas del Toro has two seasons: wet and wetter. It receives an average of 115 inches of rainfall a year. While most of that falls from April to December, it's a significant amount of precipitation.

The rain here is not like the monsoons of Southeast Asia where it can rain night and day for weeks. Days generally offer some sun and brief showers of heavy, intermittent rain. Beginning in January, rainfall is less, and picks up intensity in April.

Real estate prices in Bocas have skyrocketed and they'll probably continue to do so. A rundown, ramshackle house on the beach will cost much more than $50,000. You probably wouldn't live in it without extensive renovation. It might even be a total 'tear-down.'

Although Bocas appears ready for a boom, there are immediate problems with its infrastructure. Potable water, sewage treatment, and waste collection are all problems that must be dealt with, as they are marginally adequate today.

Some islands are privately owned and will operate exclusive resorts or retirement communities. *Isla Solarte* will be a planned retirement community. It is tranquil and surrounded by crystal blue water. This project is owned & is being developed by Americans. At the time of this writing, it is still in the planning stage. Contact: www.tropicalproperties.com

Bocas is a wonderful vacation spot. It's a little like Key West 100 years ago (or so I'm told – I missed that trip). Most people come as tourists to snorkel, dive, surf, and lie in the sun on snowy white beaches. Or snooze in a hammock strung between two palm trees.

It's a midwinter's dream for those who live in the frozen north, and who wish to prove the highest and best use of the pineapple is a frosty, *Pina Colada.*

But look it over carefully before deciding to settle in here. Remember, it's only a short flight from Panama City and David. You can be on the beach of your choice in a very short time.

San Blas Islands

The *Comarca de San Blas* is the home of the Kuna Indians, and has been granted a form of sovereignty by the Panamanian government. The Kunas are fiercely independent and dedicated to maintaining and saving their ways and customs.

For example, a Kuna woman is not even given a name until she has had her first menstrual period. Until that day arrives, the young girl responds to a nick-name. The women dress traditionally, and wear a gold ring through their nose.

Kuna Girls

There is no possibility of buying property or retiring among the Kunas. However, the San Blas Islands are a fascinating and beautiful place to visit.

Contadora Island – Pacific Coast

Long a favorite of Panamanians and Latin Americans, *Contadora* is in the Bay of Panama. It is only a fifteen-minute flight or one-hour boat ride from Panama City.

Contadora is not one of the larger of the Pearl Islands, but is considered Panama's most exclusive address. In Spanish, '*Contadora*' means counting house.

In the 16th century, slaves were brought in to dive for pearls and cultivate the land of the islands. Today, the pearl beds are not nearly so productive, but one of the largest pearls in the world, the 31-carat *Peregrina* was found here. It was the property of several of Europe's Royal Families, and now belongs to Elizabeth Taylor.

Pearling is still practiced, and the two best islands for buying are *Isla Casaya & Isla Casayeta,* about 12 km from Contadora. *Salvetore Fishing* will arrange transportation.

The beaches in the *Archipelago de las Perlas* are mostly light tan in color, like most of the beaches of Pacific waters, whether in Central America or California. The water is mostly turquoise, loaded with tropical fish swimming among the reefs, and aqueous home to leatherneck and hawksbill turtles. A snorkeler's dream.

Contadora is quite beautiful with at least a dozen secluded beaches and coves. The tradewinds here are quite regular. I talked with a California couple who recently bought a lovely condominium on *Contadora.* Two bedrooms, two baths, maid's quarters, etc., ($137,000) and while not right on the beach, they have a full beach view from their living room and balcony. They told me they have yet to turn on the air-conditioner because of the cool trade breezes. That price has undoubtedly appreciated.

Panama's only official nude beach, *Playa de las Suecas* (Swedish Women's Beach) is on Contadora, around the corner and to the south of the *Contadora Resort.* There are 12 beaches on this small (1.2 square km) island, and they are mostly unoccupied except during holidays. The permanent population is something less than 350 people.

Hotel Punta Galeón (507) 250-4134
A very nice hotel of 48 rooms. Pool, sauna, kid's pool, restaurants, bars, etc. $110/$130 night. The hotel is situated on the bay and has excellent beaches.

The Hotel Contadora Resort (507-250-4033) The most crowded beach area generally is Playa Larga in front of the Resort. This beach also affords an excellent opportunity for spotting marine life, particularly amberjacks, manta rays and both kinds of sea turtles. Snorkeling here is nothing short of fantastic. Snorkeling trips and guides can be arranged at the hotel.

The resort is large, with 354 rooms. Facilities include a huge pool, tennis courts, nine hole golf course, (all of which are free to guests) including mountain bikes, tennis rackets, and snorkeling equipment. Rates are about $80 (per person) per night, but these are open to negotiation as many guests arrive on package deals. All meals are included – buffet style.

Contadora has long been the near-exclusive playground of the wealthy. Many famous artists, writers, politicians, and executives from the world over have counted *Contadora* as their retreat, including the late Shah of Iran.

All of this plus the other accoutrements of the tropics: coral reefs, palm trees, sea turtles, parrots, and riots of tropical flora. There's one big difference here. You won't find raucous bars, wet tee-shirt contests, or a zillion students on Spring break.

There is a nine-hole golf course, two lovely (and quiet) resorts, a few shops, a new medical center, and several good restaurants. And, of course, the airstrip for the flight to Panama City.

The island is small, supply is small, so properties tend to be quite dear. Beachfront houses begin about $400,000 and up, depending on size. Properties off the beach are more reasonable: from a ball-park of $90,000 and up.

Then there's the lovely condominium units, mentioned earlier, under $200,000.

Isla San Jose

The lovely resort of Hacienda del Mar was developed by the president of Aeroperlas, Panama's commuter airline. This is truly an upscale resort of 12 luxurious cabins, with a fine restaurant. The nightly rate is $250 per cabin, with a few larger cabins available.

Isla San Jose is a good-sized island of approximately 44 square km. An excellent road system was installed by the U.S. Navy several years ago. The island has 37 beaches, nine year round rivers, and several waterfalls. The Hacienda del Mar is the only development, so each cabin could have three private beaches. Talk about a honeymoon heaven!

The resort arranges tours, deep sea fishing expeditions, and four-wheeler explorations of the rainforest with its myriads of birds, flora and other fauna.

Islas Tabogas

This group of small and close islands is in the Bay of Panama. *Isla Tobaga* is less than 600 hectares in size – about 1400 acres. It has a stormy history of pirates, murder, and sea battles.

Today, the only assaults on the island are weekending Panamanians who come to enjoy the resorts and beaches.

There is a ferry, the Calypso Queen, which leaves from Muelle 18 in the Balboa District of Panama City. The round trip fare is $7.50.

The day's entrance fee is $5.00 and entitles visitors to their free run of all beaches. The Hotel *Tobaga* rents umbrellas, paddle boats, hammocks, mats, and snorkeling equipment – all at reasonable prices.

There are no autos on the island, and besides the hotel there is only one other restaurant-bar, the Bar El Galeon. Nightlife is limited.

There is no property for sale here, but it's a fun and an inexpensive day's outing. Tobaga is a favorite of Panamanians.

Pacific Beaches

Approximately one hour from Panama City, miles of wonderful beaches begin. The coastline here is quite beautiful, and many investors (from many countries) and retirees are beginning to locate and/or invest in the properties along this stretch.

First class resorts are available where you can spend some time while investigating the area. *Playa Coronado* is little more than a one-hour drive from Panama City on the four-lane Inter-Americana Highway.

The **Hotel Coronado** is wonderful, and one of the best resorts in Panama. The *jardines* (gardens) are lovely, the staff is friendly, there's an Olympic size pool, Jacuzzi, tennis, equestrian center, spa, gym, and an excellent golf course designed by George Fazio. Restaurants are 1st class. Beaches are terrific.

Rooms are spacious with separate living and sleeping areas. About $175/night from Dec-March, less later in season. www.coronadoresort.com

This Beach area has grown in popularity over the years. Property prices are at a premium anywhere in the Coronado area, but if you shop, you can still find beach-front for about $100,000.

Further west (about 25 km) is the huge resort of **The Royal Decameron**. This is probably the Pacific Coast's most popular resort with more than 600 rooms, pools, restaurants, spa, gym, tennis, discos, casino, beach and poolside bars, etc. One of the reasons it is so popular is its "all-inclusive" price.

Less than $100 per person per day includes room, all meals, drinks (yes, drinks are included), equipment and access to everything. Friends of mine recently stayed here mid-week for $56 night. Reservations: 507-899-2111 www.decameron.com

Vista Mar

Only 55 miles west of Panama City is the new development of Vista Mar. This is a beautiful, gated community project that sits on terraced bluffs above the Pacific. Directions and signage are very clear from the Interamerican highway. This is a multi-layered project of more than 500 acres.

Multi-layered, by definition includes several choices available from raw lots, to condominiums, and single-family homes.

The condominiums are located in two towers of fourteen units each. The condominiums are a minimum of 858 square feet at $113,000 and go up to 2,255 square feet at $249,000.

The vacant lots for custom homes are located on the first terrace and are a minimum of ¼ acre – each with beautiful Pacific views.

There are clustered villas of 12 to 14 homes across the street from the golf course. They start at $135,500 for 2,000 square feet up to $160,500 for 2,450 square feet. These clustered units each share a common area with a pool, social area, and children's park.

The homes on terraces 3-6 start at $255,000 (2816 square feet) up to 3,767 square feet at $296,000.

The golf course is scheduled to be opened in April, 2007, and is considered to be world-class.

Each home or condo has an ocean view. The homes range in size starting at 1,800 square feet, with three bedrooms, two baths ($179,500) and up. Each home includes fully contained maid quarters with bath. The home designs generally place these quarters near the laundry room.

The project has an 18-hole golf course, club-house, restaurant, and 50-room hotel. The architecture is dramatic.

Amenities include tennis, pools, health center, spa, bicycle paths, and an ecological park. Satellite TV and high speed internet connections are available for all units.

The development is only five minutes from El Rey Supermercado, bank, hardware store, beauty salon – even a veterinarian.

Whether you're retiring or looking for a second home, don't miss this spectacular development. For more details, contact them at: Their website: www.vistamarresort.com

The Highlands

Not too far from Coronado Beach (19 km) is the *Altos del Maria* project. This is a major development by *The Grupo Melo, S.A.* The Melo Group is a very large company. They are the largest chicken and egg provider in Panama. Their eggs are in every store. They are also partners with Tyson for distribution in all of the Caribbean. Melo also owns the Izusu and John Deere distributorships in Panama, as well as the *Pio Pio* restaurants. The project reflects their degree of funding.

Altos del Maria is only 65 miles from Panama City, so it is easily accessed on the 4-lane, Interamerica highway. Its location is in the province of Panama, district of *Chame*.

The Sales Manager, Pedro Sarasqueta, in Panama City escorted me on a Saturday morning.

It was quite warm in the coastal area, but we climbed on an excellent road to the property and were enjoying the cool fresh air of the highlands in a few minutes. The temperature at the entrance gate to *Los Altos del Maria* was almost twenty degrees cooler than at the beach. Air conditioning definitely was not required.

The average year-round high temperature here is 68-degrees Fahrenheit. (20-degrees C) The average minimum is 61-degrees (F), 16-deg C, so the temperature is very uniform.

The landscape is lush, tropical greenery, and it's the habitat of hundreds of species of exotic birds, deer, and other small mammals. From the highest point on the project is a view of both the Atlantic and Pacific Oceans. Other views at lower elevations are almost as spectacular, but limited to either a Pacific Ocean view or of the lush valleys.

There are 350 lots in the current phase. Melo owns over 3,900 acres in these cool highlands. All roads are in (more than 27 miles of paved asphalt) with power and water to each lot.

Water is supplied from three aqueducts managed by the developer. The water source is the numerous, high quality year-round streams whose purity is exceptional.

Hutchings   Highlands View

Many lots have ocean views, and all are really well laid out. The engineering appears to be first-class and very much up to American standards.

The development takes advantage of the terrain, and rather than one large tract, there are several smaller units, each with a natural terrain separation. There are rivers, streams, waterfalls, wild orchids, and lovely scenery in this development.

Lot sizes range from about one-quarter acre to three-quarter's acre. Prices range from $25,000 to $60,000. Financing is available, and discounts apply for cash payment or the purchase of more than one lot.

Grupo Melo is <u>not</u> constructing homes. They are only selling the completed lots, but they can recommend several local contractors in the area.

Contractors are quoting $40-$50 per square foot for construction. This is for basic construction and is subject to change based on specifications and amenities. In observation of other building projects is Panama, this may be a low-ball price.

Telephone, high-speed internet, and satellite TV facilities are all available. An English speaking doctor has built a new medical clinic for the convenience of the residents. There is also a heliport on the project in the event an emergency or health evacuation is needed.

If you are thinking of buying property or building in Panama, you should definitely look at this project. There is no village

yet, but a convenience market is underway. The project is close to Panama City, close to the beach, Coronado Resort, Supermarkets, Golf, etc., yet has the fresh, cool air of the central highlands. Tel: (507) 260-4813
www.altosdelmaria.com

El Valle Anton

Somewhat farther to the west is the charming community of El Valle Anton, known to the locals as simply 'El Valle.' This small community (6,500 pop) is nested in the crater of an extinct volcano. Its eruption three million years ago created one of the largest craters in all of the Americas – nearly five kilometers in diameter. The crater filled with rainwater over the eons, but between 25,000 and 10,000 BC, the lake drained, leaving a deep floor of sedimentation.

As the area became populated with humans, they settled here and began growing crops in the rich volcanic soil. Their arrival date is not factually determined, but the best estimate of archeologists is approximately 10,000 to 15,000 years ago.

Because of its proximity to Panama City (about 75 miles) and its cool weather (about 2,000 feet in altitude), El Valle has been a long-time favorite of Panamanians wanting to get away from the tropical weather of Panama City.

It has also become a favorite because of its Sunday market. A large handicrafts market where indigenous people bring their wares has become a tradition. Woven baskets from the *Guyami*, and even the finely woven treasures from the *Wounaans* as far away as Darien province are sold here.

Panama hats from *Ocú* and *Penemone* are also sold, as well as fruit, vegetables, wood carvings, figurines, and pottery. Most items are less than $20. It's quite an affair.

Property here is less expensive than on the beaches or even further west in Boquete. If you believe, as I do, that a certain amount of expatriate community and activity is important, then you may want to think twice about settling in El Valle – lovely as it is, because the expat community is very small.

On the other hand, if you would like to come to Panama and start a nice little bed and breakfast, El Valle might be a candidate. However, to be successful in the 'B & B' business, one needs a steady flow of potential customers. El Valle seems to have that on the weekends, but during the week, it can be 'iffy.'

El Valle is a very quiet little community with limited facilities, including medical. There are a number of smaller hotels and restaurants.

Hotel Don Pepe (507-983-6425) $35-45 per night. 12 large rooms, clean, with private baths, & hot water. Communal TV and laundry. There is a good restaurant on the first floor offering several chicken and seafood dishes.

Hotel Rincon Vallero (507-983-6175) 14 A-C rooms, private hot-water baths $65-95. Very good restaurant with shrimp, seafood, and steak specialties.

Hotel y Restaurante Los Capitanes (507-983-6080) This is a nice place. Rooms are well-furnished with TV, VCRs and hotwater baths. Four rooms are outfitted for handicapped. Excellent restaurant and bar. $40-$80.

La Casa de Lourdes (507-983-6450)   An elegant hotel and restaurant in a Tuscan Villa style. Two rooms, surrounded by gardens and a pool. The excellent restaurant includes, meat, chicken, and seafood entrees.

Again, we have not attempted to list all of the places to stay and eat. There are more facilities available in both categories. If you visit El Valle and these places are full, look around.

Perhaps the greatest charm of El Valle lies in the fact it offers great walking trails for naturalists and birders.

There is also a Canopy Adventure ride for the more daring. This is a suspended cable built within the tree canopy dozens of meters above the jungle floor. There are six platforms, and the ride takes you to all six. At one point, the ride will allow you to pass and look <u>down</u> at the 250-foot high Chorro El Macho (The Manly Waterfall). This ride requires personal strength and daring. It's not for everyone.

El Valle also has a Museum and Zoo, and neither offers a lot for the visitor. Zoos in most Latin countries can be unkempt, sad places. The Zoo at El Valle offers no surprise to either feature.

The *Museo* offers little to get excited about. There are some old petroglyphs of an earlier civilization, several religious artifacts, and information about the giant volcanic eruption that created the crater where El Valle currently sits.

The Western Highlands

Gateway to the western highlands is ***David (Dah'veed)***, about 265 miles west of Panama City. This is the third largest city in Panama (130,000) and is the provincial capital. *David* is hot most of the time. And humid.

Primarily an agricultural center, *David* doesn't offer a lot of excitement as a place to settle in. However, *David* has many attractions. It is a first-rate supply center for automobiles, furniture, appliances, and hardware.

Chiriqui Province is the breadbasket of Panama. More fruit, vegetables, and cattle are raised here than in all the rest of Panama. And the coffee plantations in the Chiriqui Highlands are wonderful to see and tour.

One of the best supermarkets in Panama is *Super Baru* located in eastern David. There is also a *PriceSmarts*, an affiliate of **Costco**. They honor the Costco card, and have many of the products you'll find in Costco stores the world over.

David also has a number of good shops, two major hospitals, and a third under construction. As the provincial capital, there are many attorneys, notary publics, banks, travel agencies, an immigration office, doctors, dentists, and other professionals.

David is a major transportation hub. Buses to Panama City, Costa Rica, Volcan, and Boquete originate in the central bus terminal.

Express Buses to Panama City offer comfortable seats, and movies for about $15 (one way). The trip supposedly takes six hours, but with construction repairs to the Interamerican Highway, allow for seven.

David has an excellent airport with at least three flights daily to Panama City and Bocas del Toro. There is no bus service

from the airport to town, but taxis are plentiful and cheap
(About $2 or $3).

David is also home to one of the best deep-sea sport fishers in
Panama, *Pesca Panama.* (507-614-5850) This firm operates
off of *Coiba Island*, Hannibal Bank, which is one of the
world's great fisheries and near David. Many world records
have originated here.

Hotels in David.

Hotel Gran Nacional (507-775-2222) In central David. A
modern hotel with good restaurant, pizzeria, large pool,
casino, and parking. All rooms have 50-chan. TV, AC, & Hot
water. Four theatres are located across the street. $45-$60.
Probably the best hotel in town.

Hotel Castilla (507-)775260 Centrally located. All rooms
have AC, Hot water, Cable TV. Good value at $25-30.

Hotel Puerta del Sol - Rooms about $27. Fair restaurant,
Bar, TV, A/C. My objection to this place is its lack of
security. Door locks are the bedroom, push-button type. I
never had a problem here with theft of any kind, but it was
always a worry to leave the room.

Each March, David hosts a large, international fair (*Feria de
San Jose de David*). Every type of merchandise under the sun,
from automobiles to home furnishings, is available. The fair
is immensely popular. The horse show and rodeo are
important features.

Transportation

The bus terminal is on Avenida del Estudiante. It is crowded, and buses leave regularly to many cities and towns. If you're going to **Volcan**, the bus leaves every hour from 5AM to 5PM. The trip takes about 1-1/2 hours and the fare is $2.30

The buses leave for **Boquete** every 25-minutes. It takes about 45-minutes and the fare is $1.20.

Express buses to **Panama City** 10AM, 2PM, 10PM, and midnight take about six or seven hours ($15) and terminate at the Albrook terminal.

Tracopa (775-0585) provides bus service to San Jose, Costa Rica, departing daily at 8:30 AM from the Trapoca office at Avenida 5 Este and Calle A Sur. The trip takes about 8 hours and the fare is $12.50.

Beaches Near David

Las Olas Resort (507-772-3000) This is a large new complex. Facilities include a bar-discotheque, restaurant, gym, beauty salon and spa. Room rates are about $85. Beach front lots were offered for $35,000, and I'm told were quickly gobbled up. More coming.

Playa Las Lajas is 62 km (36 miles) east of David. Light sand and palms line this portion of the coast. Lodging and restaurant facilities are limited.

The Highlands – *Volcan*

This village lies to the west of *David*, is an agricultural community, as is most of this area, and perched on the northwestern slopes of *Volcan Baru*. At 11,400 feet high, this dormant volcano is the highest mountain is Panama.

The province of *Chiriqui* shares its border with Costa Rica, and Volcan is approximately 10-miles due east at an altitude of nearly 5,000 feet. It may be quite a good place to retire. The weather is moderate (about 68-75 degrees F the year round.) The population is nearing 7,000 (in the surrounding area) with an expatriate community of 60 families, – and growing

In addition to markets and shops, there is a medical clinic in Volcan, and the nearby towns of Bambito and Cerro Punta are also delightful. Bambito is the home of the 4-star *Hotel Bambito* with its tennis courts, pool, hot tub and sauna, horseback riding, etc. Rates are a little pricey, ranging from $120-145, but it's a lovely retreat.

There are ruins of a pre-Columbian culture in nearby *Barriles*. These ruins are on private land, so don't go traipsing across the fields without getting permission from the owner.

There's an American expatriate living in Volcan, Bill Hemmingway (507-284-4175, or 507-232-5443 evenings) who will be happy to tell you of the many advantages about retiring in Volcan. Bill arranges nature hikes, bird-watching tours, and trips through the national park and rain forest, as well as scenic drives to Costa Rica or across the continental divide to the Caribbean. He can guide you to property and brokers.

Real Estate prices in and around Volcan are substantially less than those in Boquete, but they are rising due to demand. I have a friend who lives in nearby Potrerillos who bought a few hectares (a hectare is 2.47 acres) three years ago. His land has increased in value over 500 percent.

A new highway is planned that will run between *Boquete* and *Volcan*. This is a road originally planned to be routed through a much more ecologically sensitive area to the north. There were many objections, and the route was re-designed to transit to the south.

Interesting places nearby are Cerro Punta, Lagunas de Volcan (Lakes of Volcan), and Guadalupe. The *Sendero Los Quetzals* is a famous trail through the forest which will take you all the way back to Boquete. Many people hire a guide and drive to Cerro Punta, then walk downhill to Boquete. Your chances of seeing the Resplendent Quetzal on this hike are excellent.

Los Quetzales Lodge and Spa (507-771-2182) is a 10-room lodge with restaurant and bars, with a lovely dining room. Rooms are $50-60. About 600 meters above the lodge is a beautiful orchid sanctuary, *Finca Dracula.* More than 2,000 species of orchids are grown here – one of Latin America's finest exhibitions. A modest fee of $7. is requested.

The Parque Internacional La Armistad is over one million acres in size and ranges across the Costa Rican border. This is a fabulous park. Most of the Panamanian portion of the park lies in the province of Bocas del Tore, but entrance is more accessible from Cerro Punta.

The plant and animal life in this park represent the most diverse in the entire country. If you're a birding fanatic, the park is sensational. In addition, there are several varieties of felines who make the park their habitat, including jaguars, ocelots, and margays.

In retrospect, the area west of David offers great potential for retirement. Property is more than reasonable, it's close to David, the climate is great, and there are a number of expatriate families living here.

Eastern Highlands – *Boquete* (Bo-ket-āy)

Boquete leads the pack when it comes to charm. Of course, that's not all. It leads the pack in the number of expatriates who reside here – most of them full-time.

It leads the pack in new housing and land developments.

It probably leads the pack in land prices – but they're still a fraction of what you'd pay in the States, Canada, or Europe. (Please be cautious about buying property on a whim) See *Business Opportunities.*

I spent several months in *Boquete* after being in Panama City, where the temperature was warm but not as oppressively hot as I anticipated. Panama City was a bustling, vibrant, urban metropolis. It was great. The sights, the history, the shopping, the canal, the hotels, and the restaurants will bring me back again.

I didn't know what to expect in *Boquete*, except I knew it was a small village nestled in a lush green valley. Rather than take the $1.20 bus from David, I took a taxi. I was lugging a large duffle bag, a carry-on bag for essentials (in case the airlines sent my duffle to Tierra del Fuego), and my lap-top computer.

The taxi from David airport to Boquete was $20. I couldn't help but compare that to the $50 shuttle bus fare between Newport Beach and LAX. About the same distance. Of course the shuttle driver spoke a little more English than my taxi driver, but he really didn't have much to say that I wanted to hear. The fare comparison was just the beginning of the many comparisons I was to make in the next three weeks.

After settling in at *The Petite Hotel Mozart*, I wanted to see Boquete.

Hutchings   Mozart Terrace

I called a taxi that took me into the village – about a six-minute ride. The fare was $1.25 — and while I'm at it, the taxi drivers here are sane, unlike those in Panama City, whose object in life seems to be to come as close to another vehicle as possible without inflicting major damage. However, a word here about the Panama drivers: their taxis appear to be generally undamaged – not like the wrecks seen in Mexico City.

My first stop was at **Boquete Highlands Realty** where I met
Kelly Collier, a real estate broker who had lived in Hawaii
before putting his roots down in Boquete.

Kelly was gracious and informative. He thought the climate in
Boquete was superior to Hawaii. Not as hot or as rainy,
although it showers every afternoon from May to October, and
rains hardest in November.

He told me small furnished rental homes would run about
$350-400/month. Unfurnished $250-350. (Yankee dollars)

Basic lot prices for ¼ to ½ acre were running about $20,000 to
$55,000 depending on view, available utilities, roads, etc.

New home construction would run about $45-$55 square ft.
No one had heating or air conditioning, except a few gringos
who were installing fireplaces.

A small *finca* or coffee farm would be priced in the range of
$35,000 to $60,000 per acre. The unit of measurement in all
hispanic countries is the *hectare* (2.47 acres), so multiply these
prices by 2.47 to get the *hectare* price.

Prices are getting higher in the Boquete area, so don't let
escalations surprise you.

Obviously, these are generalized prices and could vary in
value by view, micro-climate, availability of water, phones,
and power. I was to discover more about pricing.

Kelly took me out to a new development, *Valle Escondido
(Hidden Valley)*. My jaw dropped when I first saw this
project. This is a guarded-gate community, with golf course,

riding stables, a small village, an amphitheatre, and a cantina – it looked like an exclusive development in Southern California or Florida. It was immaculate.

Valle Escondido construction is stucco with red-tiled roofs, and the architecture is right out of Tuscany.

I met the developer of *Valle Escondido*, Sam Taliaferro. Sam is (was) semi-retired as a silicon chip manufacturer. He fell in love with *Boquete*, its people, and the climate.

The project is multi-layered, with duplexes, single-family residences, and building lots for sale. It is a gorgeous community. Prices start at $169,000 for a 2-bedroom, 2-bath duplex. Financing is available. They sold out of the first, and have begun construction on phase II. The prices are projected to be under $170,000.

Mr. Taliaferro's concept has been to bring an upscale development to Boquete. With a background in the high tech industry, high speed internet connections are in place as well as underground utilities.

Hutchings   Valle Escondido Duplex   Boquete

A spa, swimming pool, Jacuzzi, exercise facility, and a holistic health center opened last year.

Valle Escondido is a first-class development. Mr. Taliaferro also owns a restaurant in Boquete as well as a very fine hostelry, *Hotel Los Establos*.

Downtown Boquete is less than two minutes from *Valle Escondido*. Three years ago (2004), there were two real estate offices on *Avenida Central*. Today, there are eight or nine. A new commercial plaza has been developed as well as two new office buildings. And, Romero's Mercado (the market) has been enlarged – substantially.

The Exotic Woods

Whether for home building or custom furniture making, the choice of woods available in Panama is mind-boggling. There is no such thing as particle board or veneers. All cabinetry is Teak, Coco-Bolo, or other local hardwoods. These woods are some of the most beautiful I've ever seen. A wide range of finishes are available. The same wonderful woods are used on the solid doors. No hollow core doors here. They're all beautiful, solid paneled. Made locally, in Boquete.

Plumbing fixtures available are American Standard. Modern appliances of US manufacture are available, including large refrigerators, gas ranges, washers and dryers. Glazed Italian tile flooring is very popular. Roofs are tile, and houses are seismically structured. Average cost: $50-$60 square foot.

People coming to *Boquete* generally downsize from their homes in the States. The most popular plans seem to be in the 1500 sq ft range. The smaller homes have 2 bedrooms, 2 baths, with lots of glass and outdoor living under roof.

William Hutchings

The number of small developments is growing as *Boquete* gains popularity. There are several builders in the area, and I've interviewed several expatriates who have bought existing homes and remodeled or built new homes. Some are making the remodeling business an avocation.

With building costs about $50 per square foot, it's easy to see how one can build a 1,000 square foot home on a $25,000 lot and have a home for less than $90,000. Land prices, however, are accelerating faster than building costs.

A word of caution: *Boquete* is becoming popular, and as such, may attract a variety of real estate 'operators.'

Again, exercise caution when thinking of a raw property purchase. Hire an attorney. Before making an offer, insist on 'comparables,' and don't be rushed into an offer by the 'scare' tactics some salespeople may employ.

A local real estate attorney in Boquete is *Sra.*Victoria Romero (507) 720-1086. "Vickie" is the wife of a local physician, Dr. Leonidas Pretelt, and a very reputable member of the community. She specializes in rental and "for sale" property in the Boquete area. She is very knowledgeable.

Another attorney is Lea del R. Adames Francheschi. Her offices are in David (507) 774-4426. Sra. Adames is a full-service attorney, and an expert in Panamanian real estate and labor laws.

New Projects

Two new developments are currently being built near Boquete. Each of which is being directed to different focused markets.

Cielo Paraiso is a beautiful and exclusive planned community near Boquete with a championship 18-hole golf course. Raideep and Colleen Lal arrived in Boquete from Toronto, Canada five years ago, looking for the ultimate in lifestyle and climate. And they brought their dream with them – to develop a luxury, golf course community at affordable prices.

They bought the property for *Cielo Paraiso* and engaged one of the world's foremost golf course architects, Michael Poellot. Mr. Poellot has designed more than 300 courses the world over – in Europe, Canada, the U.S., Southeast Asia, South Africa, and Japan. Each country can boast of his more well-known courses.

To supplement the 160 exclusive building sites surrounding the course (most lots are in the ½ to ¾ acre size), the Lals hired The Warren Group from Santa Barbara, California to design a hotel and clubhouse. These exclusive facilities include the only convention facilities in the Western Highlands. They are the ultimate in luxury, and will include every amenity imaginable, from tennis courts, spa, restaurants, pool, etc. Construction began in 2005.

Nuare Boquete, Residences, Resort and Spa is another new upscale development just south of Boquete. This planned community's homes range from 2,650 square feet to 3,800 square feet. Condominiums range in size from 1,250 square feet to 2,335 square feet, and priced from $122,000 to $236,000.

All utilities are underground, with high speed internet, satellite, and telephone service available. An advance security system has been employed. Pets are welcome.

The amenities are superb – including club house, pool, Jacuzzi, tennis courts, arts & crafts studio, wood shop, exercise room, restaurant, bar, and library/lounge.

In addition, the community has been designed with retirees specifically in mind. A care facility is planned (a full-time nurse will be employed), with massage, health services, and physiotherapy facilities. Activities will include crafts, cooking lessons, dancing, and nightly movies.

This is an ambitious project and has been beautifully thought out and designed. There are only 82 lots available. Lots and homes are anticipated to begin at $150,000. Of course, the larger homes will be commensurately more. Custom lots will be available from the mid-twenties.

By the time this book is published, there will undoubtedly be more projects. Stay in touch by accessing www.boquete.org.

Exploring *Boquete*

Boquete sits in a small bowl of a valley at the eastern base of *Volcan Baru*, at an altitude of 3,200 feet. The altitude accounts for its spring-like weather the year round.

The village has good shopping. There are two large markets with a good selection of meat, produce, and most commodities imaginable. Of course, many people make the 22 mile trek to David on occasion to stock up at *Super Baru* or *Price Smarts, (Costco)* but the local markets do a nice job.

There are clothing stores, an electronics store, a computer store, bakeries, pharmacies, etc. Gift stores galore. There's also a public market with some of the best produce you'll ever crunch into. It's really inexpensive, and an enjoyable experience to attend. Locals, expatriates, and the *Ngobe-Guaymi* Indians come to the village every Saturday.

Boquete Climate

One of the biggest attractions to *Boquete* is its climate. The temperature is constant – a spring-like 75 degrees (F) almost every day of the year. However, the nights are cool – averaging 60 degrees (F). Cool enough to require sleeping under a light blanket at night. You'll also need a jacket or sweatshirt in the evenings.

The rainy season starts in May and lasts through November. A typical day during the rainy season is sunshine until noon or one o'clock. Then, clouds will gather and one or two showers can be expected in the afternoon or evening – punctuated by sunshine.

Showers can be intense, and as November approaches, can become quite heavy. But it seldom rains all day, and the temperature still remains at a pleasant mid-seventies.

Incidentally, temperatures are generally stated on the *Celsius* scale rather than *Fahrenheit.* To make a quick approximate conversion, for example, take the *Fahrenheit* reading, subtract 30 and divide by 2. If the temperature is 74 (F), subtract 30 (=44) and divide by 2 = 22 Celsius.

To calculate Fahrenheit from a Celsius reading, multiply the Celsius reading (example: if it's 26 celsius) by 2 (=52) and **ADD** 30, or 82 degrees Fahrenheit. (The scientific formula is: $F = 9/5C + 32$) It's almost as accurate to use the quick and dirty way I've described above, and much easier to multiply by two than 9/5). Using 30 instead of 32 will approximate the difference.

Back to the climate: Of course, it does rain once in a while in the 'dry' season, but infrequently. The rain is just enough to maintain the wonderful greenery that surrounds Boquete.

How About the Humidity?

Boquete is almost 3,500 feet in altitude, and humidity hardly exists. The humidity is nothing like that in the coastal areas, and not even close to the muggy, cloying humidity of Washington, DC, St. Louis, or Miami.

How About Bugs?

Panama has established a reputation for harboring mosquitoes. And, it's well-deserved if you're on the coast or in the coastal jungles where mangrove swamps and still water offer a perfect breeding environment.

I stayed in *Boquete* for almost three months and saw very few mosquitoes. Certainly not enough to even consider them as a pest. A true testimonial to this is the Palo Alto Restaurant whose dining room is roofed, but otherwise completely open, and bugs are never a problem.

Guides

One of the best things to do when arriving in a new town is to look for a guide. If you don't speak Spanish, then find a guide who speaks English.

There are several excellent guides in Boquete. There are those who concentrate on touring the coffee farms and processing facilities. **Terry and Hans van der Vooren** are acknowledged experts in the world of coffee, and they also specialize in birding and nature tours (507-720-3852).

Boquete Mountain Cruisers is operated by **Patsy Underhill**. Ms Underhill has a wealth of knowledge and experience in the travel business. She has been a resident of Boquete for several years. (507) 720-4697 or 624-0350.

Richard Livingston is an American who offers his Guide Services, which are very complete, at very reasonable rates. (507) 636-9887

Check www.boquete.org for more guide services.

Boquete is world renowned for its coffee, perhaps the finest in the world. The valley is small, and the environment is ideal – rich, volcanic soil, cool weather, and coffee farmers who have worked for generations developing the finest *Arabic* trees possible. There are a number of processors in the area and tours of their facilities are also available. If you love coffee, you'll be enchanted with Boquete.

Birding Around *Boquete*

Birding is exciting in this small valley. The resplendent Quetzal is here, among hundreds of other species. The door was open to my room one day while I sat outside, enjoying the morning sun. A beautiful, small *"perrico"* flew in for a short visit. He was a gorgeous blue-green-yellow specimen. His visit was short, and he flew out as fast as he flew in. Maybe he determined I didn't have any bananas.

If you do go off into the jungle, don't do it without a guide. Some friends went on a day hike down the Quetzal Trail (about 8 hours). It had rained all day. When the group reached the bottom of the trail where their pick-up ride was supposed to be, the bridge had washed out.

The *Rio Caldera* was raging, and it was impossible to cross. Their guide went upstream a ways and found where local Indians had felled two large trees across a narrow part of the river. The entire group nervously scrambled across the tree falls, holding on for dear life, because if someone had fallen in the torrent, it would have meant serious injury or drowning.

All's well that ends well, but they had quite an adventure, and it was fortunate no one was hurt.

Living Costs - Boquete

Living costs are substantially lower than in the U.S.

Direct TV (satellite) is less than $50 month and includes many stations from the U.S.

- Telephones: Basic land lines are about $20.
- *A DSL* Internet connection is an additional $35.
- International calling (to the U.S.) with Dial-Pad runs $0.037 per minute.
- Cell phones are in wide use and service is excellent. (I bought one for $39 and used it for three months – phone cards ($10) are used to pay for the calls.
- Electricity: about $25 per month

From local markets:

Filet Mignon	$4.00 lb
Prime Ground Sirloin	$2.00 lb
92% Lean Ground Beef	$0.85 lb
Pork Tenderloin	$2.20 lb
Eggs XL - Brown	$0.55 doz
Fresh Bread (Bakery)	$0.35 loaf
Fresh Butter	$2.00 lb
Milk (Homo)	$0.90 qt
Local Coffee	$2.10 lb

I believe the best tasting tomatoes in the world are grown in *Boquete* - even better than the ones my grandfather raised in his home garden. The price at Romero's Mercado runs about eleven or twelve cents.

Prices may be lower at *Super Baru* in *David* and the selection is somewhat greater. *Price Smarts* also has good values, but like any Costco store, you must buy in larger quantities.

Fresh seafood and fish are comparably lower – the Pacific is only 22 miles from *Boquete*. Vegetables are inexpensive and wonderful – they are raised locally, and organic vegetables are abundant. Fresh Rainbow trout are plentiful here in the cool streams.

Micro Climates

Even though the valley is small, there are several micro-climates in and around *Boquete*. As you climb out of the valley and head to the north and west, you can find yourself in the cloud-forest within three miles. At some time during the day (more prevalent in early morning and late afternoon) you will encounter a very fine, floating mist. It is called *The Bajareque (Baha-raykay)*.

When water droplets are refracted in the sunlight, spectacular rainbows are formed, known as the *Arco Iris*. Sometimes, you will see multiple rainbows. It's quite a sight. But this light mist is also one of the climatic features that makes *Boquete* such a wonderful growing environment for vegetables - and particularly coffee. In Viet Nam, a similar phenomenon is known as "rain dust."

Places to Stay - *Boquete*

As in Panama City, we won't give a complete listing of
every hotel and hostel, but enough really good ones from
which you can start your selection process. If you are
visiting for a month or more, be sure to ask each hostelry if
they have long-term rates.

Also, if you are going to be here a while, look into the
availability of short-term house rentals.

Hotels - Full Service hotels:

Boquete Country Inn, Boquete Garden Inn, El Oasis Resort,
Hotel Fundadores, Isla Verde Inn, Los Establos, Palo Alto
Riverside Boutique, Panamonte Inn and Spa, The Coffee
Estate Inn, Valle Escondido Resort Hotel, and Villa Marita.

All of the above establishments are very good. I have
personally stayed at the three establishments listed that are
asterisked:

Hotel La Petite Mozart (507-720-3764) Three rooms.
$19/26; $35; and $45 for a suite. Turn left on *Volcancito*
Road, as you come into Boquete. If you pass the large IPAT
structure on the right, you've gone 50 yards too far. Turn
left on *Volcancito* about two miles. This is truly a petite and
charming hotel serving excellent meals and wine.

Located on 2 hectares of coffee farm, the view from her
breakfast terrace is lovely. The proprietress speaks Spanish,
English, and German.

*Boquete Garden Inn (formerly Las Cabanas de la Via Lactea) (507-720-2376) This charming complex is on a beautiful piece of property that backs up to the *Rio Caldera*. The 10 lodgings consist of five 2-story hexagonal buildings, strategically located in a garden-like setting.

Rooms are large and comfortable with kitchen facilities and large baths. About $75/plus tax for two, commensurately more for larger units and more people. Long-term rates available. I stayed here for two months, under the previous owners, and have never enjoyed more attentive hosts.

Hutchings   Boquete Garden Inn

Hotel Los Establos (507-720-2685) Owned by Sam Taliaferro, developer of *Valle Escondido.* The hotel is every bit as nice as his premier development. The hotel sits high on a slope in the Palo Alto area looking down on the Boquete valley across pasture land, coffee fincas, and the village of Boquete. Elegant rooms from $165 to suites $235.
*Hotel Panamonte (507-720-1327) At the north end of town just before the bridge crossing of the *Rio Caldera*. This is the *Grande Dama* of hotels in Boquete. Built in the 1920's, it has a lovely dining room, beautiful gardens and a comfortable bar and lounge – with fireplace. This hotel is quite special with a wonderful dining room and excellent service. Rooms about $75.

La Montana y el Valle – The Coffee Estate Inn (507-720-2211) Three luxurious bungalows with complete kitchens, living/dining room and separate bedroom. This is a working coffee farm with trails leading into the forest. No children under 9. Barry Robbins and Jane Walker, Canadian Expatriates, prepare wonderful meals for guests only. Coffee is roasted daily. A bungalow price of about $90 includes brief tours.

Boquete Restaurants

Dining in Boquete ranges from typical Panamanian food to basic pizza parlors to *hamburgesas* to elegance. The pizza parlors are generally along Avenida Central. Thankfully, the closest thing to "fast food" is the Java Juice restaurant for *hamburguesas and smoothies. (It's good.)*

Bistro, a restaurant near the village center, is popular with the gringo community. The food is good. The mushroom soup ($2 bowl) is terrific. They have a complete bar and a good wine selection. Dinners from $8 - 16.

Panamonte is probably one of the nicer restaurants in all of *Chiriqui* province. Built in the 1920's, the *Panamonte* exemplifies Panama. The bar is very comfortable, and the food is very, very good. Dinners from $7. White tablecloths, silver service, and flowers are on every table. The ceiling fans add to the tropical environment. The hotel has lovely gardens and a comfortable lounge with fireplace. Even in Panama, a fireplace is great on rainy afternoon.

Palo Alto is a unique, new restaurant that serves excellent food and has a lovely selection of wines. The restaurant is located just a couple of kilometers from central Boquete on Palo Alto Road. It's dining room is open to the Rio Caldera - with the wildness of the jungle just on the opposite river bank. Try their *Beef Brochette* Dinners from $7

Restaurante La Huaca on Avenida Central. A nicely restored home serving excellent Italian food from really good pizzas to pasta. Full bar and excellent wines. A popular rendezvous for locals and expatriates. Dinners from $6

The Santa Fe just across the bridge near the center of town – opposite the flower gardens. Nice menu, but famous for its hamburgers. They're huge and delicious. The Santa Fe is especially popular with its "Happy Hour" on Friday afternoons.
Other restaurants: Amigos, Cocina Rica, Machu Pichu, Palace Argentine, Grill at Valle Escondido, Tango Sur, and El Café. At the rate Boquete is growing, this list is probably incomplete. Smaller eateries, such as *Tipicos*, Pizza Parlors, and *Hamberguesas* are plentiful.

Stores & Shopping – Groceries *(Mercados)*

There are two good markets: **Romero's** and **The Mandarin.** Each has a broad selection of products, both local and American. Each has quality dairy products, produce, and a good butcher shop. The Mandarin has other items, i.e., clothing, etc. Romero's has expanded as well by adding a deli and bakery.

General Merchandise

There are many other stores in Boquete ranging from Auto Supply, Computers, Department Stores, Pharmacies, Gift Shops, Hardware Stores, etc. There are three Bakeries in town, none of which is great.

Medical Care

Boquete and its citizens are fortunate to have two imminently qualified physician/surgeons in practice. Both speak excellent English. Clinics are open Monday through Saturday. They even make house calls! David is only 22 miles away with major medical facilities and hospitals. Most people seem to travel to David for dental care.

Spanish Lessons

I know of two excellent instructors in Boquete. **Rebecca Hill** owns the *Oasis Internet Café* and also instructs small groups. Her rates are reasonable ($6 per lesson) and everyone seems to like the sessions and profess to learn a lot.

Marie Boyd was a teacher in the Panama City school system for many years. She is married to Bob Boyd who grew up in the Canal Zone. Marie has instructed students of many corporate accounts, i.e., Sony, etc. She charges $6/hour and will come to your home for private lessons. Call 720-2539; or cell 606-3554 in Boquete.

Expatriate Community

Boquete has a large, and growing, community of expatriates from the world over. There are many from the United States and Canada, but also families from all of the Americas and Western Europe. The community is socially active, and holds regular meetings pertaining to living in *Boquete*. Everyone is welcome. *At the time of this writing, meetings were held weekly and were well-attended.*

Hutchings   Expat Gathering

Socially, the expatriates hold a monthly potluck – generally on a Sunday afternoon. I attended two events and had a wonderful experience each time. Incidentally, they were well-attended by several Panamanian residents. These afternoons were thoroughly enjoyable.

The "expats" come from all walks of life and professions, and from many countries. The Americans tend to be retirees. The Canadians and Europeans are somewhat younger and tend to be investors or simply seeking second homes.

Most have a common desire, a thread linking them together:

They all wanted to live in a place that had a wonderful climate and where they could live within their means.

After chatting with many, I invariably asked:

"Do you miss the States?" The answers were common: **"We're able to get back easily, and Panama is wonderful."**

Dan & Jeannie Miller

One afternoon Dan Miller and I were having a beer in the *Panamonte Hotel* in Boquete. His wife, Jeannie, had just flown back to the States on a family emergency.

"This is a great place to live. If we get homesick, which so far we haven't, Miami is only 2-1/2 hours from Panama City. We're no farther from home than if we were in Chicago."

The Panamonte is one of those places that seem to put us back a few years. A light rain had begun to fall outside our window. We were in the lounge area sitting in overstuffed chairs, and one of the staff was lighting a fire in the fireplace.

I asked Dan if he'd mind talking a little about Boquete. He said he'd be happy to answer a few questions.

"Dan, what was your career in the States?"

"In our working days, I was a private attorney in Washington, DC specializing in communications. I worked with the FCC getting licenses, etc. for my clients.

Jeannie had been a flight attendant for a major international airline."

"Did you retire?"

"We retired and sailed the Caribbean in our 46-foot sloop. We'd been on the boat for seven years, and came to Boquete almost by accident. *Bocas del Toro* in Panama was one of our stops in the Caribbean. The weather was hot, wet, and humid. Some friends suggested we take a break and go to Boquete. It's not very far from *Bocas,* distance-wise, but it's a world apart climatically and socially. We liked it so much, we bought a building lot."

"Was that on a whim?"

"Jeannie and I had talked a lot about making a life-style change. We love the boat, but seven years non-stop and it was time for something else. We hadn't come to Boquete for that reason. We just wanted to get away from the heat and the bugs. As it turned out, we fell in love with this place."

"That was a big decision."

"In some ways, yes. But we still own the boat and can always go back to the sailing life."

"What do you like best about Panama?"

"Lots. The country is beautiful, and you have the diversity of a first world city down in Panama, miles of beaches, and a very lush countryside. The cost of living is low, and we don't have to worry about currency devaluations, etc. The climate is great, the Panamanians are nice people, and the expatriate community here is special."

"Do you worry about medical care?"

"I've had some wonderful experiences regarding medical care in Panama. My doctor speaks excellent English, and that eases the problem of communication. Hospitals are only 23 miles away in David, and if I really felt I needed the comfort of a U.S. doctor, Miami is just a 2-1/2 hour flight from Panama City."

"What kind of a visa do you have?"

"We don't. Just the tourist card, but we're going to get a *Pensionado* visa this year."

"You're happy here?"

"You bet. I'm doing more and more writing. Jeannie has her painting, and we have three horses. They're Colombian *Paso Finos*. They are our passion. And we hope to start construction on our house in the next 60 days."

"So you're renting?"

"Yes. We have a small 2-bedroom house, furnished, and the water and gardener are included in the rent. $295 per month."

"How about electricity?"

"Power runs about $25, and the phone about $35 – we make a lot of calls to the states. We also have ADSL for our internet connection. Its another $35."

Dan and I decided to have dinner and we moved to the main dining room. The *Panamonte* really was 'old Panama.' The paneled walls were painted white, large fans whirled slowly overhead, the tables were covered in white linen, and the place settings were silver. Flowers were everywhere. On the tables and in large pots strategically placed around the room.

Dan decided on the fresh *trout almandine*, and I had some beautiful large shrimp with a sweet pepper stuffing. For dessert, I had flan and we both had coffee. With the *jubilato* (senior citizen) discount, the grand total for the two dinners was $20.45. This place has a way of growing on you.

Jim Horton & Marni

Another couple I came to know were Canadians from Peterborough, Ontario.

I asked them how they had decided on Panama in general, and specifically, *Boquete*.

"The winters in Canada can be darned cold, to say the least, and we wanted a little time in the sun. We spent most of the first part of December sunning themselves on the Caribbean side of Panama in *Bocas del Toro*, living on a rented boat. That proved a bit uncomfortable as we had to close all the hatches every night to keep the bugs out. The other problem was: there was more rain in *Bocas* than sunshine. We left Canada to enjoy the sun."

To take a break from Bocas, they visited Boquete and really enjoyed their visit. They enjoyed it so much, they bought some property (three building lots) just outside of Boquete, and hired an architect to proceed with their building concept. They knew they wanted a guest cottage, so the plan was to build the small, guesthouse first and live in it while the main house was being built. After moving to the main house, they planned to rent the guesthouse.

Under Panamanian Law No. 8, their rental guest-house qualifies as a tourism investment and means they will receive a 20-year exemption on real estate taxes for all assets of their enterprise. That includes the main house.

The guesthouse is small (about 600 square feet) but very functional. And, while there is no need for heating or air-conditioning in Boquete, they did include a fireplace. On rainy nights it will be pleasant to have a fire.

Much of the furniture will be teak (Panamanian Teak). They visited one of the custom furniture builders in Boquete and purchased the following items: four bar stools for their kitchen counter; a six-foot dining table with four chairs – two with arms; a queen-size bed; and two chaise lounges for their verandah. All items hand-made from beautiful teak. Their grand total price: $800. The design of the guest house is special. A local architect drew the plans and they contracted with a Panamanian builder.

I asked Marni about the kitchen. She bought a 4-burner gas range, a washing machine, coffee maker, toaster, 21-inch TV, and a large refrigerator-freezer. Total price: a little less than $1,000. All were new, name-brand items.

Marni & Friend

Floors, of course, are glazed tile, and the ceilings rise to 15-feet which makes the small house seem much larger. There's a lot of glass, and French doors open from the bedroom to the house-length verandah, which is all under roof.

Jim talked about their investment. He confided that the building lot, the guesthouse, the main house, and furnishings would total about $100,000. They will probably sell two of the lots over a period of time, and if property continues to appreciate in Boquete, part of their investment will be recouped.

Jim and Marni may speed up their timetable a bit. They were going to finish the guesthouse, come back next winter and build the main house. They may start the main house this spring. That means going back to Canada and probably selling their lakefront home.

I asked them what they liked best about Boquete.

Finally, Jim said, **"Maybe the question should be, what don't we like about Boquete? The weather is great, prices are good, scenery is spectacular, the Panamanians are lovely people. Maybe they could fix some of the sidewalks.**

And you have to have a little patience with the bureaucracy – like it took us most of two days to get our tourist cards renewed in David at the immigration office."

Marni smiled. "I'll second all those things. On Wednesdays we sometimes take the bus to David, shop a while, have one of those good pizzas near the *Hotel Gran Nacional,* take in a movie at $1.80 each, and hop the bus back to Boquete. The whole day, including bus trips, pizza and the movie costs us about $10. And, we've had a lot of fun."

Jim chimed in. "And the expatriate social stuff, like the potluck yesterday afternoon at the Santa Lucia Country Club. There were over 80 people there. The food was great, everyone had a good time, and we met some new people as well as renewing some old friendships. One of the neat things is that many of our Panamanian neighbors attend."

I think Jim is right. What's not to like about Boquete?

Kirt Barker - Arborist

Another interesting expat is Kirt Barker. Kirt's father, a professor at Yale, spent several years in Europe as a teaching professor. As a youth, Kirt attended school in Germany and picked up the expatriate life-style at an early age. He has lived in Central America for more than twelve years, and in Panama the last four. Kirt is an arborist, and is not retired. He received his M.S. degree in Forestry from Yale University, and after his collegiate studies, Kirt did a stint with Sailing Magazine.

He has worked in Central America for the World Bank and the U.S. State Department. Obviously, he has a great interest in re-forestation projects and now works closely with the Panamanian government to that end.

Panama, like many countries, was over-logged. Many exotic hardwoods of the tropical forests were ravaged by opportunistic loggers. Teak, coco-bolo rosewood, mahogany, and other rare trees became virtually non-existent. Not only in Central America, but in the tropical forests of the Amazon and Asia. The worldwide thirst for wood is almost inexhaustible.

When Kirt heard about Panama's re-forestation program he knew this was the place he wanted to be. The country was serious about the preservation of existing forests and the implementation of a new program to continuously replenish and grow new stands of exotic timber.

He immigrated to Panama, bought property and began a new career raising teak and coco-bolo trees. Kirt also has a small *finca* and is in the process of growing vegetables. He's found a new crop in *jalapena* peppers, and is searching for a variety of *habanera* peppers for cultivation.

I found Kirt to be a fascinating young man. He's doing what he wants to do, doing what he believes in, and is doing it in the place he loves most. Panama.

Many other of the local "expats" in Boquete were friendly, enjoyable people. Most have friends and family in their home countries. I asked each of them about their concerns of living so far away. I asked about their children and grandchildren back in the states. Their answers were unanimous.

"No real problem. We can get back to the west coast almost as fast as if we lived on the east coast. And, they can visit us. They'll love Boquete."

Summary

The journey to Panama surprised me.

Panama is a place where the cost of living was low enough to accommodate a retiree's benefits.

Panama's climate was close to being perfect.

Panama offers outstanding medical care and insurance.

Panama's people are friendly, hardworking, and of good humor.

Panama's government is willing to grant substantial financial incentives to retirees.

Panama is within easy travel distance from the States.

Panama has a safe environment.

Panama has many expatriates from all over the world.

Panama's modern cities are first world in accommodations and infrastructure.

Panama's investment opportunities are outstanding.

Panama is a great place to live.

William Hutchings

Brief History of Panama

To better understand the *Republica de Panama*, a little history is in order.

Archeologists believe the first inhabitants of Panama arrived between 10,000 and 12,000 years ago. These people were descendents of the migrants who journeyed from Asia across the land bridge of the Bering Sea and migrated southward.

The Spaniards arrived in1501. A Spanish explorer, Rodrigo de Bastidas was the first European to reach the Isthmus. In 1508, Ferdinand V, King of Spain, granted settlement rights to Spanish explorer Diego de Nicuesa. Colonies were established on the Caribbean coast, but the importance of the Isthmus began to be realized when Vasquez Nunez de Balboa led an expedition across the Isthmus to the Pacific coast. He was the first European to see the Pacific Ocean from the Americas, and it became apparent that a relatively short land journey could connect the Atlantic and Pacific oceans.

Shortly after Balboa's expedition, in 1519, Panama City was founded on the Pacific side of the Isthmus. Panama became a market center and crossroads for Spain's conquest of the Americas. Gold and silver (plundered from the Incas) were transported from Peru to Panama City, then carried across the Isthmus to waiting ships in the Caribbean harbor of Portobelo.

These riches made both Panama City and Portobelo targets for pirates. The pirates of the Caribbean, epitomized by Henry Morgan and Sir Francis Drake, preyed on cities and caravel's alike. Panama City, Cartagena, and Portobelo were targets for plunder as well as centers for the slave trade.

The Viceroy of Peru governed Panama until 1718 when The Viceroy of New Granada was created by Spain. This territory included present-day Colombia, Ecuador, Venezuela and the Isthmus.

In the mid-1800's, Spain's empire in South America began to crumble. The fever of independence swept through the colonies. In 1821, Panama declared its independence from Spain and decided to become part of the new Republic of Colombia.

For eighty-two years, Panama was treated like a stepchild. Panamanians began making their own laws, and grew distant from Colombia. They also grew apart culturally from the rest of Colombia, becoming less religious, politically more liberal, and more open to the outside influence of Britain and the United States.

Britain and the United States realized the importance of Panama lay in its narrow land mass, and began to compete for the rights to control the transit of goods and people from the Atlantic to the Pacific. The sea route around Cape Horn was long and treacherous. The possibility of a canal was born, and the preferred route was either Nicaragua or the Isthmus.

American businessmen took the lead when they financed and constructed a railroad across the Isthmus, completed in 1855. After the discovery of gold in California, transportation of goods and people flourished, and for a while the Panama Railroad was the most profitable in the world. Businesses to serve travelers boomed on both sides of the Isthmus.

In the late 1870's, French diplomat Ferdinand de Lesseps, who had built the Suez canal in Egypt, called a conference in Paris to implement a sea level design and raise money to build a canal across Panama. Work started in 1882, but the project was beset by many problems. Tropical disease, equipment delays, financial problems, and poor planning forced the project into bankruptcy.

In 1902, Teddy Roosevelt and the Congress authorized buying and rehabilitating the French route. The United States negotiated a treaty with Colombia for construction rights, but the Colombian senate refused to ratify it. Rebellions by locals in Panama against Colombian rule and violence occurred frequently. The increase in the number of U.S. citizens and businesses in the area fanned the flames.

The U.S. sent its Marines to Panama to preserve law and order, to protect the lives and property of American citizens and businesses, and to repel Colombia's military efforts to prevent Panama's independence. While still a province of Colombia, Panama was on its way to becoming a U.S. protectorate. It declared its independence on November 3, 1903.

Within two weeks, a treaty was signed giving the U.S. construction rights to build the canal. The terms of the treaty gave the U.S. a perpetual lease for a section ten miles wide, stretching from the Atlantic to the Pacific. Within this zone, the U.S. could exercise complete control, including the canal's operation and military occupation. The canal was completed in 1914.

Panama had limited resources. For years, its biggest asset was the income derived from the lease, but roads, hospitals, utilities, and schools were still built by Panama. The Republic was dependent on the canal-zone for water, jobs, imports, transportation, and military security.

Resentment of U.S. domination began to grow. Relations with the U.S. deteriorated in the 1950's, and remained strained for thirty years.

In 1977, President Jimmy Carter negotiated a new treaty with Panama that provided the canal be turned over to the Republic on December 31, 1999. The treaty allowed the U.S. to maintain a military presence, but more of the canal income would accrue to Panama during the years between 1977 and 2000. On the turn-over date, the U.S. relinquished all rights to the canal and withdrew its military.

In 1983, Manuel Noriega, former head of Panama's intelligence service, became head of the National Guard and assumed power. Noriega did not hold political office, but as commander of the military and the police, he controlled the government. Noriega used the military to imprison, torture, and murder opponents and those who disagreed with his policies. At one time, Noriega had been an informant of the CIA, but drifted into major affiliations with the drug cartels. In the late 1980's, the U.S. withdrew its support of the government.

In 1988, Noriega was indicted by a U.S. court on drug charges. He fomented riots and street demonstrations against the U.S., removed a duly elected President of Panama and nullified the election results. Tensions rose between Noriega's armed forces and the U.S. military. The U.S. invaded Panama on December 20, 1989 with the stated goals of arresting Noriega to face drug charges, restoring democracy, and protecting American lives and business interests.

William Hutchings

The invasion was controversial. It violated international law, yet it was welcomed by the majority of Panama's citizenry as the only way to rid itself of Noriega and his brutal, corrupt regime. He is now in prison, and if he ever gets out, he is wanted by the French Government.

In 1994, Perez Balladares was elected President. He instituted wide economic reform, reduced the size of government, and initiated programs to attract foreign investment. The Panama Canal Authority was formed to take over the duties of managing the canal in 2000. The U.S. and the Panamanian government cooperated fully to make the transition smooth and trouble-free.

Panama assumed control of the canal, military bases, and adjacent facilities on December 31, 1999. For the first time since the 16th century, Panama had assumed control of all of its territory, and relations with the U.S. blossomed. The resentment of America being a political and military occupier of their country has dissolved into one of welcome and friendship.

Frequently Asked Questions

Q. Can we bring our pets to Panama?
A. Yes. Check with a Panamanian attorney who will help with forms etc. Cost will be about $140. per animal.

Q. What's the best way to ship our household goods?
A. Containers – 20 or 40 foot, depending on the amount of goods. The cost will be $3,000 to $4,000 – not including packing. The best advice is to sell things before you leave.

Q. Do I have to pay duty on household goods?
A. Not if the goods are "used."

Q. Should I bring a car?
A. Shipping a car can be difficult. Duties are about eight percent unless you've obtained a *Pensionado Visa.* Some people include their car in the same container as their household goods. Ask your forwarder about 'roll on, roll off' for a car.

Q. Is it necessary to get shots?
A. No. Shots are not required to visit Panama. However, there is no 'downside' to get the big three: Typhoid, Hepatitis, and Tetanus. Yellow fever is not a problem unless you travel to uninhabited parts of the jungle.

Q. Are credit cards readily accepted?
A. Visa, MasterCard and American Express are generally accepted everywhere. Travelers Checks are something of a problem. Your bank ATM or debit card is a necessity.

Q. Do I need a Visa to visit?
A. No. Your only requirements are a passport and Tourist Card. The Tourist card ($5) is available from the airline or upon arrival in Panama. You can't get a visa other than in Panama.

Q. How about currency exchange?
A. The only paper currency in use is the U.S. dollar. The Panamanian currency is officially the 'Balboa' but it has been pegged at the U.S. dollar since 1903.

Q. Climate?

A. Panama is tropical. The year round daytime temperature in the coastal areas will average 80-90F. In the highlands, 70-75F, but at night, you'll need a sweater.

Q. Can foreigners own property?
A. Yes. They have the same property rights as citizens.

Q. Do I have to speak Spanish?
A. The literacy rate in Panama is 97%. English is a required subject in schools. It is estimated 25% of the population now speaks English. However, buy a Spanish Lesson CD before you visit, and take lessons after you arrive.

Panama Embassies and Consulates

If Panama requires you to have a visa for visiting, they can be obtained from an Embassy or Consulate. This does not apply to visas for residency, such as the *Pensionado Visa*. Residency visas can only be obtained in Panama.

At the time of this writing, the only countries which Panama requires a passport and a visa were Chad, Ecuador, Egypt, the Philippines, Peru, the Dominican Republic, and Thailand.

Visitors from the following countries need a passport and a tourist card: Antigua, Australia, Bahamas, Belize, Bermuda, Bolivia, Brazil, Canada, Chile, China, Colombia, Denmark, Granada, Greece, Guyana, Iceland, Ireland, Jamaica, Japan, Malta, Mexico, Monaco, the Netherlands, New Zealand, South Korea, Taiwan, Tobago, Trinidad, The USA, and Venezuela.
Visitors from the following countries need only a passport: Argentina, Austria, Belgium, Costa Rica, El Salvador,

England, Finland, France, Germany, Guatemala, Honduras, Hungary, Israel, Italy, Luxembourg, Paraguay, Poland, Northern Ireland, Scotland, Singapore, Switzerland, Uruguay, and Wales.

If the name of your country does not appear, call the Panamanian Embassy or Consulate nearest you or (507) 227-1448.

Panamanian embassies are maintained in the following countries: Brazil, Canada, Colombia, Costa Rica, El Salvador, France, Germany, Guatemala, Honduras, Israel, Italy, Japan, Mexico, Nicaragua, Singapore, Spain, UK, and the USA. Australian citizens should contact the Panamanian embassy in Singapore.

Some countries have Panamanian consulates. In the US, there are consulate offices in Chicago, Honolulu, Houston, Los Angeles (Anaheim, CA), Miami, New York, New Orleans, Philadelphia, San Diego, and San Francisco. The embassy is in Washington, DC.

Helpful Web Sites

www.panamainfo.com	www.panamadera.com
www.cieloparaiso.com	www.internationalliving.com
www.escapeartists.com	www.vistamarresort.com
www.altosdelmaria.com	www.boquets.org

William Hutchings

Index

About the Author

Bill Hutchings started his writing career as a technical writer, free-lancing for NEC, Texas Instruments, National Microware, Venture Software, Business Automation, and others in the high tech field.

After several years of writing about data base management applications, he wrote his first travel book, *Radio on the Road ...the Traveler's Companion.* This book has enjoyed eight editions and thirteen printings. *He also wrote The National Public Radio Directory,* which was published in three editions.

In 2007 he wrote *Promote Your Book in the Media,* a book and software program designed to help authors publicize their books.

Bill spent several months in Mexico doing research for a novel, *Treasure,* before making his trip to Panama. He fell in love with the people and life on the Isthmus. A second novel, *Counterfeit Affair,* is scheduled for completion in the fall of 2007

.

THE SUGAR
ADDICT'S
TOTAL
RECOVERY
PROGRAMME

By Kathleen DesMaisons, PhD

Potatoes Not Prozac
The Sugar Addict's Total Recovery Programme

THE SUGAR
ADDICT'S
Total
RECOVERY
PROGRAMME

Kathleen DesMaisons, PhD

SIMON & SCHUSTER

A VIACOM COMPANY

The recommendations in this book are not intended to replace or conflict with advice given to you by your physician or other health care professional. If you have a pre-existing medical or psychological condition, or are currently taking medication, consult with your physician before adopting the suggestions in this book. Following these dietary suggestions may impact certain types of medications. Any change in your dosage should be made only in co-operation with your prescribing physician.

First published in Great Britain by Simon & Schuster UK Ltd, 2002
A Viacom Company

1 3 5 7 9 10 8 6 4 2

Simon & Schuster UK Ltd
Africa House
64–78 Kingsway
London WC2B 6AH
www.simonsays.co.uk

Simon & Schuster Australia
Sydney

A CIP catalogue record for this book is available from the British Library

ISBN 0-7432-0673-8

Printed and bound in Great Britain by
The Bath Press, Bath

Mother, thank you for your continuing love. Your guidance makes it work.

Contents

Introduction

Are you a sugar addict? Have you ever wondered why you love sweet foods so much? Does chocolate run your life more than you want to admit? Do you joke about being a 'sweet freak'? Does it ever scare you to feel so compulsive about wanting sugar? The questions listed below will help you understand what it means to be a sugar addict. When I say 'sweet foods', I mean coffee or tea with sugar, biscuits, cakes, sweets, cereal, fizzy drinks, ice cream, sweet rolls, energy bars, chocolate or any food that you know is sweetened with sugar, honey or artificial sweeteners.

❏ **Have you ever tried to cut down or control your use of sweet foods?**

Have you ever picked a certain day and said, 'Starting Monday I am not going to have chocolate'?

Have you ever been secretly delighted when you are out to dinner and your friends order dessert and urge you to join them?

3

❑ **Are you using more sweet foods than ever before?**
Have you ever realized that you used to get one chocolate bar, but now you buy three at a time?

Do you find yourself stopping at the convenience store for bread and milk *and* M&M's?

❑ **If you don't have your regular 'dose' of sugar, do you get irritable and cranky?**
Have you ever been in a meeting at work and found yourself unable to pay attention to the agenda because you are thinking about your afternoon cappuccino?

Have you ever been frantic when you arrive at your friends' house for the weekend to discover they have *no* sweets in the house and you have no car?

❑ **Have you ever got upset when someone ate your special food?**
Have you ever felt silent rage and panic when you have gone to the refrigerator for the last of the cream cake and discovered someone had eaten it?

Have you ever kept a stash of chocolate in your underwear drawer and been horrified when your daughter found it?

Are you unable to keep a stash anywhere because you eat it first?

❑ **Have you ever lied about how much sweet food you eat?**
Have you ever told your kids you don't know where the last box of After Eight Mints is when you know you ate them and put the box in the bottom of the dustbin?

Have you ever said, 'I don't know what happened to it' when you know perfectly well you ate it?

❑ **Have you ever gone out of your way to get something sweet?**
Have you ever gone far out of your way to stop at the coffee shop for your favourite drink and sweet roll?

Have you ever chosen a restaurant based on the quality of its desserts even though it's an hour's drive away?

❑ **Have you ever binged on sweet or white flour foods?**

Have you ever told yourself you were going to have just a bite of ice cream and ended up eating the whole tub all by yourself?

Have you ever got a special cake for a party at the weekend and ended up eating the whole thing yourself?

❑ **Have you ever felt you had a sugar hangover?**

Have you ever crawled through the morning with a headache and crankiness that is immediately relieved when you have something sweet?

❑ **Is it impossible to 'just say no' to sweet foods?**

Do you feel inordinately relieved when you finally get your sweets?

Have you ever made a cover noise like coughing, singing or humming while you opened the cabinet door to get your sweets?

❑ **Is sugar controlling your life?**

Are you ashamed and fearful that you will always be out of control? Would you be horrified to have your friends know how you answered any of these questions?

If you answered yes to two or more of the questions in bold-face, you are probably a sugar addict. You are reading the right book. If you answered yes to all the questions, you have come home to the right place! While you may not let yourself admit openly to these secrets, you know they are true. You know that you have hidden sweet wrappers under the rubbish so no one would know you had eaten another. You know you have sneaked biscuits before the family came home so they wouldn't know who ate the last ones. You know you have lied, cheated and stolen for your 'drug' of choice. These are signs of addiction, but until now you may not have let yourself think about applying these words to your relationship to sugar.

I understand how powerful these feelings are. I would have answered yes to every question in my sugar days. I am a sugar addict like you, but now I am in recovery from my sugar addiction. This recovery has saved my life, and I want to share with you the solutions I have found. I have deep compassion for what you are dealing with and want to bring you the healing and radiance that my recovery has given me.

My father was an alcoholic and died of alcoholism when I was only sixteen. I grew up with all the classic symptoms of being the child of an alcoholic. I had to stop drinking in my early twenties, but I still had a powerful interest in sweet things. I needed them. I planned my life around them. I kept a supply, got upset if someone ate my goods, and knew the best places to get my 'drugs'. Even though until recently other people discounted the idea of a sugar addiction similar to an addiction to alcohol or drugs, I knew better. I knew my addiction to sweets was running my life.

At first, though, I thought the primary problem was my weight. I sincerely believed that if I just lost weight, everything would be okay. But over time, I came to see that the story of my weight was far bigger than just too many kilograms – was part of the story of my sugar addiction. I didn't realize it, but my sugar addiction was associated with my mood swings, depression, fatigue, fuzzy thinking, PMS, impulsivity and unpredictable temper. I had no idea that all these things could be connected to what I was eating. After all, I was just eating sugar, not using heroin or alcohol.

I finally came to understand my own addiction through my professional work with addicts and alcoholics. I moved to California in the mid-eighties after an active career in public health, looking for a way to continue my long-standing commitment to helping others. Eventually I started and became director of an alcohol and drug treatment centre, not then understanding how that would shape my own need for recovery.

Unaware that addiction treatment historically had at best a 25 per cent success rate, I almost immediately became concerned about the lack of success we were having in our treatments. Six months after we began the centre, I started looking for variables that might improve treatment outcomes. Initially, I looked at the issues that have traditionally been thought of as important in treatment: length of time in treatment; skill of the counsellor; group versus individual work; twelve-step programme involvement. None of them seemed to have any particular impact on our clients' ability to stay clean and sober.

During this time, I had changed my own eating because I wanted to lose weight. I had started on a diet that was very similar to what you will be reading about in this book: no sugar, moderate amounts of complex carbs, more protein and regular meals. The results stunned me. Not only did I lose weight, I felt incredible. My cravings went away. My mood swings disappeared. I felt focused and clear and excited about life. I stopped feeling compulsive about food and sweets. These changes convinced me that something more than weight loss was going on. I had dieted before but had never felt like this. *This* felt like recovery. As a result, I got really interested in the relationship between diet and addiction.

I started to ask my clients about their diets as well as their patterns of drinking and using. While my clients were drinking or using, few of them cared about sweets. As soon as they got sober, however, their interest in sweets and refined carbohydrates like bread and pasta skyrocketed. The more they had, the more they wanted. Although many were sober, they still acted addictively towards their sweets. Their behaviour resembled their old drinking patterns. They continued to be moody, impulsive and irritable even though they had stopped drinking. Historically, these behaviours have been attributed to detoxification from alcohol or a state called a dry drunk. Because of my own experience with diet and mood, however, I suspected they

stemmed from something biochemical. My clients were eating in the same way I had been eating. We had the same moods and emotional symptoms. Maybe, I thought, we shared a similar brain chemistry. Maybe we all were sugar addicts.

During this same time, seemingly by chance, I came across an article in an obscure journal that made a connection between alcoholism and sugar. The article suggested that there could be a correlation between diet and the ability to achieve sobriety. Because of my own personal history and what I was seeing with my clients, I intuitively felt that this connection had to be true and thought it might even be the link I sought for improving treatment outcomes in our clinic.

I followed my intuition. Drawing on my own experience, I developed a food plan for my clinic clients. When they followed the food plan, the number of people getting and staying clean and sober increased dramatically. During this same period I also maintained a private practice helping people make life changes. While the clients at the clinic were predominantly alcoholic men, my private clients were mostly overweight women who were depressed, dealing with mood swings, chaos in their lives and low self-esteem. I started to ask them, too, about what they ate, which surprised them. After all, they were there to talk about what they felt, not about what they ate. I was floored to discover that their diets were very similar to the way I had been eating before I changed my diet. They skipped meals, ate huge amounts of carbohydrates, and basically lived on sugar. But they were willing to try almost anything to get better, even if they had to change what they ate and when they ate it.

As my private clients began to use the same food plan I had developed for the clinic, they experienced the same miraculous turnaround my clinic clients and I had: their depression lifted; they became clear, focused and purposeful; and many lost weight. All were excited by the changes they experienced with what we called 'doing the food'.

I was so impressed by what I saw happening with my clients that I wanted to understand better why this plan was working so well. I decided to go back to school for a PhD. I gave up my full-time job, sold my house and moved into a one-room apartment. I wasn't at all perturbed by the fact that I was fifty years old and committing to a whole new career path. I knew I was on to something and I was willing to put my money where my mouth was.

I put together a doctoral committee of experts in the fields of nutrition, public health, alcoholism and neurochemistry, and together, we mapped out what I needed to learn.

As I read more and more scientific literature, I learned that sugar evokes a brain chemical called beta-endorphin – the very same chemical evoked by alcohol or heroin. Sugar could in fact cause the same chemical and mood effects in the body, albeit on a less intense level, as some of the most addictive substances in the world!

At the time I was doing my research, the scientific connection between sugar and addiction couldn't be found all in one place under 'sugar addiction'. There were bits and pieces and clues in the literature about alcoholism, heroin, depression, eating disorders and nutrition. So I collected pieces of the puzzle from each field. I started reading information on the treatment of heroin addiction with a different eye. Heroin is one of a class of drugs called opioids that affect the beta-endorphin system within the brain. Substituting the word 'sugar' for 'opioids' led to some powerful insights. I read this line in my substance abuse text: 'post-addict volunteers usually experience an elevation of mood and an increased sense of self-esteem' when they take opioids.

The idea that opioids and opioid-like substances such as sugar could affect self-esteem had an electrifying effect on me. I remember reading that line and feeling the hair on the back of my neck stand up. If sugar created an opioid effect, it would

enhance self-esteem. No wonder my clients and I were drawn to it! I felt as if I was building a case for a theory of sugar addiction. Sugar addiction could be a real, physiological state and changing the diet could be a way to treat it.

I also wanted to know why sugar addiction developed in certain people. I developed a theory that a condition I called sugar sensitivity could explain why certain people were more vulnerable to the effects of alcohol and drugs than others. My doctoral study focused on the relationship between sugar sensitivity and alcoholism. Eventually, I expanded the theory to include sugar addiction as a symptom of sugar sensitivity. My doctoral work and my clinical practice demonstrate that diet can be an effective treatment for alcoholism and drug addiction as well as sugar addiction. Incorporating this food plan into our treatment programme had had a huge impact on the success of the programme: 90 per cent of the alcoholic clients who used the food protocol graduated from the treatment programme, and 92 per cent of the graduates were still clean and sober many months afterwards.

After earning the first doctoral degree ever awarded in the new field of addictive nutrition, I wrote *Potatoes Not Prozac*, which introduces the theory of sugar sensitivity and explains how food can be used to change brain and body chemistry – food in addition to medication or as an alternative to medication. The book identifies all the physical and emotional symptoms that my clients and I experienced – depression, mood swings, compulsivity and weight issues – as evidence of sugar sensitivity. Friends told friends about sugar sensitivity and the book became a bestseller.

To provide a supportive community for *Potatoes Not Prozac* readers I designed a website (www.radiantrecovery.com). In the past two years, it has had more than 5 million hits – 150,000 unique visitors – and a forum with more than 10,000 pages of letters. People from all over the world continue to tell me that

the ideas in the book have changed their lives. They are thrilled with the information found on the website, but they want more – more information on what sugar addiction is and how it works; more insight on how sugar addiction is connected to sugar sensitivity; and more details on how to move out of sugar addiction. To expand our healing story to an audience of readers as well as Web users, I've written this new book.

The Sugar Addict's Total Recovery Programme gives you more of what my readers have asked for . . . more of the science of sugar sensitivity introduced in *Potatoes Not Prozac* and a road map for working with your own body chemistry. This book gives you a well-tuned version of the food plan I first created for my clients and myself more than ten years ago.

Sugar addiction is a symptom of a deeper problem called sugar sensitivity. Sugar sensitivity is an inherited condition that makes you more reactive to imbalances in your body and brain chemistry that exist even prior to eating sweets. These imbalances create cravings, mood swings, erratic energy and sugar addiction. This book will help you understand how sugar sensitivity can set up sugar addiction and make you feel crazy. It will help you:

- Understand *why* you feel the way you do
- Learn how you can fix the problem yourself – naturally
- Guide you through the process of making successful changes
- Maintain the changes you make over the long haul

The goal of this programme is not to be perfect or to go off sugar for the rest of your life. The goal is to become aware of what, how and when you eat *every day* and to be in relationship to your body. Going off sugar and white things is not like going off alcohol, drugs or nicotine. While you may pick a day to be sugar-free and go through a period of detoxing from

sugar, most likely you will not be sugar-free for the rest of your life. You will simply get better and better at the process over time. Your recovery will become a way of living as you move closer to the radiant health you deserve.

The Sugar Addict's Total Recovery Programme is simple, fun, to the point and easy to follow. It's a well-tested path to success. You will hear the voices of people just like you who have recovered from their sugar addiction. Their tips, encouragement and great-tasting recipes will help make the healing programme work for you. Concrete, specific recommendations will keep you heading in the right direction. You are not alone and you *can* heal your sugar addiction.

1

Why You Are Different

If you are a sugar addict, you can't 'just say no' to ice cream, sweets, fizzy drinks, chocolate or biscuits. If you are a sugar addict, people have been saying 'watch your calories', 'exercise more', 'clean up your room', 'stop snacking on biscuits', 'stop drinking', 'stop smoking', or 'why don't you just _____' to you nearly all your life. You fill in the blank. The message is the same, although the content may vary.

The problem is clear. You are doing something that you don't want to be doing. But the solution isn't so clear. If you could just stop it, you would! You *can't* just say no. And the longer this helplessness goes on, the more tricks you try, the more failures you have and the more hopeless you feel. On the outside you may act cool. You might even have flip responses or pat retorts, but each time you hear the 'why don't you just say no' message – even if it is subtle – you brace yourself. You ask yourself: 'Why can't I get it together and take care of myself? Where is my willpower? Why aren't I like other people?' They just decide to *do* something and then they follow

through. Again and again you decide, you make a commitment, you start – then your resolve fades. You get busy, you get overwhelmed, you get distracted, and your intention dissipates like the morning fog in the noonday sun.

Nancy is a sugar addict. She has vowed to give up chocolate almost every day of her life. Three days into her commitment to quit, something always happens and she reaches for a chocolate bar. Rosemary, who is not a sugar addict, decides that chocolate isn't good for her skin. She decides to cut it out of her diet, never buys another chocolate bar, isn't tempted, and doesn't think of it again. Rosemary's resolve may be inconceivable to you. Nancy feels like your sister.

When you are a sugar addict, saying no is *not* an issue of willpower. Your biochemistry has a direct effect on your behaviour. Your craving and desire for sugar are profoundly affected by your brain chemistry and, even more significant, by what and when you eat.

You are a sugar addict *because* you are sugar sensitive. Sugar addiction is a primary symptom of sugar sensitivity. If you are sugar sensitive and your meals are erratic, if you skip breakfast, eat lots of sweet things, drink quarts of diet soda or eat mounds of pasta and bread, then you will be depressed, moody, erratic, volatile, forgetful and impulsive. You may have a short fuse, a short attention span and a reputation for being all over the place. You may have trouble with your weight, you may have an eating disorder or you may have a problem with aggression.

It has probably not occurred to you that the food you eat could have such a dramatic effect on you. You may have figured out that sometimes you are really cranky when you haven't had your 'fix'. You have to go out and get a tub of your special brand of ice cream even if it's eleven o'clock at night. Your friends or parents or boss may have noticed that you have something like a split personality. Sometimes you are creative, cheerful, charming, funny and delightful. Other times you are a royal pain

in the neck and even the people who love you stay out of your way. You are a sugar addict.

When you first hear me talking about sugar addiction in this way, you may not be convinced that it is a real condition. You may not think it is possible to be addicted to something so 'harmless' as sugar. Stay with me while I take you through the reasoning for my position.

Criteria for Addiction

Here are the criteria the American Psychiatric Association uses to determine addiction:

- The substance is taken in greater amounts or for a longer time than intended.
- There is a persistent desire or one or more unsuccessful attempts to cut down or control use.
- Major time is spent in seeking, using or recovering from the effects of use.
- Frequent intoxication or withdrawal interferes with responsibilities.
- There is a decreased level of social, recreational activities due to use.
- There is continued use despite adverse consequences.
- There is a marked increase in tolerance.
- There are withdrawal symptoms.
- There is use to prevent withdrawal.

Let's reframe these criteria and see if we can create a list for sugar addiction.

• The substance is taken in greater amounts or for a longer time than intended.
Have you ever planned to have just one biscuit and eaten the

whole plate? Have you ever planned to have a hot chocolate once as a celebration and found yourself going back every day? Have you ever planned to have a piece of cake and eaten the *whole thing*? Can you imagine eating half a piece of cake and leaving the rest because you just weren't hungry for it?

• There is a persistent desire or one or more unsuccessful attempts to cut down or control use.

One or more unsuccessful attempts seem sort of funny to sugar addicts. Have you ever tried to control your use? Does that question make you laugh because it seems so absurd? Have you spent most of your life trying to cut down or control your use of sweet things? Once you start eating sweet things, you cannot stop.

• Major time is spent in seeking, using or recovering from the effects of use.

Do you make sure you always have a can of Coke (or even Diet Coke) on your desk? Do you make a special trip to Costco to get that *big* jar of jelly beans? Do you feel an inordinate sense of relief when your family is gone so you can eat what you want? Do you have sugar hangovers and feel cranky and irritable the day after?

• Frequent intoxication or withdrawal interferes with responsibilities.

Now at first blush, you may think that your sugar use does not affect your life. But are your bills paid on time? Is your work up to date? Do you double-book appointments? Are you too tired to function at three in the afternoon? Are you funny, charming and all over the place after you eat sugar or have your fizzy drink or sweetened coffee? Look at your behaviour with a different eye and you may be shocked at how true this is.

• There is a decreased level of social, recreational activities due to use.
Do you prefer to be alone so you can eat what you want, when? Do you get nervous about visiting your son's apartment because you know he doesn't have *anything* there for you to eat? Do you shy away from those friends who have given up sweet things? Are you drawn to the people doing the 'reward meal' on the Carbohydrate Addict's Diet because you know you will have company in eating what you want?

• There is continued use despite adverse consequences.
This is the killer – continued use despite adverse consequences. You know it's bad for you, you know it's killing you, you are in despair, and you go back for more. Hits kinda close to home, yes?

• There is a marked increase in tolerance.
You need more to get the same effect. One small biscuit won't cut it. You have to eat the whole packet. You remember not so much the high feeling, but the feeling of relief – that the world is okay, you fit, and things will be all right. But it takes more to get you there.

• There are withdrawal symptoms.
You may not have made the connection to withdrawal per se. You may simply intuitively know that you feel better if you have a cup of tea and a piece of cake. Or you know exactly how much better you will feel once you get your supply down the hatch.

• There is use to prevent withdrawal.
You know you are cranky and will feel better if you have something sweet. Your three-year-old is having a temper tantrum because you said no to her in the supermarket. You get her a fizzy

drink and pop it open and she sits there being a good girl. You take a sugar break at 3:00 P.M. because you know if you don't you will be a basket case by 3:30. You know what time the edginess will start.

Sobering, isn't it? Makes you think. When you first connect with this idea of sugar addiction, it may be a little scary to you. You may find it hard to put yourself in the same class as alcoholics or heroin addicts. You may have been conditioned to think that addiction is bad and only weak-willed people are addicts or alcoholics. This book will help you understand that addiction is a chemical reality. The reason you are a sugar addict is your unique body. You respond to sugar more intensely. You hurt more in withdrawal. You feel better when you have it. The physical dependence is real. You are not a bad person; this is not a character defect. Once you start to think of yourself as having a unique brain and body chemistry, you can start on the road to recovery.

You are a sugar addict because you are sugar sensitive. Sugar addiction is a *symptom* of sugar sensitivity. If you just treat the symptom by giving up sugar, you do not heal the real problem – the biochemistry of your brain and body – and you're not likely to stay away from sugar for life. The key to long-term healing is going to the *cause* of the symptom and balancing the systems that are now out of kilter.

Sugar Sensitivity: The Three Components

Sugar sensitivity describes a collection of three different inherited problems that can have a huge impact on how you feel and how you behave. At present, sugar sensitivity is a working hypothesis that has not been scientifically proven. You can't walk into your doctor's surgery and say, 'I want a test for sugar sensitivity.' But you *can* look at your moods and behaviours and take

a reasonable guess about what is going on. Your body and your symptoms will guide you in designing a food plan to restore your chemical balance and heal your addiction.

Let's take a deeper look of what's behind sugar sensitivity. Each of the components – carbohydrate sensitivity, low serotonin, and low beta-endorphin – has been studied in depth, and I want to share what science shows us about them.

Carbohydrate Sensitivity

Carbohydrate sensitivity is a term scientists developed to describe a volatile blood sugar reaction to eating carbohydrates. Generally, when a person eats carbohydrates, the blood sugar rises and the body releases a chemical called insulin. The insulin allows the cells to use the sugar in the blood as energy. As the cells use up the sugar, the amount of sugar in the blood decreases. The control of the blood sugar usually works very well. It stays in balance and keeps the blood sugar level.

If the person is sensitive to carbohydrates, the blood sugar increases more rapidly than it should; the body overreacts and produces too much insulin, which causes the blood sugar level to drop quickly. Carbohydrate sensitivity causes a rapid rise and fall in both insulin and blood sugar levels.

If you are carbohydrate sensitive, you use your fuel too quickly and get into trouble. You expect your breakfast to last. Toast and coffee works fine for your friends with normal body chemistry, but you crash at 10:00 A.M. and feel you could eat anything in sight. Or you might feel as if you are going to pass out. You may have diagnosed yourself as hypoglycemic and believe that you need to eat every few hours. But sugar sensitivity is not the same as hypoglycemia.

In hypoglycemia, your blood sugar level drops lower than normal. Once you eat, you are restored. If you are sugar sensitive, once you eat, you may be in bigger trouble because your

blood sugar and insulin levels will continue to overreact. If you continue to eat carbohydrates, your sugar levels will spike again and you will be on the prowl in another two hours.

As your blood sugar fluctuates, your mood will fluctuate with it. When your blood sugar is rising you may feel really good, even high. And when it falls, you will feel cranky and tired. You may experience huge highs and lows throughout the day and not make the connection to your blood sugar levels.

What you eat makes a huge difference in how severe the blood sugar and insulin spikes are. Carbohydrates affect your blood sugar more than proteins and fats will. Carbohydrates that are absorbed more quickly into your bloodstream will affect you even more. Many other things can affect this volatile blood sugar as well. The amount of fibre in the carbs and the amount and type of fats you eat will also determine how greatly your blood sugar is affected. One way to measure the expected effect of certain foods is called the glycemic index, which provides indications of how much different foods can cause your blood sugar to rise. Foods low in fibre and high in sugar – doughnuts, for example – have a much higher glycemic index than foods high in fibre such as whole grains.

If you are carbohydrate sensitive, the effect of high-glycemic foods on your body will be even greater. Sugars and low-fibre carbohydrates will make the highs and lows even worse. Potatoes have been dubbed a high-glycemic food by many diet doctors. To reassure you that they're not – if eaten *with* their skins – let's learn a little science about the history of the glycemic index.

Before the 1980s, doctors and dietitians who were working with diabetic patients recommended they eat a certain number of carbohydrates, including bread, rice, potato, cereal and similar foods. Little consideration was given to any effect that these starches might have in a diabetic's body. In 1981, David Jenkins published an article in *The American Journal of Clinical*

Nutrition describing the effects on blood sugar of certain selected starches. He gave 34 men and women 50-g servings of different starches and measured the effect on their blood sugar. He called the results the glycemic index (GI).

The foods with the lowest GI were legumes (lentils were 29 and soyabeans were 15). The highest GI went to parsnips at 97, and potatoes weighed in at 70. When measured, all the foods had been eaten alone rather than as part of a complete meal. Over the years, scientists continued to explore the usefulness of the GI.

In 1993, David Trout published a study that discussed the complexity of measuring the glycemic index. He found that a number of variables have an effect on the scores. Things like the source of the starch (legume, grain or tuber), the species of the starch, the way it was cultivated, the cooking methods and the degree of ripeness all contributed variation. In addition, the reduction of the starch particle size before, during and after cooking all affected the GI. The majority of the studies (approximately two-thirds) were being done with diabetics, and no studies were being done to compare the effect of the same foods, cooked in the same way, on diabetic compared to normal individuals. No testing was done on the different ways the foods affected men and women.

In 1995, Kaye Foster-Powell published the International Tables of Glycemic Index in which she reviewed and compiled the 73 studies that had been done on the subject. Her compilation was partially funded by the Australian sugar industry. She found great variations in the effects on blood sugar of the same foods and in some cases could offer no explanation. For example, porridge (i.e., oatmeal) varied from as low as 42 to a high of 75. Significantly, she noted that as particle size decreases, the GI increases.

In fact, because the GI was developed for use in diabetic diets, it was never intended to be used in isolation. Further, as

Foster-Powell's study shows, the total amount of the carbohydrate eaten, the amount and type of fat, and the fibre content *all* affect the absorption rate and its impact on the blood sugar. For me, this indicates that while the GI can be helpful in looking at the comparative effect of different foods, it should not be the only guide you use. *The Sugar Addict's Total Recovery Programme* will explain the more useful guide of eating brown things (such as a potato *with* the skin) rather than white things.

Brain Chemicals

The second and third components of sugar sensitivity involve two special brain chemicals. Your brain uses chemicals called neurotransmitters to send messages from one cell to another. The levels of these chemicals profoundly affect how you feel. Your brain is designed to work best when the levels are optimal and the chemicals are all in balance. The two brain chemicals most affected by sugar sensitivity are serotonin and beta-endorphin.

Low Serotonin

Serotonin is a chemical that serves as the brakes in the brain. It is the chemical that supports just saying no. If you have low levels of serotonin, you will be impulsive – you will have a hard time saying no. Your brakes don't work right. You can't 'just say no'.

Because you aren't able to say no to destructive behaviours, they may become compulsive. Compulsive patterns become addiction. Once you've started, you can't stop. You have what is known as low impulse control. Low serotonin sets you up biochemically. If you are sugar sensitive, being able to say no is not so much an issue of willpower as of low serotonin levels.

If you have a low level of serotonin you may also be depressed. Your depression can be made worse by the amount of

light in your environment. This condition is called seasonal affective disorder or SAD. In the winter, you may be more depressed and more compulsive about your eating. You can't stop and you feel hopeless.

Serotonin levels significantly affect low impulse control, depression and seasonal affective disorder. Typically the solution for low levels of serotonin has been prescription antidepressants that raise serotonin levels. Drugs such as Prozac effectively do the job. In cases of severe clinical depression, such drugs can be lifesaving. But many times these drugs are given out as a quick and easy solution to a problem that can be better handled by changes in diet and lifestyle.

In my own clinical experience, mild to moderate depression is closely tied to diet. High sugar consumption goes hand in hand with what is generally labelled as depression. I always recommend that a client try to change his diet as the first line of defence rather than the last. The solution you will learn about in *The Sugar Addict's Total Recovery Programme* is an all-natural, no-drug solution. What you eat and when you eat it can have a profound effect on your serotonin levels.

Increasing serotonin levels is a two-part process. First, you need to increase the amount of an amino acid called tryptophan that your brain uses to make serotonin. Tryptophan, like all amino acids, comes from protein. If you are eating mostly starches and sugars, your diet may be low in protein. You may not be getting the tryptophan your brain needs. Eating more protein foods on a regular basis will increase the amount of tryptophan in your blood.

However, just because there is more tryptophan in your blood, it doesn't mean it can get into your brain. Your brain is very careful about what it lets in. It has a protective shield called the blood-brain barrier to screen out things that might damage the brain. When the amino acids, including tryptophan, get up to the blood-brain barrier, they compete with each other to see

who can hop across first. Unfortunately, little tryptophan usually loses. I like to think of tryptophan as the amino acid runt. The big guys (the other amino acids) walk all over him and won't let him cross.

Science brings us a wonderful solution for the problem of the runt. If you eat a food that causes a release of insulin, the insulin goes up to the blood-brain barrier and calls the big guys. It says, 'Hey, guys, wanna come work out at the gym?' The insulin isn't interested in runty little tryptophan, so when the big guys go off to the gym, little Mr. Tryptophan is left by himself at the blood-brain barrier. Without competition, he hops across and sacrifices himself to the serotonin factory.

The combination of regular protein and an insulin-producing carbohydrate to increase your insulin level at a specific time does wonders for your serotonin levels. A potato seems to be the ideal food for the job of getting Mr. Tryptophan into your brain to raise the serotonin. This is why my first book was called *Potatoes Not Prozac*.

Even though my recommendations for eating will seem very simple, they are carefully thought out to give you powerful results with no side effects. As you get to know how and why your body functions, you can make more and more informed choices about the best way to deal with your own symptoms. Eating in the way I recommend can increase your serotonin levels and so decrease your impulsivity, reduce your depression and help you say no to your sugar addiction.

Low Beta-Endorphin

The third component of sugar sensitivity is low levels of beta-endorphin. Beta-endorphin is the brain chemical that is a natural painkiller. If you have a high level of beta-endorphin, you can go out on the football field and get bashed around and keep going. If you have a low level, you cry at the drop of a hat.

When you get an endorphin rush and feel euphoric, that is beta-endorphin being activated.

Beta-endorphin levels also affect your self-esteem, your sense of confidence, your being shy and your feeling out of the circle. If you have low levels of beta-endorphin, you can feel lonely and disenfranchised from the world. This is not merely a psychological response; it is a biochemical one.

Sugar, like heroin, alcohol and morphine, activates beta-endorphin. Because of the beta-endorphin release, all these can make you feel euphoric. But sugar-sensitive people will feel more euphoria than others do. People who are sugar sensitive have lower levels of beta-endorphin than normal people do. The sugar-sensitive brains try to compensate for low levels of beta-endorphin by upregulating – opening more beta-endorphin receptors. Because the sugar-sensitive person is in an upregulated state, she gets a bigger hit than her normal friend does. This is why she feels she died and went to heaven after a hot fudge sundae, while her friend simply thinks it tasted good. She devours a whole packet of chocolate chip cookies; her friend can eat one bite and leave the rest. He wants six beers rather than one or the whole bottle of wine instead of one glass. Sugar sets the sugar-sensitive person up for sugar addiction.

When the sugar-sensitive person tries to stop using the sugar that evokes this wonderful beta-endorphin response, the receptors start screaming. This is called withdrawal. The person experiencing withdrawal may feel cranky, irritable and out of sorts but never know it is last night's sugar binge creating the horrible feelings. Cravings loom large as the beta-endorphin receptors scream and relief is as close as a can of cola or a doughnut. The physical dependence on sugar to relieve the discomfort of withdrawal reinforces the need to use more and more sugar. The addiction grows into a real problem.

The Story of the C57 Mice

My excitement about beta-endorphin and its relationship to sugar addiction started from learning about and studying the work of Dr Christine Gianoulakis at McGill University. In doing research on beta-endorphin and alcoholism, Dr Gianoulakis found that alcoholics have lower levels of beta-endorphin than people who are not drawn to alcohol do. She also found that children and grandchildren of alcoholics are born with lower levels of beta-endorphin. This means that they are born with a genetic predisposition to alcoholism even if they do not drink. These very important findings came from many years of research working with different strains of mice in the laboratory.

Before she ever even examined people, Dr Gianoulakis worked with two different strains of mice that responded to the effects of alcohol in very different ways. Science laboratories breed different strains of mice to have different chemistry. The C57GL/6 mice had a far more potent reaction to drinking than their 'dry' brothers and sisters, the DBA/2 mice, did. Essentially, the C57s got drunker more quickly. In scientific terms, they are called alcohol-preferring mice. The DBAs are called alcohol-avoiding mice.

Dr Gianoulakis and her colleagues wanted to determine a biochemical reason that these two strains responded so differently to alcohol. They discovered that the C57s and the DBAs have very different levels of the brain chemical beta-endorphin. The C57 mice are born with much lower levels of beta-endorphin. To compensate for this lower level, their brains increase their receptivity to beta-endorphin (upregulation), which results in a bigger response to things that evoke beta-endorphin. This explains why they have a bigger response to alcohol.

The C57 mice also have a very big interest in sugars. The C57 mice prefer the taste of sweet things far more than their buddies the DBA mice do. Sugars such as alcohol evoke beta-endorphin. So the brains of C57 mice respond to the beta-endorphin effect more intensely.

Scientists also learned that the C57 and DBA mice also respond to painkillers very differently. C57 mice have a reaction to morphine thirty-five times more powerful than that of DBA mice. Thirty-five times is a huge difference. Sugar creates a response in the brain using the same biochemical pathways as morphine, and both affect the beta-endorphin system. This explains why you as a sugar addict have a far more powerful reaction to sugar than your non-sugar-sensitive friends do.

Here are some more differences. The C57 mice get hyperactive when given morphine. DBA mice do not. Scientists have not tested whether C57 mice are more likely to be hyperactive from sugar than DBA mice are, but I speculate that they might be. When the scientists say sugar does not cause hyperactivity in children, I wonder if they are testing children who are not sugar sensitive.

When withdrawing from morphine, C57 mice become lethargic and passive. Lethargy and passivity may be very familiar responses for you as well whenever you realize you need a sugar fix and can't have one! While the little mice don't actually have couches to curl up on and wait for the pain to pass, you do. But you may never have connected these feelings to the process of beta-endorphin withdrawal.

Sugar-activated beta-endorphin changes emotions as well as physical feelings. Not only does sugar reduce physical pain in C57 mice; it also reduces the pain of loss or social isolation. When baby mice are taken from their mothers, they cry. Scientists measured the number of times the babies cried in a specified number of minutes. They gave the babies sugar water and,

no surprise, they stopped crying. The 'isolation distress' was significantly lessened by sugar. Sugar creates a temporary flood of beta-endorphins, thus numbing the emotional pain of separation. You may not call the pain of loneliness 'isolation distress', but you know that sweet foods give you comfort and make you feel less isolated and alone.

Here is another fascinating finding about the little C57 mice. When put in a no-win situation, the DBA mice looked for an escape, while the C57 mice crouched and became immobile and defensive. Think of that. The non-sugar-sensitive strain got mobilized to find solutions, while the sugar-sensitive mice sat on the couch and argued about why they couldn't go for it.

Shift this information to people and just hear the DBAs saying to their C57 friends, 'Why don't you just go get a new job if you are so unhappy? That's what I would do.' Hear them ask, 'Why don't you just say no?' The DBAs decide to diet and do, and then lose 5 kg in a month. They are the ones who can have just one biscuit instead of eating the entire packet.

The scientists doing this research have not started thinking of the C57s as a sugar-sensitive strain, but I think it is only a short step from the profile of a C57 mouse to the profile of a sugar-sensitive person. In my mind, the match is uncanny. If you start thinking of yourself as a big C57 mouse, you can have lots of clues about why you act the way you do. You will also understand why your DBA friends can't make sense of your way of being in the world.

What Does C57-ness Mean for You?

You may have felt like an 'alien' if you grew up surrounded by DBAs. But now you can take comfort in the science of these mice. Just as scientists do not trash the little C57s or consider them inferior to the DBAs, you now know that the mice are simply two distinct strains with two very different body chemistries.

There is no right or wrong mouse. No good or bad one. No good body type or bad body type.

The scientific dispassion about mouse strains can teach you compassion for yourself in your own journey to healing. When you look at the C57s' tendencies as just another way of being, you open yourself to compassion for your way of being in the world. And as you learn how your sugar-sensitive body works, you can start making choices for healing.

Think of yourself as the human equivalent of a C57. You love sweets. You are comforted by sugars. You turn to sugar for solace when you feel isolated. It gives you courage when you are afraid and takes away the pain when you are hurting. Sweet foods can give you 'motor mouth'. You become engaging, funny and self-confident. Sometimes your friends wonder if you have been drinking. Often, you choose other C57s as friends, so you go out for coffee and have cake instead and really enjoy your social times. Having coffee with your cake feels like heaven. You get clear, focused and relaxed for about thirty minutes. You love that feeling. Your DBA friends actually enjoy the *coffee* and care less about the sweets you always have with it.

When you try to go off sugar you sit around and wait till the discomfort passes. You crouch like the C57s. You hunker down with your discomfort. You go immobile. You feel as if your cells are made of lead and are screaming. You feel the effect of withdrawal in your gut, your skin and your brain – wherever there are beta-endorphin receptor sites. You get so uncomfortable, you go back to the food that comforts you. You know that sweet foods give you energy. You don't realize that the sugar is resolving the lethargy of beta-endorphin withdrawal.

When you feel defeated and overwhelmed, you go into what I call 'the great sleep' – lying on the couch and not moving. Or you may act as a hero and never appear defeated at all. Outwardly, you encourage everyone else to believe that you are absolutely in control. But inside, you are holding on by a thread

and feel horrible. When faced with the same crises you find yourself in, your DBA friends get energized. Yet you feel inadequate and overwhelmed. You take Prozac; they change jobs and get a promotion. You hate this injustice and have not had a clue how biochemically mediated it is.

Being sugar sensitive is very confusing because alcohol, sugar and white things get you mobilized, make you brave, funny and self-confident. You may not have noticed that this energy lasts for only a little while. When the beta-endorphin hit wears off, you crash. You go into withdrawal, which is very uncomfortable. You become even more immobile, hopeless, demoralized, overwhelmed and tearful, but you do not make the connection to withdrawal. What you do remember is that when you use sugar, you feel okay. So you are willing to trade thirty minutes, then twenty minutes, then ten minutes of feeling okay for the rest being horrible because you are so desperate to feel okay. You will do anything not to experience the pain of sugar withdrawal.

This is why so many people who write to me lament that they cannot imagine giving up sugar. It's the only thing that makes life worth living. Now, thinking rationally, we both know that sugar is not the thing making life manageable. Yet I hear this all the time. This is sugar addiction. This is being caught in a place that is killing you, but you have no idea what is really going on. But don't feel bad about this. You *can't* see what's going on when you are in the middle of it.

Ironically, many sugar-sensitive people are very intolerant of alcoholics and drug addicts. They do not realize that sugar addiction is affecting them in the same way. Alcoholism and drug addiction are only more intense forms of sugar addiction. Addiction creates a life driven by the desperate need to feel better and to escape the terror of the withdrawal, and a life centred on getting your fix.

The Sugar Addict's Total Recovery Programme gives you a name for what is happening. It provides a vocabulary and concepts to explain your behaviour. Suddenly, your feelings start to make sense. The vague knowing you have had for a while (sugar sensitives are intuitive people!) gets a name. You don't have to think of yourself as hopeless, depressed and out of control. Your inherited biochemistry is the culprit, not laziness, lack of discipline or mental illness.

Remember to think of yourself as a big C57 mouse so that you can connect with what these mouse studies mean for you. Those things that you have considered character flaws for all this time are a function of your sugar-sensitive biochemistry. You believe (erroneously) that DBA behaviour is good and C57 behaviour is bad. Society tends to recognize and value DBA behaviour as the standard for being good, so, picking up on that attitude, you have usually judged yourself harshly. It is time to change your sense of who you are.

Sex Differences in Brain Chemicals

Men generally have higher levels of both serotonin and beta-endorphin than women do. This difference in brain chemicals can shed some light on why men on the whole are less impulsive and have a higher tolerance for pain than women do. However, some men (children and grandchildren of alcoholics) inherit lower levels of both serotonin and beta-endorphin. Their levels are more like those of women.

These are the sugar-sensitive men. They may be seen as sensitive guys because they are more aware of feelings and more vulnerable to both physical and emotional pain. Sometimes this vulnerability creates a great deal of pain in childhood for these men. I used to ask the male clients in my clinic whether any of them had been called a sissy as a child. One hundred per cent

answered yes. These men were all alcoholics and all sugar sensitive. They were more likely to have trouble with impulse control. They would get angry and shoot off their mouths. They would drink (which reduced their impulse control even more) and then would shoot off more than their mouths.

What I saw in the clinic with alcoholic men is now mirrored with what I see in sugar-sensitive men doing this programme. The similarities are striking. Sugar-sensitive men can be moody, introverted and intuitive. Their creativity and humour about being sensitive may mask deep feelings of inadequacy and low self-esteem. They may also mask these feelings by being alcoholic, abusive, angry and out of control. Or they may simply be depressed and turn to alcohol for solace.

Because the feelings that come from low levels of serotonin and beta-endorphin are so hard to manage, sugar-sensitive people continue to be drawn to the substances that seem to make them feel better. The 'feel better' substances are alcohol, drugs and sugar. Often sugar-sensitive men will be drawn to alcohol as the solution and sugar-sensitive women will be drawn to sugar as the solution. Both affect the same biochemical vulnerability caused by low beta-endorphin.

Because women are born with naturally lower levels of beta-endorphin and serotonin than men, they are more likely to be impulsive and depressed and to have lower self-esteem. Women who are children or grandchildren of alcoholics will have even lower levels of beta-endorphin. Women's levels also fluctuate each month in sync with the menstrual cycle. Beta-endorphin for women peaks at ovulation and then drops precipitously before menstruation. The fluctuations in beta-endorphin correspond with PMS symptoms. PMS brings not only physical symptoms but also feelings of hopelessness, inadequacy and a desire to isolate yourself; this is due to dropping beta-endorphin levels. Many report food cravings during this time that seem impossible to resist.

In addition, with the onset of perimenopause or menopause, the peaking of beta-endorphin around ovulation diminishes and women may find themselves in a biochemical crisis. The changed levels of beta-endorphin add to an already complex hormonal shift. They may feel even more drawn to substances that evoke beta-endorphin – sugar and alcohol and chocolate.

Women who are the children of alcoholics are even more at risk. They start off with lower levels of beta-endorphin and can be in big trouble in the second phase of their menstrual cycles because their beta-endorphin levels drop even further. They may experience severe PMS or feel increasingly depressed or inadequate, even though rationally they know these feelings are not warranted. Cravings for carbohydrates, chocolates or sweets may increase dramatically. These cravings are chemical. Low beta-endorphin means low self-esteem and cravings. The chocolate response and the sugar addiction come out of the biochemistry of sugar sensitivity.

The Three-Legged Stool

Let's put the three parts together: carbohydrate sensitivity causing volatile blood sugar, low serotonin and low beta-endorphin. Sugar sensitivity involves each of the three parts, but it is also affected by the relationship of these parts. Imagine a three-legged stool with blood sugar (BS), serotonin (5HT) and beta-endorphin (BE) each acting as a leg. A deficit in any or all three of the legs makes the stool off balance. Anyone who tries to sit or stand on it will fall.

Each sugar-sensitive person may have problems with a different leg of the stool. Sugar-sensitive people with deficits in blood sugar (BS) will be volatile and moody; sugar-sensitive people with low levels of serotonin (5HT) will be depressed and impulsive; and sugar-sensitive people with low beta-endorphin (BE) will have low self-esteem, feel socially isolated and have a very

low tolerance for painful situations. Sugar-sensitive people with deficits in more than one area would have the symptoms of both – or all three – areas.

Not only are there symptoms associated with each leg of the stool, there appear to be unique dietary habits associated with each. The BSs are likely to skip meals, forget breakfast and eat erratically. They suddenly realize they are desperately hungry and grab anything they can find. The 5HTs are drawn to sweets, bread and pasta – their comfort foods. They tend to be binge eaters or compulsive eaters and often struggle with their weight. When lack of impulse control and compulsive eating combine, the result is often serious weight gain.

The BEs are hard-line sugar and alcohol lovers. These are the ones who play with the edge, flirting with danger and squeaking by. They are the miracle workers who push deadlines and come through in a crunch, no matter the cost to their bodies. The BEs may be normal-weight men and women who are closet sugar users. They may be nervous, energetic adrenaline junkies who take great pride in not eating. When they do eat, they grab white carbohydrates and sugars to go with their third cup of coffee. Because they may not have weight problems, it is hard for them to connect with the seriousness of their sugar sensitivity or sugar addiction.

Working with All Three

Most of my own clients seem to be a combination of all three: volatile blood sugar (BE), serotonin (5HT) and beta-endorphin (BE). They get to check the box marked 'all of the above'. They are sugar addicts because they are sugar sensitive. Sugar sensitivity is a very complicated problem. Until now, solutions have targeted only one leg of the stool at a time. Trying to figure out which leg of the stool to treat and then figuring out the degree of deficit has been difficult for doctors to sort out. Few doctors

understand the relationship of all three parts of the stool, making it even harder for you to find a solution.

When you most need a solution, when you are most unbalanced, you are the least able to sort out the answer. You may not have a clue about why you feel so bad, so you settle for the first advice you are given. In good faith, you seek help and are told to do what the doctor orders. The most likely solution is a prescription for an antidepressant. The antidepressants work with only the serotonin leg of the stool. Unfortunately, drugs can be hit-or-miss, and they don't always work or keep working. The dosage needs to be adjusted. The brand needs to be changed. The depression may get better, but then it comes back. The problem remains, and the side effects are difficult. You lose weight and then regain it. You have no sex drive. You are still tired. You still have mood swings, and they are getting worse. Only now, you feel despondent because you have spent so much time, money and energy on healing. You *should* be fixed. But the other legs of the stool are still imbalanced. Low beta-endorphin hasn't been touched by any of the interventions you've tried. Your blood sugar levels still fluctuate wildly.

Because of your weight gain, you intuitively feel that if you found the right diet and lost weight, you would feel better. But until now, most of the diets, like the drugs you have tried, target only one or two of the legs of the stool. They offer you hope, and in fact work well in addressing one piece. But they are not complete.

You may feel a sense of hope as you read this book. You may feel that if you simply go off of sugar, you will be okay. **But you cannot treat your sugar addiction by simply going off sugar.** You need to treat your underlying sugar sensitivity and heal the imbalance that creates your continuing need to use sugar addictively. You need to restore all three legs of the stool. The story is far bigger than learning to 'just say no'. *The Sugar*

Addict's Total Recovery Programme will address all three problems contributing to your addiction and give you a solution that will finally work.

Why Other Eating Plans Haven't Worked for Sugar Addicts

Now that you have a better understanding of how blood sugar, serotonin and beta-endorphin are so important to the sugar-sensitive person who is sugar addicted, let's take a look at some of the dietary plans you may have tried. Look at them through the filter of this new information to understand why they worked or didn't work for you.

The Atkins Plan

Robert Atkins in *Dr Robert Atkins' New Diet Revolution* suggests shifting to a low-carbohydrate, high-protein and high-fat diet. Atkins says carbs are bad because they produce insulin, and his plan is very appealing. You can have steak, bacon, cheese, eggs, butter and cream. Staying away from desserts doesn't seem so bad in the face of the comfort of fat. And, most important to many of us, the Atkins plan promises dramatic results quickly. You lose weight. You lose weight fast. And you seem to feel terrific . . . for a while.

Atkins is right about sugar and simple carbohydrates creating weight gain, but he makes no allowance for sugar sensitivity and addiction. Just start the diet, stay on it, he says, and you will feel better. But if a sugar sensitive adheres to the Atkins plan, she will have a problem in her serotonin and beta-endorphin production. If she follows Atkins to the letter, she will minimize her insulin production. But her body *requires* insulin to move tryptophan from her bloodstream into her brain *to make serotonin*. If the insulin response is minimized dramatically, the serotonin level drops and the ability to 'just say no' will drop dramatically. She will become depressed.

Six or eight weeks into the Atkins plan, a sugar addict will be one cranky puppy. If she tries a little something sweet, her beta-endorphin cravings will awaken. The sleeping giant of sugar addiction, now roused, will take her to the bakery, the ice cream store or the bar. She will feel wonderful with the 'just a little' something, truly mellow, relaxed, hopeful and peaceful. So 'just a little' more will seem fine. Two weeks later, she will discover she is in a full-blown relapse. And she won't be able to stop. Her impulse control mechanism, which is dependent upon serotonin, will have been shot. This is called rebound, and she is in big trouble.

Trying Out the Zone and Protein Power

The Zone is more tempered in its instructions. 'Balance,' Barry Sears says. 'Seek balance.' The formula 30-40-30 became a key word for Zone dieters as many worked hard to get Sears's ratios down at each meal. Mastery of the formula promises a slim body and high energy for ever. But sugar-sensitive dieters often drift away from the rigour Sears demands. Sears also says the 30 per cent carbohydrates could be jelly beans or white bread. Even his special Zone bars have sugar in them. Sugar-sensitive dieters find themselves eating five or six bars a day and wondering why the plan isn't working. While the Zone plan does offer a masterful response to altering insulin levels and hormonal levels, it does not address addiction or beta-endorphin priming. Its very design is to reduce insulin action that over time reduces the availability of tryptophan for conversion into serotonin. It's no surprise that many sugar-sensitive people fall from the Zone within a few weeks.

The *Protein Power* diet seems more promising for sugar addicts and sugar-sensitive people. Like Atkins, Michael and Mary Dan Eades talk about the need to control insulin levels by shifting away from carbohydrates and moving towards protein and fat. *Protein Power* seems kinder and more sensible than Atkins.

While promising dramatic results, it offers a workable plan. Protein Power dieters felt better, lost weight, and kept working at it. But something was missing. Six to eight weeks into the plan, sugar sensitives started getting restless, noticing carbohydrates wherever they went. Bagels and muffins started calling to them again. Many sugar sensitives slipped, had a few servings of a favourite comfort food – and found themselves sliding into bread, biscuits or ice cream. They couldn't understand why they had fallen off the programme so quickly.

The Protein Power diet does leave sugar sensitives less vulnerable to failure than the Atkins plan, but it doesn't deal with either addiction or the brain functions affected by diet. The balanced approach to nutrition in *Protein Power* is healthier and more reasonable, and keeping the fat level at 30 per cent protects dieters from fat-induced insulin resistance. But the Zone, Protein Power and Atkins plans, when followed carefully, will contribute to a problematic drop in serotonin. The clarity and focus dieters feel for six to eight weeks on the plan dissipate. The diet starts to seem too restrictive, and once more sugar sensitives are on the prowl for something to eat that will make them feel better. This restlessness and irritability is low serotonin speaking, not a lack of willpower. With low serotonin you and your diet are in trouble.

The Hellers' Plan

Richard and Rachael Heller's *The Carbohydrate Addict's Diet* taps into many dieters' intuition that something more is going on for them in their biochemistry than for other dieters. The term 'carbohydrate addict' sounds on target. Many people *know* they feel like addicts – helpless and out of control – around carbs or sweets.

The Hellers expand on the important role of insulin in losing weight. They promise that if you have your carbs in a particular way and at a particular time of day, you can eat what-

ever you want. Their idea of a 'reward meal' is thrilling to
dieters who are also sugar sensitive and sugar addicts. Dieters
know they can do anything they have to during the day if at
6:10 P.M. they can get bread, wine, pasta and ice cream as their
reward.

The Hellers also promise that this reward meal will help to
take care of serotonin levels, which control feeling full. The reward meal raises your serotonin, thus quietening your cravings
and controlling your addiction. This is an awesome promise.
Pay attention, be rigorous all day, then get a 'reward'. You have
only to wait until evening and then you will be fine. And you will
lose weight, feel great and never have to diet again.

However, the 'reward meal' is a ticket to disaster for sugar addicts and sensitives. It reinforces the core of addictive thinking
by reinforcing the idea of cutting a deal and just hanging on
until the reward time rolls around. The deal is being able to
have anything you want if you have it within a certain time window. But when you choose your favourite reward foods, sweets
and white flour breads, you are priming your beta-endorphin
level. You will activate cravings leading your brain and body to
expect – in fact, to *demand* – more of the same. So the very thing
you believe is the source of your comfort (the reward) is actually feeding your addiction to sugars and carbs and reinforcing
your cravings.

The addictive tendency of a sugar or carbohydrate addict's biochemistry is *not* due to low serotonin, but to beta-endorphin. The
Hellers' reward meal boosts a sugar addict's beta-endorphin level
temporarily; a short while later, it sets off cravings. Eventually, she
slips off the plan. First, her reward meal may continue beyond the
allotted hour. Then the reward becomes a binge. Three weeks
later, she may wake up in shame, horror and confusion. She has
gained weight. She is out of control once again. She doesn't know
what happened. Her beta-endorphin system got dramatically out
of balance.

Sugar Busters!

Sugar Busters! is straightforward. 'Just say no to sugar,' the authors say, reinforcing the message that sugar addicts and sensitives have heard all their life. The authors write that all foods made with sugar and white flour are bad, so stop eating bad stuff. But many sugar sensitives and addicts developed headaches, irritability and serious crankiness on the Sugar Busters! programme. Their withdrawal was too quick and too intense. The diet had no support to increase serotonin. Nor does the plan deal with addiction. 'Just say no' doesn't work for most sugar sensitives and addicts.

Looking at these different weight-loss diets together, it is easy to see that none of them addresses all the components of sugar sensitivity. The needs of all three systems – carbohydrate sensitivity that creates blood sugar volatility, serotonin and beta-endorphin – have to be addressed or you will continue your life-long struggle with food cravings and addiction.

2

The Solution

The Sugar Addict's Total Recovery Programme works with all three biochemical components of the sugar-sensitive brain and body to heal sugar sensitivity and addiction. This recovery plan very simply says, 'Let's get to the heart of the problem. Let's heal the conditions that make you fat, make you impulsive and make you crazy. The solution is not *no* carb, but *slow* carb. Slow carbs contain whole grains and a lot of fibre. Not high protein, but regular and sufficient protein.' The plan provides a way to reduce your insulin overall but retain a timed response to increase your serotonin, to minimize your cravings by stopping the beta-endorphin priming and to increase your beta-endorphin production.

The Sugar Addict's Total Recovery Programme is a long-range solution, not a quick fix. The plan tells you what to do based on your brain and body chemistry and explains why you are the way you are. It teaches you what being sugar sensitive means and shows you what you can do about it starting right away, today. It also takes the radical approach that you don't need to follow a

rigid programme to free yourself from sugar addiction. Designing your own plan, knowing your own style and getting to know your own body with its unique reactions is an approach totally different from those of most popular diet plans.

You need a solution that works for you, a simple solution that you can understand and implement. You are ready to get healthy and feel better. Here is where the food plan comes in. The food plan addresses all three problems at once without side effects and at no cost. It stabilizes your blood sugar, raises serotonin and reduces the overreaction of beta-endorphin to sweet foods that creates cravings. The final part of the plan is designed to enhance your everyday level of beta-endorphin.

Because the plan is so manageable, you can focus on doing the food without having to measure, balance, calculate and adjust for each deficit. In essence, you do the food and the plan takes care of the healing. The process accounts for what seems to be the miraculous change users have reported.

Introducing the Seven Steps

I will talk about the seven steps of the plan in more detail in the next chapters, but here it is important for you to see how the steps fit with the science. Step 1 (eating breakfast with protein) stabilizes your blood sugar and sets up having enough tryptophan in your blood to manufacture serotonin. Step 2 (keeping a diary) teaches you how to read your body and adjust the rhythm and pace to your own needs. Step 2 also teaches you to see which of the three legs of your biochemical stool is most off balance. Step 3 (three meals a day with protein) stabilizes your blood sugar further and prepares for the increase of serotonin production.

Step 4 (having the vitamins and the nightly potato) increases your serotonin and gives your brain what it needs to manufacture serotonin. Step 5 (shifting from whites to browns) moves

you away from your love affair with carbohydrates. It gives your body the positive effect of carbohydrates while eliminating the part that creates craving. Step 6 (taking out the sugar) reduces the craving for sugar by eliminating beta-endorphin priming. Eliminating the priming heals the addiction. Step 7 (finding radiance, or simply getting a life) teaches you the behaviours that enhance the increase of beta-endorphin.

The seven steps work their magic. You get a biochemical body-brain stool with three solid legs. You don't have to figure out a complex healing prescription; you just do the food, listen to your body and make the adjustments to heal your own sugar sensitivity and addiction. You, not some outside expert, prescribe what is right for you. Whether you are male or female, whether you are fat or thin, whether you are depressed or addictive doesn't matter. The starting food plan is the same for all. The refinements come as you learn about your body and your needs. Simplicity makes it work.

There are also seven steps in my first book, *Potatoes Not Prozac*, but the steps in the Sugar Addict's Total Recovery Programme are a little different from the way they were first written. I originally recommended starting with the food diary. For some people, however, even that was too hard. I want you to have confidence that you can do this plan. Now I recommend starting with breakfast.

Here are the steps:

1. Eat breakfast with protein.
2. Keep a diary of what you eat and how you feel.
3. Eat three meals a day with protein.
4. Take the recommended vitamins and have a potato before bed.
5. Shift from white foods to brown foods.
6. Reduce or eliminate sugars.
7. Create a new life.

I will say more about each step as we move through the book.
The steps may seem ridiculously simple to you. They are simple,
but a bit harder to do than you may think. Notice that going off
sugar is Step 6, not Step 1. This entire book is aimed at getting
you to go slow and follow the steps in order.

Why the Steps Are in This Order

If you try to do this programme without following the steps in
the order presented, the programme won't work for you. It's
that simple. You may feel worse instead of better and decide to
give up because the 'programme doesn't work'.

If you can trust that there is a method to my madness, and do
the steps in the order recommended, you will stabilize each of
the biochemical functions involved in your sugar sensitivity and
addiction. We will stabilize your blood sugar, increase your serotonin, reduce the beta-endorphin priming and then increase
your beta-endorphin levels.

Later on, you'll have plenty of room to exercise your own
judgment and make your own choices – you'll tailor the details
of the plan to suit you. But don't tinker with the big picture.
And don't rush to the end. You do not need to be dramatic and
do it all at once. If you try to go off sugar, alcohol, drugs and
white flour – even caffeine and nicotine, for example – you will
feel terrible. Your head will hurt and you will get both irritable
and panicky. Don't do it that way. Quieten your sugar-driven
impatience and follow the steps.

Do the steps in the sequence and you will get wonderful results. That is my promise to you.

Don't Rush to the End

'Okay,' you might be saying. 'I'll do the steps in order, but I'll
do them one right after the other. Let's get on with this. If this
works, I want to heal this problem NOW!' This is your sugar

sensitivity talking. Your sugar-sensitive brain, with its love of impulsivity, wants you to do everything right away. 'Give it to me all at once,' it says.

Please don't do it!

Do one step at time. Do not proceed to the next step until you have mastered the one before it. Start with breakfast with protein. The steps need to go in sequence. Each step builds on the previous one. The food plan is designed to change your blood chemistry and improve your neurotransmitter function. It will stabilize your blood sugar level so your moods don't swing from extreme (and often unrealistic) optimism to despair. It will increase your serotonin level so you have more impulse control and are less depressed. Finally, it will optimize your beta-endorphin level so your self-esteem increases and your interest in sweets evaporates. The food plan will create changes way beyond anything you have imagined. This plan heals more of your life than just your sugar sensitivity and addiction.

So even though the steps may seem obvious and simplistic, they actually create profound physical and emotional change. Give your body (and your sugar-sensitive brain) time to get used to each change before going on to the next step.

The key to success with this programme is to go slowly and go in sequence.

Getting Ready to Start

As you get ready to start, you may have different feelings depending on what sex you are. Men and women seem to have very different styles in doing the programme. Often, the guys will write me a short note and say, 'Okay, tell me what to do, Coach.' I give them the steps and they go off and do them – and they tend to do them quite well the first time out.

Then one of two things happens. I hear from the first type a

year later. They report that the plan made a significant positive change in their lives and that is the last I hear from them. Often these are guys who are also recovering alcoholics. They have done twelve-step work and the food plan simply completes their programme.

The second type also does the programme really well initially. Then, about three months into it, they discover all sorts of unexpected feelings. And they are spooked big-time. Their food gets wobbly; they get confused and come back to start at the beginning. Eventually, as they learn to manage their new feelings, they do fine.

Women, on the other hand, often fuss for several months before actually starting. They talk about their ambivalence, about feelings, about fear and confusion. They don't want to give up their good friend Mr Chocolate; they often go out on a 'last' sugar run, which of course exaggerates everything they are feeling. And then they quietly start with the programme by eating breakfast with protein every day. Their feelings become manageable, and they get back to the plan.

Whether your feelings come before you start or several months into the programme, pay attention to them, notice them, record them in your diary, but do not get distracted by them. Simply focus on the food and use the feelings to guide your progress and you will be more successful. You do not have to understand or make sense of all the feelings for the programme to work. You simply want to learn the connections between your moods and what you are eating.

Notice your ambivalence if it comes up, write about it in your food diary, and keep doing the food. There is no one right way to do the plan. Learn your own style and rhythm of making change so you can tailor your plan to work for you.

Sugar Feelings

When sugar-sensitive people first learn about their body chemistry, they generally feel a great sense of relief. They feel as if they have finally 'come home' to a story that makes sense and puts the pieces together. They want to rush into doing the whole programme at once. You may feel this as well.

Even though you feel excited to have found something that sounds so right on, you may also be afraid that it won't really work. You may be terrified that you are being set up to hope only to fail once again. You want to do it all, and you are terrified that you will have to give up what comforts you. You may have a love/hate reaction to these ideas. And your feelings about giving up sugar may be so intense that they spook you.

Tips from the Field: You Are Not Alone

Here are some of the things that run through people's heads before they start the programme.

- **Will this really work for me?**
- **Will it help the depression?**
- **How will I remember all the details?**
- **How will I keep a diary?**
- **Does this mean I'm going to have to cook?** (I can't cook. I know how, but I am blocked. I can't seem to ever get my kitchen cleaned up enough to cook in there. And if I cook, I'll have to clean up.)

Your enthusiasm and fear are filtered through what I call sugar feelings. Sugar feelings come from an unbalanced biochemistry and the foods you are now eating. Sugar feelings distort the natural reactions you have. Sugar feelings make

things seem bigger, more dramatic, more exciting – and scarier.
Whenever you feel scared or doubtful, simply take a deep
breath, have a cup of tea and sit with the feelings. Be patient
with yourself. Do nothing. Do *not* start changing all your food
right away. Just keep reading, reflecting and tempering your desire to do everything right now. Do one step, one choice at a
time.

Keeping Things Simple

It is easy for you to get overwhelmed when you are presented
with lots of new information. That's actually a symptom of sugar
sensitivity.

My job is to keep things simple, to get you started on this programme without overwhelming you with information. The
early part of your journey will be more directive and specific.
You will have options, but the basic steps you will need to take
will be described clearly. These changes will set up your body
for success with the rest of this programme. These very first
steps you take will begin healing your sugar sensitivity – which
will make doing the rest of this programme easier.

The Sugar Addict's Total Recovery Programme includes the experience and expertise of the people who have been working the
programme over the last few years. As you may know from your
own experience, sugar-sensitive people are gifted and creative,
with a lot to say. The website has hosted exchanges that have
tested this material in an active community. I have read more
than 40,000 letters on the subjects we will be discussing in this
book. *The Sugar Addict's Total Recovery Programme* will give you
the nuts-and-bolts guidance continually being refined on the
Web by people who used to feel just as you do now, but who now
live free of cravings and mood swings.

Here is an email from someone who has been sending her
questions and comments to the website regularly:

I've been part of this community for more than a year. I think I was among the first to check it out when it got started. You wouldn't have recognized any of us back then!

The forum is so many things to me. It is a refuge, it is a library, it is a friend, it is an awakening, it is a barometer, it is a sounding board, it is a course correction, it is ideas, it is progress. . . .

I wouldn't have stayed on the journey without this community! Yet I've almost walked away several times because the pain this process would tap into was too intense. But something would happen EVERY TIME I thought of leaving that would keep me here. Somehow the support and encouragement I needed would come through.

I LOVE what this community is. I've never experienced anything like it. Thank you for being a part of my healing.

The Sugar Addict's Total Recovery Programme will take you through the seven steps one at a time. But it will also give you practical tips and advice to help you do the programme. You will learn

- What to order in restaurants
- What to cross off your grocery list
- What you can fix quickly for dinner
- What to eat when you have sugar cravings
- Why potatoes are good for you
- How to make friends with veggies
- How to get back on the plan when you've slipped

You will also share recipes, shopping lists and tips for coping with tough situations, such as a business meeting that runs past your usual mealtime. This book puts the answers to all these questions – and more – in one place.

Tips from the Field: Reaching Radiance

The thing that is different about me now is the way I feel. In my first couple of months on the programme, I felt better outside: calmer, less nervous and shaky. Now, after four and a half months, I feel better inside: more hopeful, more excited about life, more capable, more solid, clearer, stronger. I know this is the result of a balanced brain chemistry.

– D.

Because people just like you have tested so much of what is in the Sugar Addict's Recovery Programme, I know that I am giving you what you need to hear when you need to hear it. The healing process is gradual and developmental. The kind of advice you need when you first start the programme is different from that you will need four months or a year later. Your brain and body will change over time. At first you may need more structure. Often people talk about the 'sugar fog' they are in when they first get started. Your feelings and reactions may be coloured by your sugar intake or by not eating breakfast. You may go back and forth between feeling overwhelmed by the ideas in the programme and feeling wildly enthusiastic about finding an answer to your mood swings and low self-esteem.

This book is quite directive at the beginning until you are able to know and adapt to your own healing style. As you become more experienced, it will encourage you to listen to your body, understand your own rhythms, listen to your colleagues along the way and create what works for you. The programme starts by stabilizing your volatile blood sugar reactions. You will learn to eat regularly and on time. You will learn to be steady, steady, steady. You will learn to hold on through what may feel like a rather tame beginning. Next, it helps raise your serotonin levels. You will have a potato at night and experience the science

behind the programme right in your own body. You will also see why eating protein at each meal sets the stage for your body to make serotonin. And you will feel better almost immediately.

You will be thrilled and excited when you master the moods that have haunted you for so long. You will become more reflective and less impulsive. Rather than responding to problems or roadblocks with tears, you will start anticipating and solving problems. Even the way you think of yourself will change. If you thought you were 'naturally' intense and moody, you may discover that you *are* naturally intuitive and perceptive, but not nearly as moody as you thought.

You will stop craving sugar and bread all day long. You will no longer wake up feeling hungover in the morning. You will be less cranky, less reactive. Life will seem brighter and you will be able to get to the things you have put off for years. *All* these things change as you change your food! *The Sugar Addict's Total Recovery Programme* will guide you as you go.

The Best Way to Use This Recovery Programme

This book is called a recovery programme because it does more than simply address or cover up the symptoms of sugar sensitivity. It heals the underlying problem that causes the symptoms. But to make it work best for you, you will need to make it your own. Personalize your programme so that it fits your needs, your style and your interests.

Before you actually start the steps, here are some ideas on ways to use your book and make it into your own programme.

Coloured Markers – Using Yellow and Other Colours

Go to a stationers and buy yourself several different colours of highlighter pens – maybe yellow, pink, and blue. Then, as you read the pages in this book, highlight with yellow (or whichever colour you choose) the phrases and sentences that

really speak to you: things you want to remember, insights that fit for you, and so on. For example, when you come to the section of Chapter 6 about planning your food, you might want to highlight in yellow the style that best describes you. You could use pink to highlight action steps you want to take, such as buying protein powder or digging out your old Crock-Pot. And you might use blue highlighter to mark the parts of the book that will help you when you're feeling cranky or having cravings.

I like yellow as a highlighter. My brain is now trained to see yellow as the code to pay attention. My books are colour coded for my own style and preferences. Your book needs to reflect your style and your process.

Post-it Notes

Pepper your copy of this book with Post-it notes marking sections that you will want to refer to later, like 'Ten Breakfast Ideas' or 'Snacks You Can Buy at a Convenience Store'. You can write the name of the section you are marking on the part of the Post-it that sticks out – it's sort of like making your own tabs to help you turn quickly to parts of the book that you will use often. You can also use the Index for guidelines.

Flags

Another trick for personalizing your book is to mark important points or sections with Post-it note flags. You might, for example, use red flags to mark pages that have your pink-highlighted action steps, or blue flags to help you find the blue-highlighted paragraphs on coping with cravings. Or use purple flags to mark the sections you can turn to when you need inspiration or fellowship, such as one or more of the stories from others working the *Potatoes Not Prozac* plan.

If you want, you can write yourself a little note on the flags.

Writing in the Margins

Is this starting to make sense? Use the book the way I hope you will use the food plan. Make it your own. See what works best for you, then do the plan (and mark your book) that way. Let's take it one step further.

As you read, make notes for yourself in the margins. Write down any questions that you have, any personal insights that you get, any comments you have on what you are reading. *Interact* with this book. Add your thoughts and ideas to mine. Argue with my ideas. Test the principles of the programme. Record your reactions to the tips and action steps. Make this *your* book, not mine.

If you don't like to write in your books, think of *The Sugar Addict's Total Recovery Programme* as a workbook, the kind of book that is *designed* to be written in.

Setting Up Your Own Notebook

If you like to keep your books clean, you can photocopy the pages of your personal copy of *The Sugar Addict's Total Recovery Programme* that have information or advice that is important to you. Then work with and highlight your photocopied pages. Put the pages in a notebook that will become your own working version of the book.

You can divide the notebook into sections that make sense to you. Instead of making dividers labelled 'Chapter 1' and 'Chapter 2', maybe use 'Good Ideas to Try', 'Key Points', 'Inspiration' and 'Recipes'.

One advantage of making your own notebook is that you can add material that isn't in the book, such as printouts of the postings on our online Community Forum or recipes you find in

other books or magazines. Some people mark their own books *and* set up a notebook. But either way, make the book yours. Put it to work for you. It will be your most valuable companion on your journey from sugar sensitivity to radiance.

Tips from the Field: Slow Down

Many people doing this programme suffer from the same syndrome: trying to do too much too fast. It is really a form of sabotage. Even if it is from overeagerness, not self-destructiveness, it still rips the rug out from under every effort you make. Work the steps at the pace it takes for you to be able to stick to them. It is okay to be where you are – overweight, depressed, addicted, whatever. Where you are is where you start.

– D.

3

Getting Started:
Steps 1 and 2

Now that you have been playing with your book a bit, let's actually get started with your programme. The first step is to eat breakfast with protein every day.

Step 1. Eat Breakfast with Protein Every Day

Some people believe that my direction to eat breakfast every day and make sure it has protein in it is too simple. They don't think it can be part of the diet and the food plan. But this step is *hard*. It may take you months to master. Breakfast with protein . . . every day.

Don't worry about going off sugar or caffeine right now. Have toast with sausage and a cup of espresso if you want. The sausage will be your protein. Have two scrambled eggs and juice. The eggs will be your protein. Have smoked salmon and cream cheese on a bagel. The smoked salmon (and to some extent the cream cheese) will be your protein.

Why Is Breakfast a Must?

Sugar-sensitive people are notorious for not eating breakfast. My readers have said they don't like breakfast, they aren't hungry in the morning, and even the idea of eating seems horrible.

Sugar-sensitive people sometimes do seem to feel better without breakfast. That's because when they don't eat for eight or ten hours, their body thinks they are moving towards starvation mode and releases beta-endorphin to protect them. Sugar-sensitive people are more sensitive to the (temporary) euphoric and confidence-building effects of beta-endorphin. They will often not eat because it actually *feels* better. It makes them feel strong and lean. But the beta-endorphin release masks their dropping blood sugar level. This is why they crash big time at 10 A.M. and then eat anything (usually something sweet) in sight.

I want to protect your body from the stress of the crash. I also want to help you move away from using not eating as a way of feeling beta-endorphin-induced confidence. There are healthier ways to achieve higher beta-endorphin.

Just eat breakfast with protein every morning. If you can't stand the thought of breakfast foods, eat a lunch-type meal instead. Have miso or wonton soup (the kind with chicken and prawns added). Have corned beef hash. Have a grilled cheese sandwich. Have chilli. Have pizza (but be sure it has protein – meat or lots of cheese – on it).

Many former breakfast haters on this programme started out by having a Smoothie-like George's Shake for breakfast. Use the recipe that follows, make up one of your own, or order the mix from me. Just be sure it has the protein powder in it.

George's Shake

500 ml milk, soya milk or oat milk
100 ml fruit juice
2 tablespoons protein powder (choose a sugar-free one)
2 tablespoons porridge oats (not instant)

Put all the ingredients in a blender and blend on high for about a minute. If you do it for less time, you will be crunching oats at the bottom of your shake. Using raw rolled oats is best. Don't use the steel-cut oats for this shake. If you prefer not to use milk of any sort in your shake, use 500 ml water and a little juice. George's Shake works because it combines nutritious foods with plenty of protein.

Whatever you choose to eat for breakfast, enjoy yourself! And make sure it has protein. Don't worry yet about making other changes like avoiding white-flour foods or taking the sugars out, just start with a regular breakfast that includes protein. We are working on creating a steady and stable blood sugar.

Ten Breakfast Ideas

Here are some other ideas for breakfast. Make a copy of this page, fold it up and carry it with you in your wallet, appointment book or purse. Flag this page so you can find it again.

1. Scrambled eggs and toast
2. Cottage cheese mixed with fresh fruit and a muffin
3. Pancakes or waffles made with protein powder in the batter
4. Two slices of toast with peanut butter
5. Cheese omelette with hash browns (grated boiled potatoes mixed with onion and then fried)
6. Beef or chicken wrap
7. Porridge oats with milk or yogurt and fruit

8. Two hard-boiled eggs and juice to have in the car on the way to work
9. Bagel with meat (such as ham) inside
10. Corned beef hash and two eggs with a slice of toast

Fast Food Breakfast Choices

For some of you, fast food places may be your only alternative. An Egg McMuffin is better than a doughnut and coffee. A Big Breakfast is even better. And yes, these are not ideal choices. But they will get you started and they will hold you until lunch. Because you are sugar sensitive, you are actually quite capable of finding what you need. You can remember times when you have gone out at 10 P.M. to find something sweet to eat because there was nothing in the house.

You can also find breakfasts in cafés and sandwich bars. Actually, breakfast is one of the easiest meals to find on the road. Scrambled eggs, fried eggs, sausages, baked beans, cottage cheese and fruit with some wholemeal toast. Go ahead and have the ham, too. You need a solid amount of protein.

Tips from the Field: The Power of Protein

I drink a George's Shake at breakfast, which gives me a big dose of protein. If I skip it, I crave sugars all day and eat and gain weight. I aim for the right amount of protein at every meal. If I'm consistent in that, and eating at regular intervals, my sugar cravings are minimal and I am *not hungry*.

– L.

A Shopping List to Cope with Chaos

Having the food you need to eat means actually having the food *in your house*. This means going to the supermarket and getting what you need. Planning and going grocery shopping regularly is the start of your making and carrying through conscious decisions about what you are going to eat. Right now it doesn't matter whether you put doughnuts and biscuits in your trolley as long as you are also buying breakfast foods and protein.

But start exercising your grocery-planning muscles. Your foggy and impulsive sugar-sensitive brain tends to take over when you are grocery shopping, causing you to come home with two Danish pastries but without the eggs you needed.

Before you go to the supermarket, write down what you are going to buy. This is the beginning of planning, a process you will get very good at. Start by sitting down and thinking about what you like to eat. This is important. Food meets your emotional as well as your physical needs. Enjoy the planning!

Once you have some notes on what you want to buy, make your shopping list match the layout of the store. Choose the store you like to shop in. Sketch a picture of what it looks like. Add where the meats are, where the dairy counter is, where the fresh fruits and vegetables are. Then list the foods you want to buy in the order in which you pass them on your way through the store. This will keep you from being distracted and 'drifting' towards sweet foods rather than consciously buying what you need for your plan.

When you first start this exercise, you may not know where the vegetables live. You may not have a good sense of your protein options. But mapping the layout will help you get the lay of the land in your own supermarket.

Tips to Help You Shop

Here are two more tips about grocery shopping:

- Don't shop when you're hungry
- Don't shop when you're tired

Try to go shopping *after* you've had a satisfying meal and at a time when you are not feeling exhausted or rushed. Now, if going to the supermarket is not the most exciting thing in the world for you, you will have to sort of will your way through this exercise. But it's easier if you are not tired and hungry when you go.

Even with the best-laid plans, however, sometimes you will be tired and hungry *and* need to buy groceries. Plan for this. Know what you will do. Maybe you will go back to the delicatessen counter and get something to eat before you start your main shopping. Maybe you will get a meal at a nearby restaurant, then hit the grocery store. If you eat first, you may still be tired but you will not be desperately hungry – and grabbing whatever sweet foods are at hand because of that hunger. You will make better choices and stick closer to your grocery list as you shop.

Your First Grocery List

You may not have a lot of experience with making a grocery list. You may be used to simply going to the store and picking out what calls to you. This time, try to think through the kinds of food you want to get before you go. If you need some help making a grocery list, start with this one. You may include other foods as well, but this is a core list.

A dozen eggs	Bread
Cottage cheese	Cheese
Potatoes	Peanut butter
Whole grain crackers	Apples or some other fruit

After you have gone grocery shopping several times you will be able to keep this list in your head. You will have the food you need on hand. Breakfast with protein will become a natural and habitual part of your daily routine. You can explore which of the breakfast choices you like most. Some people choose one breakfast and eat that every day. Others want to have something different every morning. Find what works best for you.

As you start to feel comfortable with your daily breakfast, begin to think about getting started with a food diary.

Step 2. Keep a Diary of What You Eat and How You Feel

Your food diary is the cornerstone of your programme. It may start out being a housekeeping task, but as you move through the programme, it becomes a vital source of information about your body and your brain chemistry. Your diary is your body's voice.

Here are the basics of starting a food diary.

First, get yourself a blank book that you can carry with you. You might want to buy a diary with a zip so you can feel safer about your privacy. The most important thing is to get something you feel comfortable with. Some people use shorthand pads, some use fancy journals, some use their computers. Do whatever appeals to you most. While your computer may seem like an ideal alternative, writing your diary in longhand is better. The changes in your handwriting will give you clues about how you are doing with the programme.

Write down in your diary what you eat or drink, when you eat or drink it, and how you feel physically and emotionally. Write down these feelings not only at the times you eat, but also whenever you notice them. For example, if you feel sleepy thirty minutes after lunch, write that down.

Use a four-column format for your food diary. Using four columns, you can easily see the connection between what you

eat and how you feel physically and emotionally. Below is an example of a page of a food diary.

Date/ Time	What I Ate or Drank	How I Feel Physically	How I Feel Emotionally
April 10 8:00 A.M.	2 doughnuts	Tired	Really good
10:00 A.M.			Depressed. Feel like I can hardly function.
11:00 A.M.	2 cups of coffee with cream and sugar	Exhausted, can't stay awake	
1:00 P.M.			Really good
1:15 P.M.	Crisps Large Coke	Wired	Crabby about work
1:30 P.M.		Tense	
3:15 P.M.	2 cups of coffee with cream and sugar	Wired	Sad. How can I be sad and wired at the same time?
5:30 P.M.	2 beers	Relaxed, warm	Happy
7:00 P.M.	3 pieces of chicken, coleslaw, mashed potatoes, 2 crackers with butter		Happy, satisfied, feel great

How the Simple Act of Writing Things Down Will Help

When you take the time to pay attention and make an entry in your food diary, you are giving energy to your own healing. You are telling your body it is important. You are noticing what you are eating and what you are feeling. You may think you don't need to write things down. You 'know' what you eat. But when you actually start keeping a diary, you will be floored to discover that what you thought you knew and what you actually did were very different.

Keep the diary. It is an invaluable tool for understanding your own needs, rhythms and changes.

Why Paying Attention Changes Things

When you pay attention to your body, you are sending it a message that it is valuable. If your body feels valuable, it will talk to you more. It will give you clearer messages and you can communicate better with each other. For too long, you have dismissed what your body feels. You have either ignored its signals or responded to its cues without being aware of what they really meant. There are likely many times you thought you were hungry when you were actually experiencing beta-endorphin withdrawal. Your diary will help you sort out what is really going on in your brain chemistry and your body.

What to Do If You Don't Know How You Feel

Some people have a hard time when they first start keeping their food diary because they honestly do not know how they feel. They get discouraged because all they are doing is writing 'fine' or 'okay' or sometimes 'horrible' and 'discouraged'. This can happen because they have not listened to their bodies for so long. They have forgotten or never learned the language of feelings. Here is a list of the feelings you might experience.

Feeling Good

Able	Desirable	Playful
Alert	Determined	Pleasant
Challenged	Eager	Pleased
Animated	Enchanted	Powerful
Beautiful	Energetic	Proud
Bold	Energized	Radiant
Blissful	Excited	Real
Brave	Exhilarated	Refreshed
Brilliant	Free	Resilient
Bubbly	Full	Responsible
Buoyant	Fun	Responsive
Calm	Generous	Satisfied
Capable	Glad	Secure
Carefree	Grounded	Serene
Caring	Happy	Settled
Centred	Honoured	Sexy
Cheerful	Humourous	Shining
Cherished	Impressed	Spiritual
Clean	Inspired	Spontaneous
Clear	Joyous	Thrilled
Clever	Loving	Stable
Confident	Open	Tenacious
Contented	Patient	Vital
Delighted	Peaceful	

Feeling Not So Good

Afraid	Burdened	Disappointed
Ambivalent	Cheated	Discontented
Angry	Childish	Disorganized
Annoyed	Combative	Distracted
Anxious	Confused	Distraught
Blue	Defeated	Disturbed
Bored	Destructive	Empty

Exasperated	Imposed upon	Restless
Exhausted	Inadequate	Sad
Explosive	Infuriated	Scared
Fearful	Jealous	Selfish
Flighty	Jumpy	Shocked
Foolish	Lonely	Shut down
Forgotten	Longing	Silent
Frantic	Mad	Sceptical
Frazzled	Miserable	Sleepy
Frightened	Nervous	Strange
Frustrated	Obsessed	Stupid
Grief-stricken	Outraged	Teary
Guilty	Overwhelmed	Tempted
Helpless	Panicked	Tense
High	Petrified	Terrible
Horrible	Pressured	Toxic
Hurt	Rejected	Unclear
Impatient	Resilient	Zonked

Go through this list and use a yellow highlighter to mark the feelings that seem to fit you best. You may find that there are only five to ten that fit where you are these days. Or you may highlight more than that if you know your feelings well. You may be discouraged because you really don't have feelings other than 'fine' or 'depressed'. Keep reading the list as you keep your diary. Your ability to recognize feelings will change as your food changes.

The fun thing will be to see how your feelings emerge as you do the programme. Whatever your feelings, the important thing is to notice – without criticizing yourself – that you are feeling something. Remember, words for feelings are not good or bad. They are simply a way to help you understand what is happening. You may be angry and frustrated at having to keep a food diary. Write this in your diary. You may be bored with

your life. Write this in your diary. Your diary is your friend. It will teach you all about your wonderful body.

Remember that sugar-sensitive people tend to be people of extremes. You can feel either totally awash in feelings or totally disconnected. What you are trying to do is learn to notice and record. You do not have to sort it all out or make sense of the feelings. As you keep your diary, however, you might discover that there is a direct correlation between what you have been eating and how you are feeling.

Tips from the Field:
When the Body Speaks, Take Good Notes

Whenever I feel a strong emotion, I try to write it in the diary. Of course, some days it's one emotion after another, but generally I can identify specific strong emotions at various times throughout the day. I used to put 'hungry' or 'tired' a lot for the physical feelings that I recorded just before I ate. Then I realized I could use the physical and emotions columns any time – and, in fact, using those columns when it *wasn't* time to eat told me a lot more about myself and how food affected me. Writing in the diary at non-meal times helps me to listen to my body.

– L.

Learning to Read Your Body

Getting started with your diary will get you started with learning the language of your body. Begin to 'listen' to the tones and new words of your body language. If you are not sure of the emotional content, focus on the physical. Try to notice when you are less tired or have more energy. If you usually have headaches and then notice you don't, make sure to write this

down. If you usually have joint pains or rashes or a runny nose and notice that you're getting fewer of them, write this in your diary. If you simply use one word like 'fine' to describe how you feel, it will be hard to sort out any change in your feelings.

Start by picking three feelings from the feelings list that you can comfortably relate to. Use them in your diary, then expand your list as you go. For example, I like to use the word 'cranky' because it really conveys how I feel the next day if my food is off. It took me a while to find the right word to describe the feeling.

Doing It Every Day

Even if you hate doing the diary, do it anyway. Write down whatever you are feeling about the diary process in the column labelled 'How I feel emotionally'. If you find you are still resisting keeping a traditional diary, try a new approach. Use pictures, make a collage, draw images, use stickers. Experiment with alternatives that are less boring for you. Use a hand-held recorder and then transcribe at the end of the day. Write in your appointment book. Be outrageous.

Tips from the Field: Making It Fun!

I use Crayola sparkly crayons (crayons that have glitter in them), as well as fluorescent gold stars, pink hearts, happy faces, etc., in my food diary. It's like doing a colouring book three times a day! Takes me back to being a child – and since I had such an awful childhood, I'm getting to do kid things now that I didn't get to do then. I know some people on the programme are actually drawing in their diaries, but since I can't even draw a straight line, I rely on the neat stickers. In my emotional column I use pink or blue to reflect how I'm feeling. This really helps when I want to look back and see if there's a pattern.

– Y.

At some point, something will shift. All of a sudden instead of munching and writing and feeling mad, you will see the diary as your friend on the journey.

Managing the Intensity of Your Feelings

Sugar addicts often have volatile feelings. You may have been using sweet or white-flour-based foods to help you manage the chaos of your emotions. Your feelings may either be huge or nonexistent or swing back and forth between these two extremes. You may feel wild or numb. You may sometimes feel deeply and other times not at all. All of this is natural because of the imbalances in your brain and body chemistry. These feelings have been unmanageable because they have come without warning or pattern. This is going to change. You will discover that there are very predictable patterns as to why and when you feel the way you do. What has seemed like chaos will change into fascinating connections between your food and your mood.

It is natural for you to be scared or to want to rush ahead. You are not alone. All sugar addicts feel this way. Much of what you feel is shaped by how you have been eating. When your meals are erratic, when you are eating lots of white-flour foods and are still having a sugar life, sugar feelings – feelings of chaos and doom – will emerge. Seeing impediments rather than solutions; feeling many fears and doubts; wanting to start, being terrified of starting; being impatient, being resistant; being wildly enthusiastic – all these feelings will surface. All the feelings are real, but they are amplified by the unbalanced biochemistry. These are not bad feelings, they are sugar feelings. Be kind as you learn to identify them.

The good news is the sugar feelings will change. Your feelings will still be deep, but they will no longer scare you. They will be manageable and understandable. They will work in your service rather than making you crazy. This is one of the most exciting benefits of sticking with your plan and 'doing the food'.

You will be able to simply work the steps of the plan before you understand everything. You will learn to listen to your body and live without knowing the rationale for each recommendation while you are sorting things out. It will get better over time. What has been scary will become safe, and you will understand what you feel.

4

Getting Steady:
Steps 3 and 4

This phase of your programme is designed to help you get stable. It is about adding new foods and new ideas, paying attention, and getting into a rhythm. Don't even be thinking about what you are *not* going to be able to eat, because you will not be giving anything up until you and your body are ready. Your body will guide you as we go through the steps. First, you want to stabilize your sugar-sensitive body chemistry.

Stability requires building a firm foundation before starting to build new structures on top of it. Now that you feel you have found a solution to your symptoms, you probably want to get on with the whole programme all at once. You want to get rid of the sugar right now. Hold that enthusiasm in check and keep reading.

You may vacillate between wanting to give up all your sugar this moment and being terrified at the thought of never eating sugar again. This is natural and to be expected. Move away from thinking that *sugar* is creating the mood swings, depression and addiction. Your unbalanced biochemistry sets you up, and what

you eat makes it worse. The problem is much bigger than just the sugar itself. In this phase, we want to stabilize both your body and your behaviour. We are going to slow you down and simply begin to retrain some of your old patterns. We will harness your impulsivity, minimizing the urge to make huge changes all at once, while still preserving your delightful spontaneity. Slow and thoughtful will be our theme for this task.

Step 3. Eat Three Meals a Day with Protein

I am a patient woman who has worked with thousands and thousands of sugar-sensitive people. On the Sugar Addict's Total Recovery Programme, every client takes small steps so that the plan works. I want you to go slow enough, too, that you can master each little change. I know that every one of these changes will have a dramatic impact on how you feel. They are the foundation for lifelong change.

Hopefully, you are now eating breakfast with protein every morning, ideally within one hour of waking up. This may have been a huge step for you. Sometimes it takes weeks to master this simple beginning because it is so easy to skip breakfast. Having the protein with your breakfast makes a huge difference in how you feel. If you have been able to get started in this way, I suspect you are beginning to feel a bit better already.

The next step is to eat three meals a day with protein, at about the same time every day, such as 7:30 A.M., 12:30 P.M. and 5:30 P.M. Or 7:00 A.M., noon and 6:00 P.M. Try to have no more than five to six hours between each meal (except for the overnight stretch between dinner and breakfast). If you are going to have to go longer than that, consider having a protein and complex carbohydrate snack to tide you over. For example, if you suspect you will have to work late and not be able to get dinner until 8:00 P.M., think about this in the afternoon or whenever this suspicion first arises. Plan to get a snack of

protein and complex carbs by 5:00 P.M. You want to make sure to keep your body from crashing in a big way. (This is the exception to my usual advice of not eating between meals.)

A normal person would just get hungry. A normal person would say at 5:30, 'I'm starving. I have to get something to eat.' But our bodies respond to blood sugar depletion in a different way. Our bodies cue into the serious blood sugar drop and say, 'Whoa, starvation may be coming. I gotta protect this loved one.' And our body releases beta-endorphin so we'll feel better. We end up feeling emotionally wonderful, euphoric, relaxed, thin and self-confident by *not* eating when we need to.

You may mistakenly think that this 'good' feeling is something to strive for. But the 'good' feeling comes as your body acts to protect you from what it thinks is happening. It thinks you are starving and doesn't want you to suffer. It releases a painkiller: our friend beta-endorphin. You know how much you love beta-endorphin! However, not eating as a way to get a beta-endorphin high is a dangerous tactic. It can set you up for anorexic patterns. This is *not* the direction we want your healing to take.

Because of this particular beta-endorphin response, when you first give up your pattern of not eating, you may experience beta-endorphin withdrawal and edginess. Don't get spooked, just understand what is happening.

The wonderful beta-endorphin feeling of being able to go for ever without eating masks trouble in another way as well. You may continue to push yourself until your beta-endorphin supply runs low. Your blood sugar continues to drop. Then you suddenly realize you are in big trouble. Now the warmth of the beta-endorphin is gone *and* the pain of the blood sugar drop hits. You eat anything – sometimes everything in sight. And if you're in the early months of this plan, 'anything in sight' may well be white, sweet and trouble.

Often people say to me, 'But I don't get hungry. Why should

I eat if I am not hungry?' Sugar-sensitive people don't always register hunger the way normal people do. Your hunger thermostat may not be working properly. If it isn't, you may not feel hunger, and you may not feel full after eating. This will change over time, but in the early stages of this programme, you will need to serve as your own clock by eating at regularly scheduled intervals. You have to compensate for your own low level of serotonin. You will need to pay close attention to the time. Use your diary to help you start to notice when you are likely to get into trouble from going too long between meals.

If for some reason a meal slips from your regular time, simply shift back to your routine. Don't confuse your body. Reinforce the *pattern* of your eating. For example, if you couldn't get lunch until 2:00 P.M., still have your dinner at the regular time. Remember, consistency and regularity is what we are striving for. We are looking to get those meals into regular slots, not at random intervals.

This part of your programme will be hard. Sometimes it takes people months to really master it. Consistency and stability are somewhat alien to the typical sugar sensitive. We often put our own needs last. This characteristic seems to be a part of sugar sensitivity. This may make us good carers, but it leaves that wonderful body of ours pretty low on the list. I encourage people to think of their body as a three-year-old child's body. You wouldn't make a three-year-old skip a meal or wait too long to eat. You would stop what you were doing and make dinner for the little one. *Do this for yourself.*

Create regular mealtimes. Remember, regular mealtimes.

Regular Protein Is Crucial

Each of your three meals needs to contain a good amount of protein. This plan is *not* a high-protein plan; it is a regular and consistent protein plan. Having protein consistently throughout

the day does two key things: It helps to stabilize your blood sugar because protein is a very 'slow' food, and it creates a steady state of amino acids in your body.

Most sugar-sensitive people on the programme are eating about 140 g of a protein (such as beef, fish or chicken) at each meal. If you want to count protein grams, aim for 0.4 to 0.6 g of protein for each 450 g of your weight for your total daily allotment. If you decide to count grams of protein, you will need to get a book, table, or nutrition software to tell you the grams of protein in the foods you typically eat.

If you are a counter, be careful not to get into trouble spending all your time trying to figure out exactly what to eat rather than enjoying the eating. Food contains things such as water and fat, so it is often hard to sort out the exact amount of grams of protein in a given food.

I encourage people to start simply by using an easy 'eyeball' method. Simply make a fist. That is about how much protein you want to have at a meal. Two eggs, a good-sized piece of fish, a good-sized breast of chicken. (This is more than the traditional 'pack of cards' portion size used in some weight-loss programmes.) If you have a bigger fist, you will eat more; if you have a smaller fist, you will eat less.

We are working really hard to shift your awareness about food. I want you to think about what you are eating rather than simply wolfing down your food unconsciously. I want you to be thinking about the enjoyment of the chicken breast rather than whether it is 125 g or 155 g. We sugar sensitives sometimes get stuck on little things and forget about the why of eating.

Do not count anything but protein foods as your protein. For example, don't count the amount of protein in bread or breakfast cereal as part of your daily protein. Even though they contain some protein, bread and breakfast cereal are carbohydrates,

not proteins. Don't think of milk as protein either. Yes, I know it has protein in it. But it is pretty light on the protein scale and won't really hold you for very long.

A good way to start with making sure you get enough protein is to make a list for yourself of the foods you like and generally eat as your protein foods. Protein foods include things such as eggs, dairy products, cottage cheese, peanut butter, lentils, tofu, beef, lamb, chicken and fish. (If you are vegetarian, you can surely do the plan, but you will need to pay close attention to what you are eating to make sure you get enough protein.)

Figure out the portion size for those foods to get the grams of protein you need per meal, then use that list for planning your meals. For example, my list contains things like this:

- Two eggs
- 140-g turkey burger
- 140 g of salmon fillet
- 200 g of cottage cheese
- 225 g tofu (soya is less dense as a protein than animal foods)
- One medium chicken breast
- 140 g of minced beef in spaghetti sauce
- 170 g of tuna salad (one can of tuna)
- Two veggie burgers (I never looked at the box to read the protein count – it just feels right)
- A 2.5-cm slice of meatloaf
- 350 ml of a protein shake (24 g of protein provided by 2 tablespoons of protein powder)

Now, how do I figure out what 200 g of cottage cheese looks like, or 140 g of minced turkey? I buy the turkey in 225-g packages and eat a little more than half the package at a meal.

I know that cottage cheese comes in 225-g tubs, so I leave some and I put it on my dog's dinner. I read the size of the original salmon fillet and cut off what looks like 140 g. By now you may have guessed I am not a counter-type person. But I have found what works for me. Your job is to sort out what works *for you.* We want it to be fun and easy.

Protein is key for your body to repair itself. Also remember that protein provides your body with tryptophan, the amino acid that your body needs to make serotonin. If you aren't eating protein, your serotonin factory will have to go on layoff status.

Tips from the Field: Making Protein Easy

For protein, I use chicken breasts, turkey breasts, steak, eggs and bacon and minced beef. When I get home from the supermarket, I separate the breasts into individual plastic bags and freeze them, so I can grab one at a time if I need to.

When I cook them, I usually cook about four servings at a time, eat one and keep the other three in the fridge or freezer.

I've used minced beef for meatloaf and cabbage rolls that I make without the added sugars and white flour, instead adding more veggies. I always try to make extras so that I have something for lunch or breakfast or for those dinners when the whole family is off on their own activities.

– *M.*

So pay attention to the protein at your meals. And remember, we are not talking about high-protein meals here. We are talking about regular and consistent meals centred on protein.

The meal needs to contain other things as well as the protein. A balance of protein, complex carbohydrates and fats is important. But at this stage, we are only working on getting protein into each of your three meals a day.

What Is a Meal?

Let's take a look at what you will be eating with your protein. What is a meal? A 'meal' is eating two or more nutritious foods at one sitting. At a minimum, a meal should consist of a complex carbohydrate and a protein. Here are some meals:

- Tuna fish and salad with vegetables (lettuce alone is kind of light)
- Eggs and toast or an Egg McMuffin with hash browns
- Chicken breast and green beans
- Three tacos
- Hamburger and corn-on-the-cob
- Cottage cheese and tomatoes
- Chilli on brown rice
- A bean-and-cheese wrap
- Fish cakes and a baked potato
- Lentil soup and a baked potato
- Beef stew with carrots and peas in it
- A bagel with smoked salmon and cream cheese
- Club sandwich, celery, crisps
- A protein shake made with milk, fruit and protein powders based on vegetable, soya, egg, or whey or a combination

Now, you may be shocked at some of the 'meals' I have listed. Remember, I told you that I am patient. I want you to succeed on this plan. I want you to start where you are, not where I or

anyone else thinks you should be. Start with your lifestyle. As you feel better, you will begin to want to make more informed meal choices. Besides, if you start to feel like I am taking away everything you love to eat, you will either resent me or not do the programme (or both). What I want is for you to start with what you can do.

Have Sweets with Your Meal and Don't Worry About It

As we are starting to talk about meals, you are probably wondering when you have to give up the sugar stuff. You know it's coming sometime and you are no doubt giving that fear a lot of energy. You may be going back and forth between being raring to go and dumping it all and being terrified that I am going to take away your support. Actually, at this stage, we will do neither.

At this point in the programme, don't even think about giving up your friends, the sugar foods. For now, simply eat your sweets as part of your meals. If you usually eat a chocolate bar in the afternoon, just eat it earlier with lunch or later with your dinner. If you have an almond croissant for breakfast, just have it with a breakfast that contains protein (such as eggs) and a complex carbohydrate (such as wholemeal toast). The other foods in your meal will slow down the effect of the chocolate or sweet foods. You will have less of a hit or rush from the sugars you eat with meals, but you can keep your friends at your side for now. Remember, though, they are now an add-on, not part of your meal. I once had someone ask me if a hot fudge sundae counted as a meal since it was two or more nutritious foods and included foods with protein in it (ice cream and nuts). She was serious. Only a sugar-sensitive person would think this way. We are so creative in finding a way to keep our beloved foods. The answer is, a sundae isn't a meal.

Tips from the Field: If You're Overdue for a Meal

If I find myself getting past the time when I should have a meal and I just can't (for any reason) get it together to make myself a meal, I either eat what I can get (a hard-boiled egg, a hunk of cheese, cottage cheese, maybe a piece of fruit – usually fruit and cheese or nuts are best to perk me up when I am crashing) or drop everything and go to a restaurant.

– D.

Why Only Three Meals? And Why No Snacks?

What's wrong with having a snack? Like cheese and crackers in the late afternoon, or half a protein shake mid-morning? Some people have even been encouraged to maintain an even blood sugar level by having six small meals a day rather than three big ones. Why do I say to eat three times a day?

You and I have a special sugar-sensitive body chemistry. Saying no is not our strongest suit. It is very easy for us to go from having 'just a little snack' to grazing throughout the day. We start eating and forget to stop. I am teaching your body how to start and stop. When you end a meal and consciously *stop eating*, you are helping your dear, sweet addictive body to learn something new and good. Stopping is healthy.

For most of us, having no control – not being able to say no and being impulsive – is a problem. We have huge pain and shame around it. It is behaviour we want to change. I have found that if we make simple choices and quieten the old negative messages we have about what we should or should not be doing, we can change old patterns. Three meals (starting and stopping) seem to do this really well.

Of course, there are a few exceptions to the recommendation of only three meals. As you follow this plan, you will start to

see that we are not working with rules so much as guidelines. I want you to be thinking about what is right for you. I want you to understand *why* I recommend certain changes.

However, if you are pregnant or nursing or engaging in major athletic activity or you are a growing teen, you will *need* to snack. And if you have to go more than six hours without a meal, have a planned snack.

Choose snacks that combine protein and a complex carbohydrate. Here are some sample snacks:

- A hard-boiled egg and a cut-up orange
- Mozzarella sticks with corn chips and salsa
- Whole grain crackers and bean dip
- 25 g of Cheddar cheeses and an apple
- A slice of whole grain toast with peanut butter
- String cheese and spicy V-8 juice

Don't fret a lot about this; just choose the best snacks for your lifestyle.

What About Diet Cola, Tea or Coffee Between Meals?

As you start to work with the idea of three meals a day, you will wonder about what to drink between meals. Just start to pay attention to the between-meal time. You want to be careful not to drift towards substituting coffee or fizzy drinks for the foods you used to eat during the day.

You also want to pay attention to your social times. So much of our social culture revolves around having something to drink together; it may seem hard to imagine life without it. At this stage in your programme, don't stop drinking anything. Don't even think of giving everything up today. Do not spook yourself.

Just start noticing your pattern – what you drink and when you drink it. Notice the triggers and the amounts. Write about the drinks in your diary.

Grocery Shopping

In order to manage having three meals a day with protein, you will need to go grocery shopping. When we live in sugar chaos, we often just eat what is in the house, or we grab something on the way home, or we go grocery shopping when we have already missed a meal and are 'off the cliff'.

All of these conditions contribute to chaos and will not support stability and consistency in your plan. I want you to begin to learn to plan what meals you are going to eat. I am going to show you how to prepare a shopping list so you have what you need to make those meals, and then actually go into a supermarket when you are neither tired nor hungry and purchase what you need. You are smiling, aren't you? You *know* this will be a radical change from your usual grocery behaviour.

Getting Ready to Go Grocery Shopping

Let's start with planning. Think about three meals a day for the time period you will be shopping for. Do you shop once a week, every day or once a month? Whatever suits your pattern, sit down and think through what you will need for those three meals a day. If you don't have a shopping pattern at all, I suggest you plan to shop once a week. Plan to get the basic food you need. You may go out for a meal during the week or you may stop quickly at the market to add to what you've already bought, but doing your main grocery shopping once a week will give you the basic foods you need to stay safe with your food plan.

Sit down and make a little chart for yourself. Make seven columns and then draw two horizontal lines across them. This will give you twenty-one spaces – three meals a day for one week. Fill in what kinds of things you think you might eat at each time of each day. This is *not* a food plan. It is simply a realistic assessment of your week. If you eat lunch from the sandwich bar near

your office every day, that's fine. Write in 'sandwich lunch', and you will know you don't have to shop for those meals. If you usually go for a cappuccino and something in the morning, just figure on whether the something includes enough protein. You may just be adding a hard-boiled egg. Then you will add eggs to your shopping list.

This is neither rocket science nor the thirty-day *Family Circle* meal plan. It's a quick sketch to help you figure out what to buy. After you have filled in the boxes, look at your chart. Start writing down the ingredients for the foods that you have filled in. This may include porridge oats, hamburger, soup, bread and brownies (remember, you can have your sweet stuff – you are just going to be eating it *with* your meals). Then go see if you already have any of the things on your list. If you have plenty of porridge oats, you don't need to buy more.

You may find you would like to begin experimenting with things that are a little healthier than those you have been eating. If you want to do this, it's great, but you don't have to.

Make sure your list includes emergency food. I always get cottage cheese, for example, even though I may not have it on my eating list. If I get home late one night and feel run over by a truck (usually because it's way beyond mealtime), I can fix a baked potato in the microwave, add some cottage cheese, and slice a tomato for dinner. Other emergency foods for when there is no time to cook are canned tuna, whole grain or rye crackers with tuna and veggies, cheese sticks and veggies, natural peanut butter on a wholemeal tortilla or bread, or a ready-prepared salad with ham and cheese.

Not ideal, but functional. If you have a potato for dinner, it doesn't count as your evening spud. If you eat late, you may want to cut your dinner potato in two and save half for the evening spud. Remember, the evening one before bed should have no protein foods with it.

A Sample Grocery List

So let's look at what you might have on your shopping list.

Proteins

Tuna   I always keep several cans of tuna in my cupboard.

Chicken   I usually get a combination of regular chicken breasts to bake and some boneless, skinless cutlets to use for a stir-fry or something. I usually get a whole chicken to roast on Sunday. Takes me back to my early days as a young wife. And makes the kitchen smell good.

Minced meat (I get either turkey or beef)   I have them package it in the weight that is the right amount for a meal. Then I can stick them in the freezer and know I am prepared. Having it minced makes it easy to use for different things: in spaghetti sauce, on the grill, in meatloaf, etc.

Fish   I generally get several different kinds of fish and put it in the freezer. Before I freeze it, I package it in individual serving sizes and label it.

Eggs   I always have eggs.

Cottage cheese   This is another staple for me.

Tofu   Again, I always keep some around because it is so easy and quick to fix.

Dairy things such as **cheese** and **plain yogurt** can be very helpful for your plan. They provide comfort and nourishment. Get **milk** if you drink it. It can be a good base for protein shakes if you decide to use them. Choose regular cow's milk or soya milk or oat milk. Stay away from rice milk, because it tends to be very sweet and may trigger cravings.

Vegetables

Ah, vegetables. I know that many sugar-sensitive people don't exactly thrive on veggies. But there are a few that you can start with no matter what.

Get at Store

Tuna: 2 big cans	Spinach
Chicken breasts	Lettuce
Whole chicken	Lentil soup
Hamburger: 1 kg	Bread
Salmon	Porridge oats
A dozen eggs	Potatoes
Cottage cheese	Carrots
Butter	Coffee beans

Potatoes   Make sure you have enough for your evening spud. Have fun with potatoes. Try different kinds; choose different colours and shapes. You are going to start noticing different tastes in potatoes. King Edwards are very different from Pink Fir Apple potatoes. Some people swear that organic baking potatoes taste best. Become a potato connoisseur.

Go to the frozen food section. See which vegetables seem okay to you. **Peas** and **sweetcorn** are fine. You don't have to eat Brussels sprouts. (The frozen ones are pretty bad.) Don't make yourself cranky about this. Don't go faster than you can go. If the only vegetables you eat are peas and sweetcorn, that's okay.

After you are finished in the frozen food section, wander down the fresh vegetable aisle. Get a bag of **lettuce**. Get a little bag if you live alone; we want to minimize things turning brown and wilted (and becoming unappealing!) in the back of your refrigerator. Consider a salad. Maybe just lettuce, **tomato**, and **carrots**. Think about what you might like. See which vegetables call to you. They may be thrilled to meet you. They may clamour to hop into your trolley and go home with you.

Fruit

After you have looked at the veggies, move over to the fruit section. We know fruit will sing to you: **oranges, apples, bananas, peaches**. Choose the ones you like. Try different kinds and colours. Don't even think about whether the fruit is right for your plan. Just get what appeals to you. If you don't know how to pick out ripe fruit, ask the person in charge of produce.

Staples

Now you are going to walk around and get the staples that are important for your own plan. This may include **porridge oats**, **soup** and **frozen entrées**. Use your list to guide you. Look around the supermarket and find food you are drawn to and will eat. Do *not* choose based on what you think is good for you. Choose what you like and will eat.

I had one client who could not master breakfast. He did this exercise and found something called cha-cha chilli in those cardboard cups you add hot water to. He started having cha-cha chilli for breakfast and felt 100 per cent better. So look for things that are fun that you may not have noticed before. For example, if you get tortillas, you can make all sorts of meals wrapped in a tortilla. If you are choosing cereals, begin to hunt out the ones that are a little lower in sugar. Shredded Wheat and Cheerios will hold you better through the morning than Sugar Puffs. Porridge is the best.

Identifying Your Own Lifesavers

Identify a few lifesavers for yourself. Pick out a few things that you will always have on hand in case you get into trouble with your food. For example, I always have **potatoes**, **porridge oats**, **cottage cheese**, **eggs** and **rice cakes** at home. So even if I am not diligent, or I forget to get to the supermarket and it's the sixth day and I am tired and cranky, I can make a meal of scrambled

eggs and rice cakes. Everyone will have different lifesavers. But identify yours and get them at the store. And pay attention. If you use them up, make sure to get more! Your food lifesavers are as important as keeping extra toilet paper in the house. (Put that on your grocery list as well!)

Avoiding Fuzzy Foods

When you are shopping, think carefully about what you are getting. We want to avoid fuzzy food syndrome. If you find that some food you thought was going to be a big hit ends up in a plastic container in the back of your refrigerator with fur on it, don't keep using this food.

For example, I love the look and feel of aubergines. I used to buy an aubergine every week. And every week it would get spotted and soft, then mushy, and I would throw it out. I did this for many months until I figured out that I love to eat aubergines but hate cooking them. Now I eat aubergines at an Italian restaurant. Well, sometimes I bring the leftovers home and *they* get furry, but I am sure you understand what I mean. The bottom line? Stop the fuzzies. If it has been there for three days, throw it out.

Step 4. Eat a Potato Before Bed

Okay, let's assume you are now eating breakfast with protein every day. You may also have started to get to the supermarket regularly. You may even be doing some planning. This is a terrific beginning. Let's add Mr Spud to your routine.

Have a potato (with its skin) every night just before bed. This may sound simple, but it will help your body raise your serotonin level and make you feel more confident, competent, creative and optimistic. Big results from a single nightly spud, huh?

You can eat your potato baked, boiled, mashed, roasted, cut

into oven fries or grated into hash browns. Just be sure you eat the skin. And you can top it with anything you like *except* foods that contain a protein. (Protein eaten along with the potato at bedtime will interfere with your serotonin-making process.) Good toppings are butter, margarine, salsa, mustard, spices, olive oil or flaxseed oil. Toppings you should *not* use are cheese, soured cream, bacon bits or cream of chicken soup.

Your nightly spud does not have to be a big potato. It can be a Maris Piper, a Ratte, or a little Jersey Royal. Experiment. I use a medium Yukon Gold with its skin on. If you find that you are having wild dreams on the nights you have your potato, this is a clue that you have low serotonin. This means you are getting a bigger hit of serotonin than you want right now. The bigger hit means your levels are very low. You need the serotonin, but it is better to go more slowly. Ease into it and let your brain catch up. Have a smaller potato, or eat just a half or even a third of it. Your body is talking to you. Listen.

You may believe that a potato has a high glycemic index and will make you fat if you eat it before bed. Poor Mr Spud has been given some bad press in the past few years. Recent books that suggest you use the glycemic index as a way to decide what to eat tell you potatoes raise your blood sugar very high. Potatoes are not bad, however.

Mashed potatoes *without* skin do have a very high glycemic index. Baked potatoes *with* the skin have a lower glycemic index but still have a glycemic punch. This is exactly why baked potatoes are perfect for the job. They evoke a glycemic response that causes a release of insulin to get that tryptophan into your brain to make serotonin. If you choose a carbohydrate that is too slow (that is to say, one with a very low GI), you will not get the desired effect. We will talk about potatoes and why they work more in Chapter 5, where I answer virtually every potato question you might have ever thought of.

When you get further along in the programme, you'll find out all sorts of options and choices about making your nightly potato more exciting. For now, just keep it simple. Eat a potato and its skin before bed.

Tips from the Field: Potato Particulars

I have found that a small spud is all it takes. You can bake it, pan-fry it, oven-fry it or make potato salad from it. You can use leftover skin-on mashed spuds and make potato pancakes if you wish. Yes, you must eat the skin and you may use butter or oil on it – just no protein like cheese or soured cream.

– S.

Take Three Vitamins

Vitamins play an important role in helping your body through the sugar detox phase, and we'll talk a lot more about them later. For now, as part of Step 4, take these three:

1. Vitamin C: 500 to 5,000 mg a day (depending upon what you are used to).
2. Vitamin B complex: choose one that is a 50-mg-a-day dosage. You might want to use a liquid formula because you can split the dose if you need to. Don't take it on an empty stomach or in the evening. If you feel a little buzzed by it, take less.
3. Zinc: 15 mg a day. Make sure to take your zinc with food. It can make you feel sick to your stomach if it is taken on an empty stomach. (Sucking on a zinc lozenge helps slow down and ease cold symptoms. If you are getting sick, you can increase the dose to 30 mg a day.)

If you're already taking a daily multivitamin, read the label and see if it contains the vitamin levels listed above. If so, simply keep taking it every day without any added supplements. If not, you may want to buy additional vitamins to make sure you are getting this baseline.

Many people ask me about taking more supplements, herbs, amino acids or other minerals in addition to those in the plan. If you have identified a need for many of these things in developing a well-balanced and healthy life for yourself, you need not stop taking them. However, often people who are addicted are very fond of taking something rather than eating meals and making life changes. To change these behaviour patterns, I encourage you to 'do the food' as your first and primary commitment. After you have mastered the seven steps, then you can explore additions to your plan.

5

Getting the Details Sorted Out: Answers to Your Questions

Usually when people are starting out on their food plan, they have all sorts of questions for me. The sugar-sensitive brain is generally smart and curious. When it comes to food, it is even smarter and more curious. In addition, most people who follow this plan have read many books on diets and nutrition before finding this one. They may have lots of questions about how sugar sensitivity and diets work.

That's why I am devoting this chapter to answering the questions I hear most frequently. Some of the questions (and answers) may not be relevant for you yet, but they will iron out ahead of time some of the wrinkles you will probably be faced with as you progress through the programme.

Is This a High-Fat Diet?

No. It is a moderate, healthy-fat plan. Your body needs fat for some of its most essential functions. The kind of fat you use has a huge impact on your health. Increase the good fats like olive

oil, flaxseed oil and fish oils, and reduce saturated fats found in foods such as meats and cheese. If you have been focusing on low-fat for a while and counting fat grams, this will be a change. That's because low-fat generally means high-sugar. I am trying to take the sugars out and increase the fat a little by steering you to the healthy ones.

Some people do find themselves eating more fat when they start the programme. Fat, like sugar, is linked to the beta-endorphin system. Sugar-sensitive people may well have a beta-endorphin release in response to eating fat: they feel confident, competent and optimistic after they have a meal higher in fat. This can be a good thing. Raising your beta-endorphin without getting a blood sugar spike (and its resulting steep drop) can help tide you over.

However, if you find yourself dreaming about high-fat foods, you will need to be careful that you don't transfer your beta-endorphin interest from sugar to fat. If your meals start drifting to nuts and cheese and more nuts and cheese, you know fat is calling you.

Isn't This Too Much Protein?

No. This is *not* a high-protein plan. It is a regular and consistent protein plan. The amount of protein I recommend is only a bit higher than the recommended daily allowance (RDA). The RDA calls for 54 g of protein a day for a 68-kg person, or a little less than 0.4 g per 450 g of body weight. I recommend that sugar-sensitive people on my programme have between 0.4 and 0.6 g per 450 g of body weight, depending on their health needs. In the early stages of your recovery, your body may have more repair work to do and you may need to eat more protein. You would be eating at the upper end of what I recommend. Later, as you feel better, you can reduce the amount.

But overall, I try to move people away from counting, whether it's grams of fat or grams of protein. Counting has played such havoc with our bodies. Counting has been the centre of most diets. I would prefer that you use the size of your fist to guide you in determining how much protein to eat at each meal. (It works like this: hold out your hand and make a fist. Look at its size. Then eat a fist-sized portion of protein at each meal. Obviously, if you weigh more or have a bigger fist, you will need to eat more protein.)

Why Don't You Call This Plan '*Protein* Not Prozac'?

The protein is essential, but so is the potato. This is a *two-part* biochemical healing process: first the protein, then the potato. The protein gets tryptophan into your bloodstream. The potato before bed gets that tryptophan across the blood-brain barrier and into your brain, where your serotonin factory is located. More tryptophan means more serotonin, which will increase your optimism, your creativity and your ability to concentrate. (If you want more details, read the next question.)

Questions on How Eating the Potato Works

What is the potato doing for my neurochemistry?

The potato is simply creating an insulin response, which has an effect on the movement of the amino acid tryptophan from your blood into your brain.

Why do we care about that? Because your body uses tryptophan to make serotonin. Serotonin is the brain chemical that makes you feel mellow and happy. It also helps you to 'just say no' to sweets and other things by putting the brakes on your impulsivity.

Tryptophan is a kind of amino acid that comes from protein. When you eat protein foods (meats, cheese, eggs, poultry, etc.), they are broken down into amino acids. These amino acids go

into your bloodstream and try to get into the brain as brain food. One of these aminos, tryptophan, is a little runt. The other amino acids, the big ones, compete with him and won't let him get across into the brain.

But there's an exception. When you eat a food (like a potato) that causes an insulin reaction, the insulin grabs the big amino acids and carries them off to your muscles as muscle food. The muscles don't really care about the runt, tryptophan, so he gets left behind in the bloodstream. Without the competition of the big aminos, little tryptophan can hop across the blood-brain barrier into the brain, where it will be used to produce serotonin. Thus, your serotonin levels rise.

So I want you to eat protein with dinner, then three hours later have something to raise your insulin level. A potato seems like a better alternative than a chocolate bar.

If you eat a bigger potato, will you get more serotonin?

Lots of people ask this. Then they take it a step further and ask, 'If you eat lots of protein *and* the big potato, will you get even more serotonin? Is there a limit to this? If one is good, two must be better!'

If you have had good protein at dinner three hours earlier, it is likely that a big potato will stoke the serotonin factory more. However, seeking a bigger hit is not the aim of the potato task. Bigger protein amounts and larger potatoes are not the goal. A hit of serotonin that is too much may cause you nightmares and give you a hangover. This is definitely not a 'more is better' thing. You're just after a good night's sleep and a gentle rise in your overall serotonin level.

If you are already taking an antidepressant, you may find that you do not need to use a large potato. In fact, if you do, you may increase the side effects of your antidepressant. Your sleep may become restless, you may have a headache, or you may find you are less able to have an orgasm. You have two options: decrease

the size of the potato or talk with your doctor about decreasing the amount of antidepressant you are taking. If you decide to do this, do it slowly and carefully.

If I don't notice any differences in my mood, should I eat a bigger potato the next night?

Play around a bit and see what happens. The effects from food usually aren't as dramatic as the effects from drugs. They are often more subtle and build over time. But most sugar-sensitive people love to experiment. It's harmless with the potato.

Why do I have weird dreams since I started eating the potato?

The potato is increasing your serotonin level, which is related to REM sleep and dreaming. These changes in your dreams mean the spud is working! This should change in a week or so. If the dreams disturb you, use a smaller potato.

The potato seems to give me a headache. Why?

You might need to decrease the amount of potato you are eating. Too much serotonin can cause a headache. This may be a clue that your 'dose' is not right.

Are there any other ways I can increase serotonin by using food and/or timing?

Once you understand the principles of the protein/carbohydrate timing, you can work out a plan that best suits you. Master the basics of having regular, consistent protein and a timed carbohydrate.

If I want to get more serotonin in the winter (I have SAD – seasonal affective disorder), should I eat a potato three hours after lunch and after dinner?

For people who are severely depressed, I will sometimes recommend that they actually have a second (or even a third) car-

bohydrate snack (three hours after each meal). This is simply to maximize the serotonin effect. Experiment to see if it helps. You don't need to eat a lot of potato, but do pay attention to *when* you eat it.

Will the potato let me stop taking my antidepressants?

The potato helps raise your serotonin levels. Some people have found that doing the food plan (not just the potato at night) has a huge impact on how they feel. They ask me whether they should just stop taking their medication. My recommendation is to do the food plan for at least six months. If you feel you are ready to reduce or stop your medication, talk with your doctor to plan a gradual taper. Some people are able to go off their medication with the food plan. Others are able to reduce their dosage. And others keep taking their medication but find it works more effectively. Your job is to understand the biochemistry of your body and your needs and then use the food plan and medications to get the result you want.

Is the potato considered one of my three meals?

No. The first phase of the programme is to eat three meals a day with protein, *plus* a potato before bed. The potato is not a snack so much as a medicinal intervention.

Can I eat potatoes with meals as well?

Of course. Just be sure to eat the skin.

What should I do if I miss the potato?

If you mean for one night, don't worry about it. If you start forgetting a lot, figure out what you can do to remind yourself. It is an important part of the plan.

Does it have to be a potato?

Well, yes and no. The potato is ideal. This is why I called my

first book *Potatoes Not Prozac*, rather than *Apples Not Prozac*. Also, potatoes are a very good comfort food. Think of the spud as number one. If you simply can't do the spud (some people are allergic to them), here are some good alternatives:

- Baked sweet potatoes with butter, cinnamon and nutmeg (without skin)
- Ryvitas with butter
- Brown rice with butter, cinnamon and nutmeg
- Porridge
- Oven-fried sweet spuds (without the skin)
- Skin-on sugar-free potato salad
- Brown rice cakes with some butter

Remember, as with the spud, don't have any protein with these nighttime carbohydrates.

What if I'm diabetic?

If you are diabetic, don't use the white potato; use a sweet potato or one of the alternatives above.

Don't potatoes have a high glycemic index? Won't they spike my blood sugar?

Yes, potatoes do evoke insulin, although when they are eaten with their skins, they raise the blood sugar far more slowly than what is reported as the glycemic index, which was developed with mashed potatoes (without skins and without butter). But remember, we *want* a timed insulin response to get that tryptophan from your blood into your brain!

You really do not have to worry about the glycemic index of one potato. Going off all the sweet foods you have been eating will create a hefty impact on your health.

The skin protects you further. It is mostly fibre and dramatically slows down the absorption process, which your blood

sugar really appreciates. Eating the potato at bedtime has been carefully orchestrated to change your brain chemistry.

Will eating potatoes be bad for my arthritis?

There have been some reports that plants in the nightshade family (which includes potatoes) do make arthritis symptoms flare up. Try a small potato and see if it bothers your arthritis. If it does, use one of the substitutes listed above, but please don't give up on old Mr Spud without first seeing how it works for you.

If I am going into menopause, should I use sweet potatoes or yams instead?

If you feel this would be valuable for you, you can substitute them for the potato. However, you will lose some of the insulin effect because of the lower glycemic value.

Do I still have to keep eating the potato after I've been on the plan all these months?

Yep. What's more, you don't *have* to keep eating the potato for ever and ever, you *get* to. It offers you benefits that you would be foolish to give up. We're not only talking about balancing your brain chemistry, but keeping it balanced. What a concept!!

Your sugar-sensitive biochemistry isn't going to go away. But you can keep it in balance and hold it steady. The spud helps. Don't discard the spud!

Questions on Choosing and Preparing Your Potato

What kind of potato is best to eat?

Any kind of potato is fine, although a mammoth one weighing a kilogram may be a little more than you can handle before bed. Choose a spud that suits you. Have fun; explore the wonderful world of potatoes.

Potatoes are classified by shape, skin colour, and use. Reds are good for a variety of uses but are best for roasting. Whites

are best for either boiling or frying, and small red and specialty gourmet potatoes are ideal for boiling. 'New' potatoes (small potatoes that are dug early before the skins have set) are best boiled or steamed.

How large or small a potato should I eat?

Experiment until you find what works for you. You could start with a small new potato, for example. The bottom line is, let your body decide.

There will be many variables that will affect this choice. If you're hungry, eat a big one. If you are a little person, have a small one. Pay attention to the effect and adjust the size to get the results you want. Most of you will probably find yourself using a small- to medium-sized Desiree, King Edward or Maris Piper. Be sure to eat the skin, too.

Can I eat the potato with butter, salt and pepper?

You can have anything that is not protein. Olive oil, salt, pepper, spice, butter, flax oil, salad dressing, mustard, salsa or curry sauce. Be creative.

Can I use mashed potatoes with butter and milk in them?

Stay away from the milk, because it has protein. You can mash the potato with oat or rice milk, however, and be fine. Make sure your spuds have the skin on them when you mash them.

Can I slice the potato into thick french fries and bake them?

Yes. You can bake them with a little olive oil sprinkled over them, seasoned with salt and pepper. They are quite good. One of my favourite ways of frying potatoes is on a non-stick pan with olive oil: slice them thin and fry them with thin-sliced onions and green peppers. Heavenly!

In fact, there are many, many ways to prepare Mr Spud. You can make fries like these, you can make a potato casserole or

soup and have a little each evening, or you can make potato skins. This does *not* have to be boring. Use your imagination and your cookbook. Ask your friends. Be creative.

Are the eyes of the potato toxic? Should I cut them out?

Eyes are not toxic; however, sprouts are poisonous. Choose potatoes that are well-formed, smooth, and firm, and without discolouration, cracks, bruises or soft spots. Avoid potatoes with green-tinted skin. Green potatoes have been exposed to light and can have a bitter taste.

Where do you buy purple potatoes?

Many stores that carry organic produce have these now. They tend to be seasonal, however, and are not always available in the summer.

Questions on the Timing of Your Potato

I'm uncertain about when to apply the potato at bedtime since I'm doing the three-meals-a-day plan.

The plan is three meals *and* a baked potato. Eat the potato three hours after dinner and before you go to bed.

Should I wait three hours from the beginning of supper or three hours from the end of supper to eat the potato?

It depends on how long your meal is. The ideal interval for the potato effect is three hours after having protein. Use your own judgment.

I rarely have three hours between dinner and the potato. It's more like one to one and a half hours. Am I wasting my time eating it? (Even at that rate, it still acts like a stimulant and I have trouble falling asleep, and sometimes I feel worse the next day.) If so, should I do the potato/slow carb three hours after lunch instead?

You are either eating really late or going to bed really early. Something is out of sync. Certainly try having the potato after lunch. But the stimulant effect will quieten down in a few weeks and you should be fine.

When I'm at work, I have a tea break at about 5 P.M., but my shift doesn't end until eleven, and then I need to unwind for an hour or so before I sleep. If I eat the potato at about 8 P.M., in the middle of my shift, will I feel mellow and sleepy? Or will I just work away the effects, so it's not as useful? And if I wait until I get home, is it too late to be effective?

I gather you are working the 3 to 11 P.M. shift. Is your tea break for tea or for your evening meal? Eat your meal and have the potato three hours later. You can take Mr Spud in a plastic bag. The 'sleep' effect doesn't seem to kick in until later on when you are in REM dreaming state (about 3 A.M.). You will simply feel more relaxed and focused in dealing with a crisis. Spud is not a drug; he's a food! Just relax and make sure you have dinner.

I work/sleep a crazy schedule. Please give me advice/guidance/rules on how to work the potato in.

The practice of figuring out what is right for you is part of your own healing. Sometimes, sugar-sensitive people work and sleep in crazy schedules because they are so out of balance. As they do the food plan, things start to shift. They start actually *planning* on the fact that they need to stop and eat dinner. Or they realize that staying up until 3:00 A.M. to study is crazy. These changes are not psychological but come with the change in brain chemistry.

Work to get three meals with protein at regular intervals. Do the best you can. Visit the Community Forum on the website and ask for help with this. Take a baked spud in a plastic bag with you and eat it even if you are on the run or are eating it at your computer. Things will get better.

What if I can't eat the spud exactly at three hours? Is it okay to eat it one or two hours before or after the three-hour time frame?

The three-hour interval is not absolute, simply ideal. Do the best you can.

Can I eat a raw potato instead of having to cook one?

No, raw potatoes do not give you the effect we are looking for. Raw potatoes are pretty indigestible and have little nutritional value. Cook those spuds!

Is it okay to cook seven potatoes all at once for the whole week?

Many people have found that preparing the potato ahead makes it easier to have one. Others simply pop a spud into the microwave each evening. Find what works for you. But I wouldn't keep leftovers any longer than three days.

Questions on How to Make the Plan Work

Once I eliminate sugar, how long will it take for my mood swings to level off?

The mood swings actually can level off *before* you go off of sugar. Remember, going off sugar is the sixth step of the plan, not the first. Having breakfast with protein, eating the potato at night and having three meals at regular intervals will all have a positive effect on your mood. Later in the plan, after all those other steps, you do your sugar detox. Once you have completed your sugar detox, you can expect pretty dramatic changes in a week or so.

Is your plan in line with OA (Overeaters Anonymous)?

Absolutely. I attend twelve-step programmes and I think they can provide a wonderful support to anyone with a sugar-sensitive body (and therefore an addictive biochemistry). Doing my programme and OA together is a pretty unbeatable combination.

I disagree, however, about having to be rigid with rules and about the twelve-step definition of abstinence as *no* slips or you start all over. I prefer a kinder approach that acknowledges the person's commitment to healing.

If I exercise a lot, is it okay to snack?

If you are in training for athletic events or you engage in strenuous physical activity or exercise, it is realistic to add more food into your plan. Try one of the following for between-meal snacks:

- An apple, two cheese sticks and a handful of almonds
- A baked potato with cottage cheese
- A turkey sandwich on whole grain bread and a pear
- Chinese foods like chicken and broccoli – ask them to leave out the MSG and sugar
- Egg salad and a whole grain bagel

Also, you may find that if you have more protein and really complex carbohydrates at your meals, you are less frantic after exercise. If you need a snack during a long run or bike ride, I would try having a George's Shake (see page 57) made with oat milk, which will keep without refrigeration.

What if I can't afford this plan?

People who are homeless and people who are very rich are on this plan. You can definitely design a plan that works for you and your budget.

Fish as a protein does cost more than macaroni and cheese. But don't scare yourself. There are many, many protein foods such as eggs, lentils, kidney beans, chicken thighs, turkey, yogurt, tofu, peanut butter, tuna and cottage cheese that can work for you if you are on a careful budget.

Also, as you progress with the plan, you won't be buying all sorts of junk food and snack food. Your food budget will stay the same, but what you buy with it will change.

What if I hate to eat alone?

Part of being sugar sensitive is feeling isolated. When we feel isolated and disconnected, doing things alone is harder. Eating alone can be a real drag because you have to buy the food, prepare it, eat by yourself and then clean up. This is no fun for any of us. Find ways to have meals that are easy to prepare and don't require cleanup. Read a book while eating. Watch TV while eating. I know that all the experts tell you not to do that, but they aren't people who live alone. Create what will work for you, because having three meals a day is really important.

What if I am too busy to cook?

Many of the people I talk to who are succeeding with the programme have had to deal with this problem. The most popular solution seems to be to set aside time after grocery shopping to clean and chop vegetables, cook some meats in advance, boil eggs, and so on. That way, when they're caught up in the rush of their day-to-day life, they can open the fridge and grab stuff.

Other people have done detective work at their local delis and restaurants and come up with lists of things that they can buy there, such as

- Tuna or egg salad sandwiches on whole grain bread
- Caesar salad with grilled chicken
- Fajitas
- Baked potato with cheese and veggies from the salad bar
- Chef salad
- Meat- or bean-filled wrap

There's another aspect to this problem that you should consider, however. Being too busy can reflect an unfocused and scattered mind, which is one of the symptoms of low serotonin. You may find that by taking the time to make changes to your food, you end up being able to get everything done – and in significantly less time.

Is taking St John's wort okay on this plan?

St John's wort can be a nice addition to the Potatoes Not Prozac Programme, but follow directions on dosage and be careful about sun exposure. Also, pay attention to foods that are high in the amino acid tyrosine (such as red wine and mature and blue cheese), because they may cause an adverse reaction.

People have also asked me about using 5HTP. I am extremely cautious about using supplements for which we have little factual information and whose processing standards are not regulated. By using this supplement, you are cranking up your level of serotonin without letting your body find its own level. As you might guess, my bias is always to use the least harmful method first – that is, eating food rather than taking supplements or medication.

Isn't having a little red wine every day good for the heart?

I have to admit that I have a bias against red wine or any form of alcohol as a way to improve heart health. Red wine acts as a really quick sugar for sugar-sensitive people. The health benefits obtained from red wine can be achieved in other ways. Alcohol is a solvent and achieves its relaxation effects by melting the lipid layer of the brain. For some people a little alcohol is great, but for many of us, it is not so good. I have a great life without alcohol, and I encourage you to do so, too.

Can I drink a George's Shake as a meal twice a day?

Once a day is fine, but please, please don't rely on supplemental foods (even those I recommend) to replace your regular meals. Remember, we are also working towards behavioural changes that include taking care of yourself and fixing yourself real meals. Be cautious with other commercial shake mixes, because they generally have lots of added sugars, often disguised as complex carbohydrates. Read labels. And remember, any shake should contain *both* protein and complex carbohydrate.

What about my comfort foods, like nonfat cappuccino with Sweet'n Low?

Until you have reached Step 5, when you switch from browns to whites, you can keep eating your comfort foods, whether they are muffins, chocolate cake or French bread. In fact, you can continue to eat sugar foods until you have done a sugar detox as part of Step 6. Just eat them with a full meal, *and as you do so,* notice your own emotional attachment to them. See if you can tease out what part of your enjoyment comes from the biochemical response these foods temporarily give you and what part of your enjoyment comes from what you associate with what you are eating. Did your mum cook pancakes on Saturday mornings? Did you always have chocolate cake and ice cream for your birthday?

Also, think about what other kinds of foods – nutritious ones – would comfort you. Some people love hot soup or butternut squash cooked with nutmeg and butter. Also take a look at the recipes at the end of the book. There are several there that might fit the bill, including Cottage Cheese–Cinnamon Pancakes, Pizza with Whole Wheat Crust, Whole Wheat Lasagna, Cornbread, Yam and Cheese Strudel, Pumpkin Cake with Cream Cheese–Peanut Butter Frosting, and Carrot Cake.

As to your cappuccino with Sweet'n Low, can you substitute an unsweetened decaf filter for it? Or try having a soya milk cappuccino. I am very leery of the effects of artificial sweeteners.

Finally, consider our trusty friend the potato. When people were asked to rate various comfort foods as to how full and satisfied they felt after eating them (see the box below), the humble potato came out miles ahead!

Food	Rating on the Satiety Index
Potatoes	323
Popcorn	154
Biscuits	120
Pasta	119
Jelly beans	118
French fries	116
White bread	100
Ice cream	96
Chips	91
Doughnuts	68
Cake	65
Croissant	47

6

Creating a Routine

Now that you have been working with the programme for a while, you need to spend a little time holding steady with your new skills. This may be anywhere from a few weeks to a few months. Steady means firm, unfaltering, unflappable and unwavering. Steady means driving in cruise control. Steady is what this phase of your programme is all about. If you compare this phase of your programme to the days before you started, it may seem kind of quiet. The idea of steady may seem boring to you. Let's listen to some friends from the forum.

Here's what Denise writes:

Steady is perseverance with the plan, taking it on faith and starting to see the light at the end of the tunnel. Steady is believing that this has worked for others and it will work for me because it feels like the right thing to do. Steady is getting back up if I slip because I know this is the direction I want to head in. Steady is not letting myself get sidetracked by frustration and other emotions. Steady is an accumulation of good days!

Phyllis puts it this way:

Steady is how it feels when I'm giving my body the right stuff and staying away from the wrong stuff. It's part of the initial learning stage, where you begin to hear what your body is trying to tell you. You're not off sugar yet, but you are beginning to make the changes that lead to it. As you do so, you begin to feel things differently.

And here is Annette:

Steady is boring – and that's good! I was so accustomed to struggling through my life, I have had to re-evaluate how I look at everyday tasks and events. What happened was that getting stable with my eating and diary keeping began to open my mind to the possibilities of everyday living. Steady gave me enough clarity to see that I could approach things differently, less emotionally.

Doing Regular Life

Let's review the five things you are working on:

1. Eating three meals with protein at regular intervals
2. Having your potato at night
3. Taking your vitamins
4. Planning your meals and shopping for them
5. Keeping your food diary

At this point in the programme, this is *all* you need to do. Five things. One for each finger on your right hand. Nothing more. Do not try to make huge changes to your food right now. Make sure you eat enough. Don't be thinking this is a diet and you need to cut back on your food. You may waver while you are learning new tools. Keep writing in your diary. Keep reading

what you have written. Look for patterns, make adjustments and listen to your body.

Enjoying the Routine

Your whole life you may well have fought against 'boring' and yearned for 'exciting'. I want you to discover a new concept in this phase. If you get your food consistent and stable, your life will start to get more *interesting*. When this happens, the drama that you looked for in making all the changes in what you are eating will come through in your life. You will notice emerging creativity, humour burbling up, positive changes in your job and changes in your interests – all sorts of things you never thought were connected to what you are eating. It is hard to describe, but it *will* happen.

Tips from the Field: No Fear

My task in life used to be struggling to get past my fears, insecurities and self-hatred to do what I wanted to do in my life. More often now, my task (my privilege!) is to enjoy observing all the wonders that happen around me, knowing what I want to do, then saying and doing what I feel without fear. I won't kid you and tell you that I feel this every minute of every day, but even when I am feeling cloudy or anxious, I know that it will pass if I continue to 'do the food'. Miraculous! I love this! This is what it's all about!

– D.

Refining the Plan

Getting steady with your plan does not mean making huge changes, it means making small ones. Refinements. For example, maybe you will figure out that dinner works better for you

at 6:00 P.M. instead of 7:00 P.M. Or you may find that breakfast at 7:45 A.M. works really well for you. Remember, this is an individualized plan. It's not about getting it right in terms of what I want you to do. It's about getting it right for you, for your rhythm and your body.

Get so steady about doing your meals, food planning and grocery shopping that you don't have to think about them any more. They will become automatic. They will become part of the fabric of your life and you won't be thinking about food all the time.

This is the time to just do the programme and create the refinements that work for you. But don't mess with the programme's basics! Don't ask if you can skip breakfast or have juice instead of a potato. Or have a can of Slim-Fast instead of a George's Shake. Try not to argue about the order of the steps of the programme. I have designed them to support your finding your way out of sugar addiction. The steps are the map for your sugar-sensitive body. Eat the potato and keep the diary!

What to Do If You Slip

After you have been steady for a while, you may be distressed to find yourself in a slippery place. You may forget to have breakfast or stop writing in your diary. You may start having a croissant and cappuccino as breakfast or a glass of wine while cooking dinner.

Some people find that while they may slip, they notice it right away and simply get back on track. More often, one slip becomes a little wobble and then the wobble gets bigger and you wake up and realize you aren't feeling so well. The fog has crept back in; you are tired or cranky. Go back to your food diary and take note of what has been going on. You may have thought it was the stress level of your in-laws visiting, but a trip through your diary may tell you that the meal at the restaurant on the evening they arrived started with homemade Italian bread and

then went to pasta, wine and dessert. Maybe what you thought was stress was really all the bread and lack of protein.

The most important thing is kindness and tenderness. All of us, including me, wobble from time to time. It is part of the process. I admit to having a weakness for eggnog lattes. They call me every Christmastime. Part of being steady is being able to notice the wobble and make a correction. If you can go back to your process and your body with humour and tenderness, you may find that the slips give you wonderful information about the most vulnerable places in your programme. Use them, learn from them, and build on them.

Check back in your food diary for where you first started to veer off the programme. It's likely that smaller slips, like not having enough protein with your breakfast, preceded the big slip that got your attention (say, skipping breakfast for two days and snacking on sugar in mid-afternoon). Or you let more than five or six hours go by between meals. Also, take a look at the feelings you recorded at the time. This programme is about listening to your body and learning how what you eat affects both your feelings and your behaviour.

Sometimes the start of the slip is not keeping your food diary. As you get steady, you may feel that you 'know' what you eat and how you feel. Please, please, please keep doing the diary. It will keep you safe in troubled times and will guide you back when you wander off.

Coming Back After a Full Crash

You may fall off the programme big time. Twelve-step people call this relapse. You can call it crashing. You may find that even the idea of giving up sugar and sweet things is propelling you to eat more of them than you used to. This is a natural response to that stress; everybody goes through it. Don't be alarmed. Just keep having three meals a day with protein.

If you do crash, the first thing is, don't beat yourself up.

Learning to stay on the programme is part of the healing. No one takes a straight line to the end. The power of your recovery comes with how well you deal with these crashes. Be kind, be gentle and be firm, too. Take a deep breath and go back to Step 1. Keep it really simple. Just focus on eating breakfast with protein every day. Eat the potato. Keep the diary. Then three meals a day with protein and complex carbs.

The good news is that coming back gets easier each time. You know the drill. If you can keep from criticizing yourself about failure, you will be fine. You have the skills to return to the programme and start anew. Use your slips as an opportunity to learn and grow. Over time, you will get steadier and steadier.

Tips from the Field: Compassion in Troubled Times

When my food is off, I am the least clear and compassionate with myself – and this at a time when I need the *most* compassion in order to carry out the detective work and find the source of my crash.

It has been a lesson in letting go of the old self-punishing diet mentality and continuing to grow in compassion. When I slip badly and feel worthless and ashamed, I try to view myself the way a friend would see me – lovingly, forgivingly. Then I go back and highlight parts of my diary and make concrete plans on how to change things.

– A.

Writing in Your Diary Every Day

If you think keeping your diary is boring, it's an important clue. It may mean that you are not using your diary to discover what your body has to say. You may be dutifully logging your food, but not listening to your body.

The value of your diary comes in *using* it. When you really understand that your diary is a way for your body to talk with you, everything will change.

If you see your diary only as a log to record how well (or how poorly) you are doing, it will get old really fast However, if you work with your diary as a living dialogue with your body, it can be a joy. You will *want* to write in it. You will want to read it and use it to understand what your body needs.

Your body wants to be in relationship with you. It wants to talk with you about how it feels. It wants to teach you what it needs, but it can do so only by giving you its symptoms. Symptoms are the language of your body. If you are feeling better, things are working. If you aren't, you will need to adjust your process and your food. But you can't know the adjustments without your diary.

If you came to my office for a private session, you would bring your diary to research your body's story. These are the questions we would explore together:

- How are you feeling when you wake up? Are you energized? Excited about the day?
- Do you have a hard time waking up? A healthy, rested body wants to get up after sleeping. Even a 'night person' will want to get up – albeit more slowly and in increments. When your body is balanced, it is pleased to have another day. If getting up is really hard for you, simply make a note of this. It will change as the food changes.
- When you wake up, do you want to eat breakfast? Are you hungry?
- Are you having breakfast with protein *every* morning? Is this enjoyable?
- Have you developed a breakfast routine that you like? Is it easy and pleasant?

- Has breakfast become automatic and simply a part of your morning without a big hassle?
- Are you having three meals with protein?
- Are you eating enough? Are you eating too much?
- Are you enjoying what you are eating?
- Are you getting the vitamins every day?
- Are you having your evening carbohydrate?

Sometimes people forget the vitamin part. But the vitamins are directly tied in to the processes that convert tryptophan into serotonin. Skip the vitamins and you shortchange your healing. If you will listen, your body will speak to you. Your body has waited through all those years of sugar. It has been forgotten and hidden in shame. Your body wants to talk with you. If you come home to it, your body will respond with a degree of cooperation that will shock you.

Your body loves you. Even if you haven't loved it, it adores you and wants to serve you. It wants to be connected. Spend time; listen to your blessed body. The diary can be your body's voice. Think of that when you read your diary or write in it. Your body has a voice – finally.

Tips from the Field: Learning to Listen

When I first started the programme, I kept a diary for about a week. Then I forgot about it. But now I am remembering to do it, because *finally* I really want to remember. I really want to hear what is going on in my body and with my food. Before, it was just something I would have to do and which I did not think I needed to do.

– A.

No More Fighting – Mastery

This programme works really well, but only if you do it. Stop fighting with the programme. Worry about the big picture and let go of the tiny little details like how much sugar is in your ketchup. Sugar-sensitive people have a whole lifetime of guilt and shame about their food. More times than they can count, they have tried some new programme, resisted it, then given it up – and tried the next new programme to come along.

Try to just settle into your routine and master it. It's very simple. Not dramatic. But you do have to do it.

Allowing the Optimism and Feeling Better

Go for gentle optimism as opposed to wild enthusiasm about this programme. Wild enthusiasm is what sugar sensitives usually feel when we discover a new programme. We think, *Oh my God, I'm gonna do the whole thing. I'm gonna go off sugar, I'm gonna change everything I'm eating, I'm gonna plan my menus, I'm gonna do everything I need to do* . . . Then we end up in the dumps once again – because we can't do it all.

The way to succeed in this programme is to just plug away at having three meals a day and eating a potato. Soon you are going to start feeling better and you are going to think, *You know what? Maybe this will work.* Gentle optimism is much more likely to succeed than wild enthusiasm.

Planning Your Food: What's Your Style?

The key to planning your food is to remember that you are not doing *the* Plan, you are doing *your* Plan. And one of the ways you are going to refine the basic plan is to adapt it to your cooking style.

My own style around food is pretty functional these days. I am happy choosing from three or four meal options. It makes

my life less complicated. When I was younger I used to cook with energy and enthusiasm. Now, because I have so many other things I want to be doing, I don't really take time to create the kind of fancy meals I once did.

Here are some styles that seem to fit sugar-sensitive people. Take a look and see if one fits you.

The Functional/Factual Type

These people have six choices they use and simply rotate their meals through them. Their foods are simple, relatively un-adorned and very easy to make. Some functional/factual types have a set for breakfast, a set for lunch and a set for dinner. They have two eggs, a piece of wholemeal toast and some juice every morning for breakfast. They eat a tuna sandwich on rye from the sandwich bar every day. And for dinner they have the same frozen meal.

The 'I Don't Want to Change' Type

These people eat the same breakfast every day and then vary their other two meals from two or three choices. They like ritual and predictability. They have been eating the same breakfast for ten years. This is a simple approach that works very well with the programme.

The One-Pot/One-Meal Type

The one-pot people put everything they are going to have for the day into a stewpot, a casserole dish or a baking pan. They eat from this pot until it is done, then start again with a new and different concoction. This works fine as long as you don't fish all the protein (chicken, beef, tofu, whatever) out of the pot at your first meal. In fact, you may want to wait to add the protein – say, 115 to 170 g of cooked chicken – into each serving you give yourself. That way you know you'll be getting enough.

The Salad Type

Salad people usually skip breakfast (which we know is not good!), then have all their meals consist of lettuce with different things added to it. These people can succeed with the programme if they don't mind eating salad and protein for breakfast instead of skipping it and if they are willing to accept that lettuce doesn't count as a vegetable (not enough bulk to it). The lettuce can be the backdrop to the real salad of tomatoes, cucumbers, carrots, shredded cabbage, courgettes, red onion, red and green peppers, jicama, celery, cold cooked green beans, broccoli, asparagus, and so on! If you add protein to your salad via hard-boiled eggs, cooked chicken, tuna, anchovies, even cold grilled steak (it's heavenly on a salad!), you'll be fine.

The Eat-on-the-Run Type

These are the people who eat in the car, eat standing up, find something on the run, and have snacks in the glove compartment. This type can stay on the programme if (and only if) they or someone who is taking care of them cooks or buys the food they are going to eat on the run. You cannot successfully eat on the run if you don't pay close attention and *plan* what you are going to eat and when you are going to eat it.

One tip: pack last night's dinner leftovers in plastic containers and eat them on your way in to work. Or on your way back to your desk after using your lunch hour to work out. Or whilst watching your son's football match. Eating on the run can work if you have access to good food.

The 'I Eat If You Fix It' Type

These are the people who eat cereal or cheese and crackers unless someone else makes them a meal. You can only succeed as an 'I eat if you fix it' type if you have someone to do the fixing. If you have a good fixer, you will do very well (like Oprah with her

personal cook). If you don't, you are in trouble. Eating cereal won't cut it on this plan. You may be able to get by if you have a good deli or supermarket that makes good takeaway proteins and things like salads and grilled veggies. But you will have to go get them. And later, when you get further into this programme, you will have to be sure there is no sugar in the sauces or salad dressings!

Frankly, if you are this type, I recommend that you choose a new style. Pick the one that is easiest for you and work on it.

The Cooking Type

These are the people who actually use cookbooks and prepare meals. They enjoy it. And the cookers have subtypes ranging from Delia Smith Miss Homemaker of Tomorrow (that was me in a past life!) to gourmet cooks to just your mother (or your father) in the kitchen. These are the people who read recipes for enjoyment, who like to shop and make meals. If this is your type, you'll sail through this programme!

A Little Exercise Always Helps

Everyone tells us we should exercise, right? Right. So there must be a good reason! What they don't always tell you about exercise, though, is that once you get used to it, your body will want to do it. You won't have to use discipline any more to get yourself walking or bicycling or swimming. Just as you will gradually need less and less self-discipline to eat the right foods for your sugar-sensitive body.

Exercise has an essential role in healing sugar sensitivity. In the first place, it evokes a nice slow rise in your beta-endorphins, those wonderful neurotransmitters that boost your self-esteem and make you feel optimistic, competent and compassionate – in short, a credit to the human race. What a great feeling! The second key thing that exercise does is make your body more

sensitive to insulin. This helps in moving the sugar from your blood into your muscles, where it can be used as fuel. When you are overweight, your body does this less efficiently. Exercise helps to repair this problem.

If you think you can't exercise, see if you can start by committing to exercise *one minute more* a day. If you are doing no exercise now, that means that on your first day you are going to do only one minute. Walk to the end of the driveway and back in one minute. That's it. The next day you are going to add a second minute. Keep going one minute more each day.

If you get up to five minutes, but six minutes seems too long, do five minutes until you feel like you can do six minutes. Do it for three days. Do it for a week if you need to. At some point, you will realize that you *can* do six minutes, and you will. Then keep increasing it one minute at a time. You are aiming for thirty minutes a day. You might need only a month to get there. You might take three months. Slow but steady wins the race. I just started doing this at the gym, and I've gone from five minutes to fifteen minutes in two weeks – with no pain. My body is thrilled.

So the bottom line on exercise is this: it doesn't work if you don't do it. And it works if you do. The key is to start – one minute at a time.

Water, Water All the Time

Drink lots and lots of water. Fill a litre bottle with water and carry it with you. Sip it all day long. Put a slice of lemon in it if you want. Try to have two whole bottles (or eight glasses of water) each day. If you weigh more than 90 kg, drink more than that.

You may think that if you drink this amount, you will have to pee all day. But a funny thing happens. As your body gets used to more water, your need to pee will be less frantic. If you're

over fifty and having problems with urinary incontinence, it actually will get *better* over time as you increase your daily water intake. If you are exercising, it will get better even more quickly.

Our bodies love having plenty of water. Water carries nutrients to our cells, carries toxins back out of them, and keeps our skin moist. In addition, it aids in the working of neurotransmitters like serotonin and beta-endorphin. Our brain functions with electricity. Water conducts electrical signals. If our brain is dehydrated, the electrical signals won't get transmitted properly. Drink water.

Remember, increase your water intake, not just your fluid intake. Juices, coffee, milk, tea and fizzy drinks *do not count* as water. In fact, coffee, tea and cola are diuretics and make your body *lose* water. If you do drink them, in addition to your 8 to 10 glasses of water a day, drink an additional 350 ml, for example, for each 350-ml can of fizzy drink.

Many sugar-sensitive people have a hard time remembering to drink more water. 'I just am not thirsty,' they say. It seems that for many people, the thirst signal, like the hunger signal, doesn't work the way it should. You don't notice thirst until you are in big trouble. Drink water by the clock rather than by your thirst. And note in your food diary how much water you have had for the day.

Tips from the Field: Water, Everywhere

I treated our family to an in-home water cooler so we have cold water on hand all the time. They drink more, I drink more. I also keep a couple of half bottles of water in the freezer, so when I need to go out for the day, I fill the bottle of ice to the top with water and it stays cold for the rest of the day.

– M.

Why Some Stuff Will Help

My readers have suggested a number of kitchen appliances that can help you find the road to steady. People started to spontaneously vote for their favourites. Here are the appliances that were voted tops by our community.

Indoor Grills

These are little grills that open up and allow you to place your food between the grill plates. They were originally designed as 'lean meat' machines because they are shaped to let the fat drain off. But they are easy to use and clean and make the food taste great. They got the majority vote.

Combination microwave oven

These ovens can handle many, many tasks, ranging from cooking the spud to reheating yesterday's leftovers or cooking a frozen dinner. They are easy to use and a great resource for turning a cold meal into a hot dinner.

Crock-Pot

The one-pot people all know the miracle of the Crock-Pot. The rest of you will be delighted to discover that hot chilli can be waiting to eat right when you get home from work. No waiting, no cooking, just sit down and eat. Chilli, soup, stew, beans, roasts – you name it; the one-potters make it.

Rice Cooker

Sometimes you shy away from making real rice – long-grain brown rice – because you feel it takes too long. You really have to keep an eye on it so the pot doesn't boil over and slop that wet rice stuff down into the burner pan. A rice cooker lets you set it up, then go take care of the rest of your life while you are waiting for dinner. And the rice comes out perfect every time.

Blender

Ah, the joys of the blender. Use the blender to mix your George's Shake for breakfast. Use the blender to make something quickly if you are over the cliff. Every sugar-sensitive kitchen needs a blender.

Your Oven

A shocking thought – cook food in the oven! Roast a chicken, putting two potatoes in the pan along with 450 g of chopped carrots, and voilà! Dinner in an hour – no hassle. And those potatoes baked in the oven taste mighty fine.

Use Your Freezer

If you make good use of your freezer, you can cook once a week and have things to eat all week long. Store individual portions in plastic bags. No preparation needed, just heat it up and eat. Make your own TV dinners.

Trying New Foods – Starting to Explore

Many sugar sensitives know how to make only bread, muffins, biscuits, brownies and good things like that – you tend to be masters at making 'white things'. It's time to learn to grill a steak, roast a chicken, make fabulous salad dressing, stir-fry veggies and sauté cabbage (then bake it in soured cream). Be outrageous. Go to the supermarket and try something new every week. Ask your friends who cook (you might have one or two who do) to teach you about new foods. Take a cookery class.

Veggies Are for Real

When you think of vegetables, do you groan and make a face? Does the thought of broccoli make you ill? Many sugar-sensitive people feel (or used to feel) that way. You remember

being told that you couldn't leave the dinner table until you ate the sprouts. Couldn't have dessert until you'd at least *tried* the cauliflower au gratin. And now that you are adults and can control (or think you can) what you put in your mouths, the only vegetables you eat are french fries, iceberg lettuce and sometimes sweetcorn.

Tips from the Field: Veggie Detente

You can change your relationship to vegetables! I grew up eating no veggies. There was always semi-mouldy iceberg lettuce in the refrigerator. I, like President Reagan, counted ketchup as a vegetable. I guess I have a 'kid's appetite' in not liking vegetables. But I have friends (many) who LOVE veggies.

Since being on the programme, I have tried to add more veggies to my food plan. I started off for a few months having 3 to 5 veggies PER MONTH (no kidding!) I actually got up to one veggie per day, which is great for me. I can't say I got to the point where I love them, but I definitely improved.

– L.

The best suggestion for people who dislike veggies is to cook once (or twice) for the week. One week, for example, you could buy a prime rib roast marinated in garlic that might give you five or six meals. Cook lots of vegetables (carrots, onions and potatoes with skins) with the roast. You'll find yourself *loving* those vegetables! The garlic helps.

Use the leftovers to design different 'quick' meals. Mix some of the meat with brown rice and veggies in a stir-fry; or top a whole wheat pizza with some of the meat shredded on top of the cheese.

You can also cook a meatloaf and eat it for the week. You sneak veggies into your meatloaf. Grated carrots, green and

red peppers, peas, anything you can find. One of my clients had a 'meatloaf marathon', and made three different kinds of meatloaf. (See Chapter 11 for numerous recipes.) She froze two of the kinds of meatloaf and ate the third until it was almost gone. Then she defrosted the second and ate it. She said it was fun, and because of the different recipes, she never got bored.

Great Vegetables to Get Started With	
Cooked	*Raw*
Carrots	Carrots
Peas	Red peppers
Butternut squash	Yellow peppers
Sweetcorn	Jicama
Yams	Mushrooms

Here's another idea for getting started with vegetables. Begin with the sweeter varieties. Your sugar-sensitive tongue will like them better. Take a look at the vegetables in the box above. Don't even think of starting with Brussels sprouts. They will scare you. Start with the vegetables that seem friendly to you.

Another way to make vegetables tastier is to melt cheese (Cheddar or Gouda) on top of them or use a sauce. One of my broccoli-loathing friends actually ate a dish of lightly cooked broccoli and cauliflower covered with a peanut-soy sauce that he found in a Japanese cookbook. The flavour of the sauce was strong enough to tone down the flavour of the veggies.

Another really helpful thing to try is to go to a market or farm shop and get fresh vegetables. You will not believe the difference in taste between a Brussels sprout from the stalk in late November and those nasty frozen ones.

Tips from the Field: Making Friends with Veggies

I try to cut up fresh veggies and leave them in the fridge to grab. I eat them more often if they don't have to be cut and cleaned each time. I also hard-boil a few eggs to leave in the fridge to eat when I need that quick protein boost.

– T.

I blanch my veggies by submerging them in boiling water for a minute or two, and then I make them into salads with dressings. I use broccoli, courgettes, green beans, red and green peppers and spuds. My favourite dressing is mustard mixed with mayonnaise. I also toss blanched or raw veggies into quiche, egg salad or baked potatoes. I nearly always have coleslaw with mayonnaise in the fridge. Sometimes I just add the raw veggies to that. I love my veggies now, but I used to struggle with them big-time.

– S.

Trying New Recipes

The next time you are in a bookshop or library, browse through the cookbooks. See if you can find one that appeals to you. If you are fairly new to cooking, keep it simple! Don't try gourmet cookbooks or elaborate recipes for foreign foods. Stick to the cookbooks for quick or easy-to-make meals. There's even a cookbook out there that is devoted entirely to recipes that require only three ingredients. Take a look at kids' cookbooks, too. The directions are simple, and the recipes are usually pretty yummy.

Ask Your Friends for their Best Recipes

Don't do this recipe stuff alone! Your friends may have favourite simple recipes that they love. Ask them! Stress that you are not looking for recipes fit for the queen of England, but for someone (you) who wants a few new, easy ideas for putting meals on the table. Remember that people who love to cook also love to share what they do.

Planning for Downtimes

It's inevitable. There will be times when you are on the run and can hardly remember your name, let alone your food plan for the day. Ironically enough, the key to handling these danger times is to plan for them. If you know you will have a meeting through lunch, bring something with you to have before the meeting. Know the meal choices in your local convenience store so that the raisins or chocolate bars don't hop into your mouth while your blood sugar has crashed and you are falling off the cliff.

Stocking Your Cupboards

Remember this idea from Chapter 3? It is *important*. It works. If you haven't done it yet, go back to page 59 and read this section again. Get your basics in place. Don't go skipping the early stuff because you think it doesn't apply to you.

I make sure I have some core foods on hand. My list includes minced meat, chicken breasts, canned tuna, frozen salmon, eggs, cheese, cottage cheese, natural peanut butter, almonds, potatoes, porridge oats, rye crackers, frozen veggies and bananas. This means that when I forget the time and haven't planned, I always have something on hand to use for dinner.

Tips from the Field: What Not to Run Out Of

I quite often cook the meats ahead and microwave the rest. I use one of those plastic divided plates. I fill up the plate from my bags of frozen veggies, precooked meats, leftover skin-on mashed potatoes, and so on.

Even if I don't have any precooked meat or leftover potatoes, at least I can fill my plastic plate with frozen veggies straight from the bag, add a dash of olive oil, salt and pepper, and grab a can of tuna.

– *D.*

When You Crash and Don't Know What to Do

If you skipped lunch and it's 4:00 P.M., you may figure out that you are in trouble. But sometimes sugar-sensitive people actually need to eat more than they let themselves when they are in diet mode. They may think they are doing everything right, but they often don't eat enough lunch and by mid-afternoon are really foggy or cranky – way beyond being hungry. I call this falling off the cliff. It is a sign of a serious drop in blood sugar. It has a desperate quality to it: you have to eat something right now!

These are the times you reach for sugar. These are the times an alcoholic in early recovery will grab something to drink. You have to have a plan in place before you get to this point. This is sort of like having a fire drill with your kids. You teach them how to get from the bed to the window. You have them practice going down the fire ladder. You don't wait until there is a fire to do the drill.

So in preparation for an over-the-cliff emergency, keep a high protein/low sugar bar in your dashboard. Keep a box of Ryvitas under the car seat. You can always scout up some cheese sticks and have a good snack on hand. Know where the

fast food places are. Know the choices so you don't have to think. It's a good idea to keep a list handy (maybe in your car) of foods that you can find in your local convenience store when you can't stop for a meal and are desperate for something to eat. The key is that your food needs to include protein. Don't reach for crisps and a Coke. Here are some suggestions of what you might choose from the convenience store:

- Mozzarella cheese sticks, Ryvitas, and milk or V8 juice
- Slices of meat (ham, turkey, etc.) wrapped around sticks of mozzarella or string cheese and milk or V8 juice
- Hot dogs and V8
- Peanuts, cashews or sunflower seeds, an apple or orange (if they stock any fresh fruit), and milk or V8
- Ryvitas and bean dip with milk or V8
- Mozzarella sticks, corn chips and salsa
- Ryvitas spread with peanut butter and milk

When You Get Hit with the 9:00 P.M. Munchies

Ah, the munchies. This is the time to stop and listen to your body. What are you actually feeling? Are you truly hungry, or are you feeling tired or having withdrawal from the sweet things you had at lunchtime? Are you bored and on the prowl? Write whatever you notice in your diary and see if you can sort it out.

Then go and eat your nightly potato. If you're bored, put salsa on it. Or make a hot potato salad by steaming, then slicing your potato and tossing it with your favourite salad dressing.

Foods to Carry With You

It helps a lot if you keep some food with you, either at work or in your car in case of emergency hunger. Here are some of the things people on the plan have kept handy:

- A box of whole grain crackers. (These will fill you up and feel more satisfying than crackers made with white flour.) Don't forget to add some protein to your crackers.
- Nuts such as raw or roasted peanuts, almonds and pecans. Pick a kind you *really* like so you'll feel emotionally satisfied when you need to grab a handful.
- Sandwich spreads that don't need to be refrigerated, such as peanut butter.
- Salad dressings that don't need to be refrigerated. My favourite is vinaigrette made with sherry vinegar. When I grab a chef salad at a fast food place and pour my special dressing on top, it turns into a yummy lunch.
- Some George's Shake (see page 57) mix packed into a big plastic glass with a lid so you can add juice or milk, shake, and drink!

Tips from the Field:
Protein to Ward Off Hunger Pangs

I used to have a problem with getting hungry at 11:00 A.M. and 3:30 P.M. Then I discovered that if I used *two* scoops of protein powder in milk instead of one after I eat my morning porridge, the problem is solved. The hunger doesn't come until lunchtime. The less milk I use, the better this works.

– *B.*

What to Do If You Miss Lunch Away from Home

This is not the time to beat yourself up or grab a chocolate bar; this is the time to get thee to a fast food place or a restaurant. At McDonald's you can always get eggs with bacon and potatoes or a grilled chicken salad or chef salad. Other fast food places

offer baked potatoes. Make your own mental list of the places in your neighbourhood that will support you in a crunch. I go to the local New Mexican restaurant and order huevos rancheros – eggs and beans and chilli. Does it every time.

7

Halfway There: Step 5

You have been working on the foundation of the Sugar Addict's Total Recovery Programme: eating three meals a day with protein, eating them at regular intervals, taking the vitamins, drinking lots of water and exercising daily. By now, you are probably pretty steady on doing those things as well as keeping your food diary, regularly planning your meals, and going grocery shopping with a list. You have mastered important parts of the programme and are ready for taking things further.

This next step will firm up this foundation and get you all set for starting to cut down on sugars. It is about substituting whole grains for the white-flour products you now eat. As you'll see, there is a huge (and delicious) variety of whole grain breads, muffins, cereals, pastas, waffles and even tortillas on the market today.

Step 5. Shift from White Foods to Brown Foods

One of the simplest ways to grasp this step is to see yourself shifting from eating white things to brown things. It is easy to remember these simple images as you make your food choices. White things are white because the grain or rice they are made from has been refined to remove its brown part, which – ironically – is also the nutrition-packed and fibre-rich part. Food processors do this because they think white things are more visually attractive. They are also sweeter, without fibre to slow down their absorption, so white things are absorbed into your bloodstream much faster than brown things – almost as fast as straight sugar. They cause your blood sugar to spike and set you up for a big fall, both biochemically and emotionally. (A potato eaten with its skin is a brown thing. Eaten without its skin – as most french fries are prepared – it's a white thing.)

Here are some examples of white things. Check off the ones that you regularly eat:

____	Bagels	____	Macaroni
____	White bread	____	Noodles
____	Cake	____	Pancakes made with white flour
____	Cereal	____	Pasta
____	Biscuits	____	Pastry
____	Crackers	____	Pie
____	Croissants	____	Waffles
____	Flour tortillas	____	White rice

How many did you check? I would have checked all of them before I changed my own eating patterns. Sugar-sensitive people *love* white things – sometimes even more than ice cream or other sweet treats. When you eat them, you want more. For some people, these addictive foods are the obvious ones, like chocolate, ice cream, biscuits, French bread. For others, the

foods that call to them are pasta, milk, popcorn, cheese, chips, even Diet Coke.

As diverse as these foods are, they all have a soothing emotional effect. They make you feel safe, comfortable and loved through their taste or feel or the emotional cues attached to them. Eating them provides you with a safe haven that draws you to them again and again. But they also create havoc in your body and your brain.

You may get spooked by the thought of not eating white things any more. White things are the foods that most often represent love and comfort. You cannot imagine life without macaroni or white bread. Be gentle with yourself. Take a deep breath. No one is going to take away your favourite foods. The idea is for you to *move towards* using more brown things, to shift towards using them more often, but the shift happens as gradually as you feel comfortable having it happen.

The World of Whole Grains

Nowadays, food manufacturers are heeding the words of nutrition advocates and are starting to offer brown breads, bagels, waffles, crackers, pitta bread, and more. Whole grains not only help keep your blood sugar level stable; they also give your body a solid, consistent fuel to draw from.

You will need to do some work to learn which foods are indeed whole grain. Sometimes breads that appear to be brown are actually refined white flour with brown colour added. The clue is the weight of the bread or grain. Fibre is heavy. So if you pick up a loaf of bread that looks brown but feels light, make another choice. And always read the labels.

Brown Things

Brown things include foods higher in fibre, such as whole grains, seeds and beans. Here are some examples of what I call brown things.

Whole grain bread

Whole grain cereal

Whole grain pasta

Whole grain pancakes

Whole grain tortillas (corn
    or whole wheat)

Muesli, no sugar added

Brown rice

Porridge oats

Sunflower seeds

Potatoes with skin

Sweet potatoes

Refried beans

Kidney beans (used in chilli)

Flageolet beans

Chickpeas

Hummus

Lentils

Millet

Pumpkin seeds

Quinoa

Soyabeans

Polenta

Yams

I have included some choices that also have protein in them (such as beans and lentils). If you are a vegetarian, you will be counting these as part of your protein. But if you are looking for slow carbohydrates, the bean things will work well. They are hearty, nutritious and comforting.

Many of these foods you can find in your supermarket. Others you may have to buy at a health food store. As you shift from eating white things to brown things, you'll start noticing big changes in your sense of well-being and your energy level. When you look at your food diary, you will see the connection between your new way of eating and your feelings. You may remember the difference between having optimal or low blood sugar. Brown things support optimal blood sugar levels.

If it is hard to make the shift from white to brown, start by having your white things only with a meal. Try giving up your mid-afternoon snack of toast and jam and have it for lunch. *Make change at the pace that works for you.* Go slowly enough that you don't get spooked, but make change. Work towards solid long-term success, not dramatic short-term results.

Balanced Blood Sugar	Low Blood Sugar
Energetic	Tired all the time
Tired when appropriate	Tired for no reason
Focused and relaxed	Restless, can't keep still
Clear	Confused
Good memory	Trouble remembering things
Able to concentrate	Trouble concentrating
Able to problem-solve effectively	Easily frustrated
Easygoing	More irritable than usual
Even-tempered	Gets angry unexpectedly

This step may be hard. You love white things because they represent comfort and love. Mince pies at Christmas are the centre of the celebration. But as you do your homework and progress through this recovery programme, you are going to find ways to keep the positive emotional attachment to the foods that are good for you and let go of the problem foods. It may seem like an impossible dream now, but it will happen! You can have whole wheat pasta or brown rice and be fine. You can have a whole grain bread instead of a croissant and have all the emotional enjoyment of the ritual. You can make a birthday cake with wholemeal flour that may actually even taste better than the traditional yellow/white cake you usually make. (You might want to bake any recipe made with substitutes before the big day to make sure you don't end up with a disaster that tastes like cardboard.) This shift from white to brown does not have to create panic. It just takes practice.

A Thousand Types of Bread

As I mentioned earlier, many store-bought breads contain refined white flour even though the bread is labelled 'brown' or 'whole grain'. As you read the food label, look for the amount of fibre. Look for 2 or more grams of fibre in each serving. More fibre means more brown.

Also read the label to see if there is sugar added to the bread. It is a common misconception that yeast needs added sugar in order to make dough rise, but yeast can use the sugars already in the flour just fine. Keep looking until you find a bread that is made without sugar. Many of my readers have discovered the joy of making their own bread. Check out some of the recipes in Chapter 11. Try them and discover that brown can be a mighty fine alternative to white.

Tips from the Field: An Alternative to Wheat

I have been using spelt flour and spelt products in place of white flour. I add the flour to whole grain pancake mix for pancakes or waffles, and use it in cornbread batter. My local health food store also carries spelt tortillas and various spelt breads.

– J.

Cereal Options

When you are slowly shifting your food from white things to brown things, don't forget that this shift applies to your morning cereal as well! White cereals include Rice Krispies, Coco Pops, Frosties, Sugar Puffs – all the things your children want and you eat at night in front of the TV.

Brown cereals are the boring ones. Here are some examples:

Porridge (unsweetened)
Other hot cereals like millet and oat bran and buckwheat
All-Bran (Kellogg's)
Shredded Wheat

If you aren't ready for 'full' brown, start by shifting to the cereals that are lower in sugars, like Cheerios (not Honey Nut Cheerios). Look for cereals that have less than 10 grams of sugar per serving.

Have your children help you on this treasure hunt. When you decide to switch cereals, be careful to read the nutrition labels. Many cereals, like breads, are labelled 'all natural' and look brown, but they are filled with sugars. Even though we are not focusing on cutting back on sugars in this step, why *add* something sweet to your diet that you'll need to take away later? Commercially made muesli is often like this. It sure looks good for you, but it has grams and grams of sugar. Or it has huge amounts of dried fruit added, which is concentrated sugar. Do not use dried fruit, but you can use some fresh or frozen fruits in moderation. Do not use sweetened frozen fruit.

Some natural foods stores now carry unsweetened muesli. Muesli is a wonderful cereal option to learn to make. You can make it without sugar (or honey) and have a delicious, chewy option for breakfast. I often take a whole grain muesli and cook it to make a hearty serving for breakfast. It has a wonderful nutty flavour and is very comforting. You can adapt almost any muesli recipe by simply taking out the sugars – things such as honey, golden syrup, raisins and other dried fruits.

Porridge oats: The Wonder Food

Porridge oats are a wonder food because they have it all: they're inexpensive and easy to cook; they contain protein, soluble fibre, no cholesterol and no sugar; and are low in sodium. Oats will not only help to maintain your optimal blood sugar level,

they will minimize your cravings. You can add protein powder to them or eat them with eggs for a solid breakfast. You can put cinnamon, nutmeg, fruit and/or milk on them. The Scots add milk and butter, which tastes yummy. You can cook them in milk, soya milk, or apple juice instead of water.

When you buy porridge oats, look for whole grain oats. These are also known as Scottish milled, and they are the best kind for you. You can toast them lightly in the oven or in a frying pan on the top of the stove before cooking; this changes the flavour to an interesting nutty taste. Whole oats take much longer to cook. They are the top of the 'slow' list. If you don't have that much time, use regular rolled oats. Even instant oats will do in a pinch, but stay away from the flavoured ones that are chock full of sugars. Try putting butter, salt and milk on your porridge rather than brown sugar. You may really like the Scottish way.

Tips from the Field:
Getting Creative with Porridge Oats

I fix my porridge ahead of time and put each portion in a separate microwavable container. Then, in the morning, I just pop the container in the microwave and it's ready in 3 minutes. I stir in some milk, peanut butter, almonds and protein powder. Read the directions on the box for the best cooking time.

– M.

I use whole grain oats and dress them up with butter, cinnamon, nutmeg, a splash of vanilla, 1 tablespoon ground flaxseed, a heaped tablespoon of sunflower seed for flavour, crunch and added protein, and either a few blueberries or strawberries. I can cook the oats while I'm in the shower, and by the time I am finished, they are ready to be doctored up. I love the texture and the flavour, and they hold me over to lunch better than the quick oats.

– C.

I like my (precooked) oats heated in a frying pan with the egg mixed in, and a little spray margarine and salt and pepper, sort of like a Scottish matzo brie. On Sundays I cook up two batches of whole grain oats. Then each morning I either nuke and season a serving of it or fry it in a little margarine/butter. Then I scramble an egg, pour it over the oats, and mix the whole thing up.

– J.

Try porridge with cottage cheese mixed in. First make the porridge, then add the cottage cheese. You may have to heat it some more if you want the cheese to melt. Add some cinnamon and nutmeg, too!

– B.

I make plain instant porridge every morning (no sugar). Right when I add the boiling water I mix in a tablespoon of cashew butter (or sugar-free peanut butter). Then I add a chopped apple and a sprinkle of cinnamon. I get my protein, fruit and complex carbohydrate all in one satisfying tasty bowl.

– A.

For a filling breakfast, I put 4 egg whites in a bowl and microwave them for one minute. Then I stir the egg whites, add 45 g uncooked oats, stir again, and microwave another minute or until cooked. I also sprinkle some raw nuts such as walnuts or cashews on top and a little nutmeg.

– S.

Pasta Alternatives

Many people have found solace in using whole wheat or brown rice pasta. Don't use the green pastas, because they are simply regular white pasta with spinach added. If you do use the brown pastas and find yourself craving more and more, you need to stop using them. When I eat whole wheat pasta, I start dreaming about a thousand different ways to have it. If I use brown rice pasta, however, (available from health food stores) it is a

nice, comforting, satisfying meal and I have no craving for more. Listen to your own body to know what is right for you.

Don't Forget the Potato!

Don't let the extra effort it takes to shift away from eating white things distract you from the importance of your nightly potato. That humble potato is helping your brain manufacture more serotonin, which will set the stage for the important change to come: cutting down on sugars. With plenty of serotonin, you will approach this otherwise scary step confidently and creatively. An optimal level of serotonin will also lower your cravings for sugar and will actually *increase* your appetite for healthy foods.

You can vary the type of potato you use; you can eat less than a whole one or choose a little one. If you find yourself having wild dreams or insomnia after trying out the potato, have a smaller one. The wild dreams are a sign of the activation of your serotonin system; they mean the potato is working. You need it, but you may need less than you have been eating. If you are very low in serotonin, you will get a bigger effect from the potato.

Some people just don't like the idea of the potato and will never eat one. Others are allergic to potatoes or potatoes aggravate their arthritis. I try to be realistic. While the potato is best, if you just can't or won't do it, I am willing to negotiate an alternative.

Choose a different slow carb. Try Ryvitas or a sweet potato or porridge or wholemeal toast or an apple. Just remember not to add anything with protein in it or you will defeat the biochemical purpose of your bedtime carb.

Sometimes people get scared about calories and they skip the evening potato. Think of the evening potato as medicine. Food as pharmacology. The potato (three hours after dinner) is the very thing that is going to help you be able to say no to the things you don't want to eat any more. It will reinforce your sense of being steady or having discipline.

Have It Your Way, But Have It

The wonderful people on our online Community Forum have
come up with lots of creative ways to cook their bedtime potato.
Here are some of their simpler suggestions:

- Slice and bake on an oiled baking sheet to make oven fries
  (it's a lot faster if you have already cooked the potato).
- Grate it with some onion and fry it up, like hash browns.
- Use leftover mashed potatoes (with skins) to make potato
  pancakes.
- Cube your potato and microwave it.
- Try any of the above with red potatoes, white potatoes or
  purple potatoes (when available). Also, some people swear
  that organic baking potatoes taste much better than the
  regular ones. (They're also smaller.)
- Rub butter or margarine on the outside of your baking
  potato to get a wonderfully crispy skin.

How to Have Fun When You Get Bored with Mr Spud

This is the time to dig out your cookbooks, ask your friends for
ideas and poke around in the library or on the Web for new and
unusual recipes. I have found several potato cookbooks. The
only restriction on fixing the bedtime potato is that the recipes
must not include protein. Even if your new recipe calls for peel-
ing the potatoes, don't do it! You need that brown skin to make
your nighttime snack a brown thing!

Oven-Fried Sweet Potatoes

*This is a recipe for one person, suggested by Cheryl, a reader. Try this
as your before-bed potato. If you want to make these as part of a
meal, use one potato per person.*

1 sweet potato
Vegetable oil
Salt and pepper to taste
Onion powder to taste
Garlic powder to taste

Wash and peel the potato, then cut it into french-fry-size pieces. Put a little oil on a baking sheet or in the tray of your combination microwave oven, and dump the fries on it. Turn them to coat all sides with oil. Then sprinkle with salt, pepper, onion powder and a little garlic powder. (Or substitute nutmeg for onion and garlic powders.)

- If you are using a conventional oven, bake at 230° C, gas 8 for 15 minutes, turning once so the bottoms don't burn.
- If you are using a combination microwave oven, bake at 220° C for 20 minutes, turn them (the bottoms get nicely brown), then turn off the oven and let them sit for another 10 minutes.

Ten Toppings for Your Baked Potato

1. Olive oil
2. Salsa (try several varieties)
3. Salad dressing (not blue cheese)
4. Chives
5. Mustard
6. Toasted onion
7. Pesto sauce
8. Butter
9. Pepper
10. Curry sauce

What to Eat in This Phase

Now that you have mastered Mr Spud, let's go back to the bigger picture. The white-to-brown shift is not all that hard to do

logistically. It's a good time to try experimenting a little with what you are having. Take another look at your breakfast and lunch menus. These may have included some white or sweet foods as you were learning the routine of breakfast every day. By now they should be including brown things as the carbohydrate part. Let's look at some good ideas that have come from *Potatoes Not Prozac* readers. These are people just like you who are trying new foods and sharing their new adaptations. Let's see our revised breakfasts first.

Ten Breakfast Ideas from the Field

Earlier in this chapter we talked about brown cereals you could have for breakfast, including several delightful things you could do with oats. Here are some other ideas from people in our Community Forum. (An asterisk indicates that the recipe is in Chapter 11.)

1. Crustless Quiche* with whole grain toast
2. Yogurt Ricotta Delight
3. Brown rice (leftover rice works fine) fried with two eggs
4. Porridge oats with Grape-Nuts, raisins and peanuts (optional: add protein powder and cinnamon)
5. Miso soup with tofu, seaweed, spring onions and bean sprouts
6. An egg-and-cheese in a whole wheat tortilla
7. A whole grain waffle with protein powder in the batter, apple sauce and plain yogurt on the top
8. Cottage Cheese–Cinnamon Pancakes*
9. Split pea soup and whole grain toast
10. 170 g chilli served over brown rice

Five Fast Dinners for the Ridiculously Busy

1. Barbecued or roast chicken (bought from the deli), frozen green beans with almonds (5 minutes in microwave), brown basamati rice (reheated from the big batch you cooked on the weekend)

2. A whole wheat tortilla with refried beans and cheese (and leftover chicken or beef if you have it around), nuked for about 45 seconds, and served with soured cream and salsa
3. Scrambled eggs with sliced tomatoes and whole grain toast
4. Brown rice spaghetti (available from health food stores), crumbled hamburger in tomato sauce, and frozen sweetcorn
5. Sautéed tofu and garlic, steamed broccoli and a potato baked in the microwave

Five Elegant Dinners

Cooking lavish dinners for company (or for yourself!) is no problem on the food plan. Try these menus – complete with appetizers or soup, main course and desserts – or invent your own, substituting brown things for white things wherever possible.

This is a great menu for a festive winter dinner:

- Roast Sticky Chicken*
- Larry's Famous Green Beans*
- Sweet Potato Puff*
- Whole grain biscuits

Here's a dinner with an oriental flavour:

- Asian Salad*
- Grilled salmon steaks served with lemon wedges
- Stir-Fried Lemon Asparagus*
- Fried Brown Rice with Onions, Almonds and Cumin*
- Pumpkin Tofu Cheesecake*

Try this summer dinner when artichokes are in season:

- Feta Frittata*
- Jumbo prawns sautéed in garlic and olive oil, served on a bed of brown basamati rice

- Steamed artichoke with mayonnaise seasoned to taste with curry powder
- Salad of baby organic mixed greens served with vinaigrette made with balsamic vinegar
- Carrot Cake*

This could be a New Year feast!

- Roast Chicken with Garlic*
- Oven-Fried Sweet Potatoes*
- Peas with mint
- Brown rice and wild rice cooked (separately) in chicken broth and/or beef broth and mixed before serving
- Squash Pie with Peanut Butter Glaze*

Here's a good one for people who like their food plain and simple:

- Roast Chicken with Garlic*
- Roast Potatoes*
- Apple Carrots*
- Fresh-baked wholemeal bread
- Fruit salad with a dollop of plain yogurt, topped with roasted almonds, whole or sliced

One-Pot Meals

- Ratatouille cooked with slices of turkey, minced beef or chicken. Serve over brown rice, if desired.
- Beef Stew*
- Feta Frittata*
- Chilli Layered Casserole*
- Asian Salad*

Your Friends the Vegetables

Many sugar-sensitive people are not all that fond of vegetables and drift to the white side of the grocery store rather than the vegetable side. But you need to get to know the vegetable options. Start with the ones that seem most familiar or with a vegetable you love. Try having it fresh and see the difference. You could even do something really outrageous and get some peas to shell. Put the fresh peas in your salad.

Corn-on-the-cob is an easy vegetable to love. Try it combined with chopped sweet red peppers and steamed young green beans. Or get peeled, cubed fresh squash at the supermarket. Steam it and serve sprinkled with grated cheese and nutmeg – you will be stunned at how good it is. Try grilling veggies that you have brushed with olive oil on the barbecue grill – on skewers or not or on your lean, mean grilling machine. Peppers, onions, carrots, mushrooms and courgette slices taste entirely different when grilled.

Stir-fry your veggies in olive oil. Get a packet of ready-to-stir-fry fresh vegetables at the supermarket. Cook them so that you can stick a fork in them, but don't let them get mushy. Sprinkle them with onion salt or roasted garlic.

Try eating your vegetables raw; put them in your salad. Arrange them on your plate. Play with your food. Be bold!

Finding New Comfort Foods

Now that you're shifting away from foods made with white flour, you may need to pick some other foods to substitute for comfort foods like pasta, bagels, French bread and doughnuts. There are two ways to go with this. Sometimes it is easy enough to substitute the whole grain version of the food for the white version, such as substituting whole grain bagels or waffles or pizza dough for the kind made with white flour, or swapping Ryvitas for Ritz crackers.

Take care that you don't develop cravings for the whole grain foods. Another option is to see if entirely different foods can provide comfort when you need it. Some of these foods might be soups like cream of chicken or split pea, dishes like chilli, quiche, frittata, Yam and Cheese Strudel, or Sweet Potato Pie (recipes for these two are in Chapter 11).

Sometimes the comfort comes from the ritual surrounding having the food. I used to *love* pizza – not so much for the pizza as for the treat. Pizza meant not having to cook. Pizza meant sharing with friends, being goofy, the smell of the pizza place, and of course the cold beer with it. I don't go into pizza places even now because all the sounds and smells trigger a desire for pizza. But I do make an adapted pizza to eat at home, and that works just fine. The recipe is in Chapter 11.

Let's take a look at how you feel about your own comfort foods. In the space below, write down your current comfort foods. Then write down what you might have instead – for example, bran muffins or Oat Muffins (recipe in Chapter 11) instead of blueberry muffins. You may need to make a trip to your supermarket or natural foods store to see what your whole grain options are. There are more than you think!

Old Comfort Foods	*New Comfort Foods*
_____	_____
_____	_____
_____	_____
_____	_____
_____	_____
_____	_____

Unfortunately, there are no whole grain options for things such as croissants, doughnuts and white cake. The very idea of a whole grain doughnut makes me laugh, since there is no way it

can be the same as those airy things with the chocolate frosting. But there must be another food that would satisfy you instead. What about warm brown rice topped with butter, wholemeal bread spread with peanut butter, Oat and Apple Pancakes (recipe in Chapter 11), a cappuccino (remember, this means a cappuccino without special sweeteners). Go on a hunt for comfort foods with your friends and see how many different ones you can come up with. You may find alternatives that work just as well as your old favourites. Our friends on the website have this discussion every few months. It's a hot topic for all of us. Food as comfort is high on the list.

Think about what kinds of foods might comfort you so you can make them when you need them. Start by identifying the specific characteristic of your comfort food that is comforting. Does your comfort food need to be warm? Does it need to be soft in your mouth? Here are some things that our readers have reported using as comfort foods instead of white things. Recipes for foods with asterisks are in Chapter 11.

- Italian Frittata*
- Crustless Quiche*
- Pizza with Whole Wheat Crust
- Cornbread
- Oat Muffins*
- Cottage Cheese– Cinnamon Pancakes*
- Sweet Potato Pie*
- Ricotta-Fruit 'Pudding'*
- Tomato soup made with milk and topped with basil and a pat of butter
- Split pea soup (add bacon bits)
- Cream of chicken soup with extra chicken added
- Oven-Fried Sweet Potatoes*
- Oat and Apple Pancakes
- Chilli Layered Casserole*

Also take a look at the dessert recipes in Chapter 11.

Figure out your list and then make sure you buy what you need when you go to the supermarket. If your comfort food is in your cupboard or refrigerator when you want it, you are less likely to go on a prowl and find the real thing.

Desserts That Work for You

Yes, you can keep your commitment to brown things and still eat dessert. Did you notice the desserts suggested in the section above on elegant dinners? There are dessert recipes in Chapter 11, too. They include Squash Pie, Carrot Cake, Pumpkin Tofu Cheesecake and Pumpkin Cake with Cashew Butter Icing. It is important that you sort out whether or not you will be okay with desserts. Some people take great comfort in brown desserts, find them a useful addition to their plan, and like making them. Others have found that dessert of any kind reminds them of the old days of sugar-laden foods. They are a major trigger food for them. Even healthy dessert alternatives serve as a trigger – just thinking about dessert makes them want more and more of the real thing. Your job is to sort out what is right for you.

Tips from the Field: Try This Treat

Sometimes for dessert I will have fried bananas. Melt some butter in a nonstick frying pan, add walnuts and cinnamon, and cook until nuts are toasty. Then break a green banana into chunks and add it to the pan. Cook until it is nicely yellowed and coated with the cinnamon butter.

– C.

8

Taking the Sugars Out:
Step 6

You may feel ambivalent about the next step of your programme – taking the sugars out. You may swing between dreading giving up sugars and barely keeping yourself from leaping ahead and chucking everything. Or you may have ignored my earlier advice totally: ditched all sugars the second day of your programme, felt horrible, and started over again. But either way, we have now come to Step 6.

If you've been doing the steps in order, going off sugars is the logical next step. You may find it isn't all that dramatic. It will be just one more adjustment to your carbohydrates so that you eat as few simple carbohydrates (sugars and white things) as possible. And you will be making that change in the context of being consistent with your three meals a day with protein, your nightly spud, your food diary, your browns vs whites.

Being stable is the first of the three keys to success with this step. The second is understanding the big picture about you and sweet foods. You may have already started to see this by studying your food diary and looking at the relationship be-

tween your feelings and the foods you eat and identifying any addictive relationships you have with sweet and white foods.

In the next three chapters, we will work on practical ways to take sugar out of your diet and heal your emotional cravings for food as love. You will learn a mental exercise called reframing. Rather than associating eating milk and biscuits with love, you will consciously start noticing other alternatives, not associated with food, that are better for your body. Sugar as love will no longer be the marker and measure of your life. When you start this process, this idea may seem pretty far-fetched, but I promise that over time, it will begin to make more sense.

Having the plan work for you in this phase will require paying attention in a deeper way. You will learn to recognize those foods that can set you off. You will learn to spot a food with covert sugar in it a mile away. This phase of your food plan will teach you to read labels, recognize sugar's many aliases, and choose to eat foods that are not filled with sugars. Step 6 has two parts. The first involves going off what I call overt sugars – the sweets, cake, pie, fizzy drinks and biscuits that you love so much. The second involves taking out the covert sugar – the sugars like high-fructose corn syrup hidden in other foods. You can choose to do both at once or to ease into it by doing the overt sugars first and then tackling the covert sugars.

By now, you eat whatever sugars you are still having with your meals. Your sugar binges are probably a great deal less intense. You may have found that you have already significantly and naturally reduced your sugar intake. As you know, sugar affects you like a drug. If you think of going off sugars as a drug detoxification process, you can help your mind and body minimize the discomfort of the transition. You can keep the detox in perspective. Your beta-endorphin receptors will not be happy about your taking sugars out. They will tell you in no uncertain terms by creating headaches, irritability and edginess. I will guide you through the sugar detox process and help you teach your

beta-endorphin receptors to quiet down and adjust to your new sugar-free life.

Let's take a look at the three parts to a successful long-term sugar detox:

1. Be really consistent with the earlier steps of the plan: the stronger the foundation, the easier going off sugar will be. If you have taken a sufficient amount of time to allow your body to adjust to the changes you are making, your sugar detox will not be difficult. If you rush things, you can get into difficulty. I generally encourage people to spend at least eight to ten weeks getting solid with the programme before they consider a sugar detox.

2. Understand the emotional cues (like love) that you associate with certain foods. For many people, especially women, sugar foods are strongly connected to feeling safe and loved. Your detox may evoke feelings of abandonment and sadness. You may feel as if you are giving up your best friend. Do not dismiss or make light of these feelings. If you don't honour them, they will sabotage your commitment to be sugar-free.

3. Keep an eye on the details of how much sugar is in the foods you eat. Sugars are hidden everywhere. Once you have shifted to a sugar-free state, your body will be far more sensitive to the drug effect of sugars. If the foods you eat are loaded with covert sugar, you can activate your craving for sugar without intending to. You will need to protect yourself from using sugars when you don't want to.

Tips from the Field: Time to Go Back to Basics?

As I work with the programme, I continue to get new revelations. First of all, it took me a while to realize that one step at a time means one step at a time. After several setbacks, I realized that I had never really achieved the three meals a day before I moved on. Looking back at the steps, it suddenly hit me in the face: 'It won't work if you don't do the steps'.

– P.

Setting the Stage

Let's make sure you are ready for this next phase of your programme. There are several ways to go off sugars:

1. Slowly decrease the amount of sugars you use until you no longer wish to
   have any.
2. Go off overt sugars all at once and then gradually decrease the amount of
   covert sugars you use.
3. Go off all sugars all at once.

Which of these three you choose will depend upon your own
style. The second method seems to be the easiest approach for
most people. The actual sugar withdrawal or detox from overt
sugars takes about five days. If you are not using huge amounts of
covert sugars at the same time, it is a reasonable and manageable
transition. As you may have already learned, if you are using a
great deal of sugar and stop abruptly, you will be miserable.

But whichever way you choose, we want to ensure that the stability you have created up to this point will hold you through
your sugar detox. Your first task includes a little housecleaning –
both physical (in your kitchen) and emotional (with your family
and friends). Let's start with the easier one.

Cleaning Your Kitchen

Go into your kitchen, open your cabinets and take out all
the foods with obvious sugars in them. This includes leftover
Easter eggs or other sweets, high-sugar comfort foods, fizzy
drinks, sugary cereals such as Frosties – you know, all the high-
temptation stuff. Throw it away or give it away. Ideally, see if you
can get every last bit of it out of the house.

If your family will go nuts if you give away their sugar foods,
arrange with them to put all the sweet things into one place.
Choose a cupboard or cabinet that you do not usually use. Call

it the sugar stash. You will know what is there, but at least you can make the choice whether to go and look at or eat what is in the cupboard. By separating the sugar stash from the other foods, you will at least minimize your bumping into such foods while you are trying to be 'clean'.

Talking to Your Family and Friends

The next step is an emotional housecleaning. So far, your family and friends have probably seen the positive change in you as you progress with this programme. They may have seen that overall you have more energy, are more upbeat, relaxed and sympathetic. They know you aren't 'fixed' yet, but they are interested in the change that is taking place in you. Some family members may have rolled their eyes at first when they heard you were on another diet, but they have probably changed their tune by now.

But now that you are going to stop eating sugar, their reactions may well change again. They may be worried that you are going to expect them to stop eating sugar, too. They may be fiercely resistant or totally uninterested in anything that has to do with your eating more regularly and giving up sugar. They may even actively subvert your commitment to the plan. Your husband may ask, 'Are you still doing that stuff?' as he orders chocolate mousse for dessert. Your kids may unconsciously try to sabotage you as well. Remember, sugar sensitivity is inherited. The chances that your family is sugar sensitive are really high. You know this. They know this. And they may not be in the same place you are, ready to move towards a sugar-free life.

You may also have close friends who are sugar sensitive. And friends who are still very attached to sugar and white things may warn you of the dangers of a 'high-protein diet'. Telling them that this food plan is not a high-protein diet will have no impact, because the concern isn't really about protein. They are

worried that if you change, they may feel pressured to change as well. And many people are not ready to. You can't clear out your husband or unsupportive best friend the way you can clear out your cabinet, but you can be clear with them and clear in your own mind and commitment. And you can actively add other people to your support group.

You need support from people who understand your programme. Talking with people who are supportive is absolutely critical to your success. You could do this by doing the programme with a friend, joining a Potatoes Not Prozac support group or finding a way to get online and talk to the great people on the website. However you choose to find support, make a real effort to do so! It will make a world of difference to the success of your programme. Having a personal connection to others doing the programme will help you stick with it.

Tips from the Field:
The Drawbacks of a Husband Who Cooks

When I started on your plan, I was reminded of Al-Anon, which tries to help families understand the changes that their newly sober spouse/parent is going through. The difference is that 'I've lost my drinking companion' translates to 'It's no fun to eat ice cream unless you do.'

For example, my husband loves to prepare meals, but I have to spoil some of his menu plans. This morning he was looking forward to us having a rich coffee cake he had bought, and I had to beg off. He's trying to be very cooperative, but just doesn't understand yet. I guess the secret is to ease the family into change.

– A.

Having Second Thoughts

As you start getting ready for your sugar detox, you may have second thoughts about whether you really want to do this. Feelings of sadness may emerge. You may wonder if you really want a sugar-free life. You may feel really sad that you will never have sweet things again. Sweet foods are so much a part of celebrations, of holidays, of family togetherness. How will you manage this?

This is a natural feeling. All of us know it well. Usually it is far more intense at the very beginning of doing the programme than at this stage, because in later steps you already have had the experience of feeling so much better thanks to the programme. Your brain and body know this is the right plan for you. But the feelings of loss may remain. This loss is real and valid. Our culture uses sugar to celebrate special events, to show love and to provide comfort, so it can be difficult staying sugar-free in such an environment.

But alternatives do exist. Making special Christmas tree ornaments can take the place of baking and icing Christmas biscuits; giving flowers can replace giving chocolates; soup and an offer of comfort can be given instead of bread. Your old 'food as love' associations will change over time. Just be gentle with yourself.

Holding the Sadness

A key part of getting ready to take the sugars out is acknowledging the intensity of the emotional cues associated with sugars in our culture. Many of your childhood memories of support and love are connected to food, usually sweet or white foods. They hold a very big emotional charge for you.

But the foods you think of as providing comfort are the very things that have contributed to your problems. In other words, often the reason you *need* comfort is due to the very sweet or white food you are eating!

This is a very difficult concept to explain to someone who is still using comfort foods. When you are caught in the middle of these foods, it is almost impossible to understand how big a problem they are creating.

An alcoholic who is still drinking will often tell me, 'I would stop drinking if I could just get my life sorted.' And she will struggle and struggle and struggle to fix her problems, but they still surround her and create her need for a drink. Using sugars and white things acts in exactly the same way. I used to feel I needed a hot fudge sundae every night after work because my work was so stressful, so demanding and so tiring. I had no idea that it was the hot fudge sundae that was significantly contributing to the stress of my life. My sugar-laden brain could not in any way make that connection.

Because you have been doing the plan for a while now, I know this concept is starting to make sense to you. You can see more clearly the huge effect that these sugar foods have on you. You recognize that your down sides are directly correlated to what you are eating. So on an intellectual level you are ready. On an emotional level, though, you may continue to be scared about having to give up things that have so much tenderness associated with them.

After all is said and done, ultimately you will be making a choice about what you want more. I still miss those green-iced Christmas biscuits. I still want them every Christmas. Time has not made it easier. But experience has. I want my recovery more than I want the *illusion* of comfort that those biscuits would give me. You will grow into this place, too. The longer you do the programme, the more this will make sense to you.

Planning for the Big Day

Detoxing from sugar will call upon you to use all your knowledge about giving your body the right foods at the right times to

keep your sugar-sensitive brain chemistry balanced. More than ever, you will need to eat regular meals with protein, and you will need to do so with consistency, day after day, week after week. This is where the stability you established earlier in the programme really pays off.

When you decide you are ready for a full detox, remember that it will take five days and you may experience some withdrawal symptoms. If you get really uncomfortable during this time, have an apple with some protein as a snack. But take care not to start eating a whole lot of fruit. Fruit contains a sugar called fructose. Different fruits have a different sugar impact. The intensity of the effect is related to the amount of fibre in the fruit. Strawberries, raspberries and blueberries will affect you far less than mangoes and papaya. If you have fruit, have it with protein. Eat fruits with skin and slow down the sugar effect. More fibre gives you a slower sugar effect. Some fruit may work for you, but it may trigger cravings. Be attentive, use your diary and, as always, ask your body what is best.

This is one of the many new ways in which you will need to pay attention to the details of what you eat and the effect it has on your mood and your body. Some people, for example, are triggered by the sugar found naturally in milk (lactose). Others (like me) get triggered by whole wheat pasta, but have no trouble eating brown rice pasta (available from health food stores). You will have to discover for yourself what your trigger foods are. Let your food diary help you do this. Continue to record your food and your feelings, and when you think you have spotted a trigger food, look further back in your diary to see what effects that food had on you earlier in the programme.

Rigorous vs Flexible

When you were just starting on your programme, it worked better to ease into sugar awareness and cut down if you were able. As you move into the detox phase of your recovery, you will

want to be more attentive to sugars in their many forms. How much covert sugar you will use will be determined by listening to your body. If you eat a certain food during detox and you find yourself wanting more of it, planning to go to the store and buy it, keeping a stash of it in the house, thinking of new ways to cook it, it is probably a food you should avoid! Read the label and make a choice.

Some people ask me, 'How many grams of sugar *can* I have?' If you have a number, then you will continue to calculate grams rather than working with your body. There is no absolute value to use as a guide. The more you can connect with the idea of being a sugar addict, the easier this process will be. But ultimately, your recovery is about your being in relationship to what your body is telling you. You can now discern what is right for you.

Be sure to note all your reactions to food in your diary. And don't just write down the feelings you have at the moment you are eating. Write down your feelings whenever you notice them. If you don't happen to have your diary with you, write down what you are feeling on any piece of paper that's at hand. Include the date and time. Then you can transfer this information into your food diary when you have time.

Spotting Sugars

Overt Sugars

Whether you have decided to do your detox slowly or all at once, you need to know your sugars. Overt sugars are the ones that look like sugar. You may have classified some overt sugars as healthy ones. For example, you may have thought that honey was better for you than white sugar because it comes from a natural source. Your sugar-sensitive body does not make this distinction. Whether the sugar is natural or refined, your reaction will be the same. And the more intense the sugar, the more intense your reaction.

Here are the sugars usually classified as overt:

White sugar	Honey
Brown sugar	Treacle
Powdered sugar	Maple syrup
Turbinado or	Golden syrup (also known as high-
raw sugar	fructose corn syrup)

The hard-line sweet foods you all know so well are the ones that are high in overt sugars. These include Coke, ice cream, doughnuts, chocolate bars, cake, pie, biscuits, etc. I have never met a sugar-sensitive person who was not an expert on overt sugar foods.

Covert Sugars

Covert sugars are those that are hidden in processed foods. They can be highly concentrated and make up a large part of a food or they can be a small amount added for 'taste'. They range from the high-fructose corn syrup found in many processed foods to the hidden sugar in canned vegetables or ketchup. It sometimes requires a little detective work to find them. Read food labels and learn to identify foods where covert sugars are hiding.

You will find that many packaged foods also have covert sugars in them. Check the labels of things such as tomato soup, bran muffins, barbecue sauce, Power Bars, fruit drinks and even frozen dinners. Check your box of salt. You will be floored to discover where our covert friends appear. Sugar is everywhere.

The sugars listed below are some of the sugars that wait in processed foods to ambush your recovery. The sugar industry has creative chemists. Sugar sells.

Some marketing ads will make claims that a certain product made with sugars has a low glycemic impact. These sugars may

affect your blood sugar/insulin response differently. But the sweet taste evokes beta-endorphin, which primes you to want more and more sugar. Even a sugar that is lower in its glycemic response may have a huge priming effect on your sugar-sensitive brain. Be attentive to labels. And, even more important, be attentive to your body. If you find yourself feeling crabby and out of sorts, go back to your diary, see what you ate, and then go read the label. If you are craving sweets or white things, you have been primed. Something has sneaked in and activated your sugar-sensitive system. Pay attention if you are craving or noticing sweet things. You may discover one of these covert sugar products in the foods you have eaten:

Amasake	Dextrose
Apple sugar	Diglycerides
Barbados sugar	Disaccharides
Bark sugar	Evaporated cane juice
(Zylose)	Florida crystals
Barley malt	Fructooligosaccharides (FOS)
Barley malt syrup	Fructose
Beet sugar	Fruit juice concentrate
Brown rice syrup	Galactose
Cane juice	Glucose
Cane sugar	Glucitol
Cane syrup	Glucoamine
Carbitol	Gluconolactone (may be found
Caramel colouring	in tofu)
Caramel sugars	Glucose
Caramelized foods	Glucose polymers
Concentrated fruit juice	Glucose syrup
Corn sweetener	Glycerides
D-tagalose	Glycerine
Date sugar	Glycerol
Dextrin	Glycol

High-fructose corn syrup

Inversol

Invert sugar

Isomalt

Karo syrups

Lactose

Levulose

'Lite' sugar

'Light' sugar

Malt dextrin

Malted barley

Maltose

Maltodextrins

Maltodextrose

Malts (any)

Mannitol, sorbitol, xylitol,
     maltitol

Mannose

Microcrystalline cellulose

Molasses

Monoglycerides

Monosaccharides

Nectars

Neotame

Pentose

Polydextrose

Polyglycerides

Raisin juice

Raisin syrup

Ribose rice syrup

Rice malt

Rice sugar

Rice sweeteners

Rice syrup solids

Saccharides (any)

Sorbitol (aka Hexitol)

Sorghum

Sucanat (evaporated cane juice)

Sucanet

Sucrose

Sugar cane

Trisaccharides

Unrefined sugar

Zylos

It is also important to understand how food labels work. Legally, if the chemical structure of a carbohydrate has more than two sugar molecules, it will be called a complex carbohydrate on a food label instead of a sugar. So the label may show that a certain food has no sugar and 35 grams of carbohydrate. But if that carbohydrate is maltodextrin, your sugar-sensitive body will respond to it as a sugar. Read the food labels in detail, and pay attention to the ingredient list rather than the grams of sugar listed to learn the subtleties of where sugars are hidden.

Low-fat products often hide a lot of sugar. When food manufacturers take out the fat, sugars are used to enhance taste. Also,

take a close look at foods that proclaim 'no sugar'. Remember that in the land of food labelling, 'no sugar' simply means 'no sucrose'. Food manufacturers use different kinds of sweeteners to mask how much sugar is in products marketed as 'healthy' or 'low fat'. The labels on these foods may show five different ingredients, such as malt dextrin, raisin juice or fructose. These all sound healthy, don't they? They are all sugars. Your taste buds and your addictive body chemistry will recognize them as sugars even though the label may say 'sugar free'. Read labels carefully.

Pay attention to where sugar is hidden in restaurant foods as well. Chinese food and Thai food, for example, are both very high in sugar. If you have gone through a sugar detox and then go out for a nice 'healthy' stir-fry with prawns and pak choy, you may find yourself with inexplicable cravings the next morning. There was sugar in the stir-fry sauce. I have had this experience even after asking the Chinese restaurant to prepare my food without sugar. You'll find more information on dining out in Chapter 10.

Artificial Sweeteners

I do not encourage your using artificial sweeteners as an alternative to sugars for a number of reasons. The *taste* of sweet, whether from table sugar, corn syrup or aspartame, evokes a beta-endorphin response in your body. This reaction will create cravings. Essentially, artificial sweeteners, while not evoking the same insulin response, will prime your brain to want more 'sweet'. This sets you up to go back to the sugars.

In addition, most sugar-free products use aspartame (Nutrasweet) as a sweetener. Aspartame is made from phenylalanine, which is an amino acid. Having a lot of phenylalanine can be a problem for a number of reasons. It is a precursor to dopamine (the same way that tryptophan is a precursor for serotonin). Dopamine is the neurotransmitter that creates a

feeling of brightness and excitement in your brain. You like the dopamine effects in your brain. They are considered potent reinforcers. Dopamine is the neurotransmitter affected by cocaine.

I have observed that a very large number of sugar addicts are dependent upon sugar-free products. My hypothesis is that the phenylalanine evokes dopamine and creates an upper-like effect. I suspect that sugar-sensitive people get a bigger reaction to this than do people who are not. This drug effect can be addictive, sometimes as addictive as sugar. Caffeine in diet fizzy drinks heightens the effect even more.

Do not switch to sugar-free products as a way to ease into a sugar-free life. If you are already strongly attached to them, work on holding your 'dose' steady while you detox from regular sugars. You can then work on a sugar-free detox down the line. I do not recommend going off sugar-free products all at once. Cut down over time and use your diary to guide your progress.

Being Attentive to Your Plan

Detoxing from sugar will call upon you to use all your skills and knowledge about giving your body the right foods at the right times to keep your sugar-sensitive brain chemistry balanced. In the detox phase, more than ever, you will need to eat regular meals with protein, and you will need to do so consistently, day after day, week after week. This is where the stability you established earlier in the programme really pays off. Pay close attention to your food diary. And to make your detox easier, increase your vegetables a lot *before* you start it.

Here's why. Vegetables are carbohydrates. They are actually very slo-o-o-o-w sugars. They will give your body a sense of being satisfied without cravings. They will not prime you to want

more and go on a quest – no one goes out to the convenience store in the middle of the night to find some frozen peas!

Also pay attention to your vitamins and the other supports (water and exercise) to your programme.

Let's just check in on your vitamin plan:

- **Vitamin C.** 500 to 5,000 mg a day, depending on what your system needs. Doctors skilled in vitamin C supplementation often suggest a 'bowel tolerance' dosage. That means starting low and adding a little more vitamin C each day. If you find yourself having gas, diarrhoea or stomach distress, cut your dosage back by 500 mg at a time until the symptoms subside. You may find that the lower dosage works just fine for you unless you are getting sick. Then increasing the dosage would be warranted.
- **Vitamin B complex.** 50 mg a day. You can take the B-complex in either tablet or liquid form. I prefer the liquid because it allows you to take a smaller amount several times a day. This reduces the likelihood of stomach upset. Do not take B-complex at night, because it may keep you awake.
- **Zinc.** 15 mg a day.

Why these three vitamins for your plan? Vitamin C, a B-complex vitamin and zinc are traditionally used in alcohol detox. Since sugar addiction is so closely linked to the metabolic pathways of alcoholism, this triple package can work wonders for your healing process.

Vitamin C is the busiest of the plan vitamins. It:

- Speeds detoxification by acting as a scavenger that consumes free radicals (by-products of toxin activity within your body).

- Helps your adrenals recover from adrenal fatigue coming from stress and the high levels of sugar.
- Helps convert the amino acid tryptophan (found in the protein you eat) into serotonin.

The B vitamins are essential in breaking down carbohydrates so the body can burn them as fuel. One of the B vitamins, niacin, is critical to the conversion of tryptophan into serotonin. B vitamins affect many functions in your body. Each B vitamin does a slightly different task. They work best when in balance and working together. Some people attempt to choose a particular B vitamin to maximize the given effect. I encourage you not to split them up. Take a complex of B vitamins. It will work better in your body.

Zinc affects a wide variety of functions in your body. The most intriguing are its effects on glucose tolerance and insulin sensitivity. Adequate levels of zinc make a huge difference in how your body utilizes glucose. Good zinc, good absorption. If the sugar in your blood is actually used and burned, it is less likely to be stored as fat in your body.

Don't Forget the Water and Exercise

Sometimes as people get further along in their programme, they backslide a bit on some of the basics like water and exercise.

Drink eight to ten glasses of water each day. (If you weigh more than 90 kg, drink more than that. Use a rough guideline of drinking one litre of water for every 30 kg of body weight.) If you have drifted away from drinking enough water, get started again! It will be even more crucial as you start your sugar detox.

I find it hard to fill up my water glass and drink it down eight times a day. But I can fill my 1-litre plastic water bottle a couple of times and simply sip from it throughout my day. Find whatever works for you and do it.

I am often asked to suggest alternatives to drinking fizzy drink. I say, 'Drink water.' 'But, Kathleen, water is boring,' people reply. And I say, 'Yup, water is boring.' But that boring old water will help to heal your sugar addiction. Drink water. Add a slice of lemon if it makes water more interesting to you. Try different herbal teas. Discover the difference in flavour of the mint teas.

Exercise is particularly helpful during detox. Sugar-sensitive people seem to either not exercise at all or exercise compulsively. While I certainly do not expect that you will remake your entire exercise programme before doing your detox, being consistent about it will help in going off sugars.

At the very least, get out and walk every day for twenty minutes. Ten minutes out, ten minutes in. And if you can get to the gym and do a little workout, that will be even better. Cranking up your exercise enhances every part of your body and your programme.

Tips from the Field: Call It 'Movement'

I work with a personal trainer once per week, as this is very motivating for me. One thing she has really helped me with is substituting the word 'movement' for the word 'exercise'. Any movement is exercise! What a liberating thing! If I get up and change the TV channel vs using the remote, that's exercise! If I take the stairs instead of the lift, that's exercise. If I talk on the cordless phone and walk around dusting while I'm talking, that's exercise. It is amazing how much movement can change our lives, no matter what our size. (I am overweight by 45 kg – and on my way down!) I do a lot of water aerobics, because we weigh only 10 per cent of our weight in water (yippee) so there's a lot less stress on our joints.

– L.

The Sugar/Alcohol Dilemma

A number of sugar-sensitive people use alcohol to relax and deal with stress. Some of you may be dependent upon alcohol. Since alcohol is a sugar, going off alcohol will be part of your sugar detox. If you are alcohol dependent, you will be going off of alcohol as a part of your sugar detox. If alcohol is part of your sugar addiction, you will need to do some extra planning.

Often people will ask me how they can know if they have a problem with alcohol. In a clinical setting, we can assess whether you have a problem with alcohol, and if you do, determine the severity of the problem. If you don't have access to that kind of evaluation, you may be having a few drinks before dinner or wine with dinner and not know if it is a problem.

The simplest way to find out is to try to stop. If you find that you want to stop but find it difficult, you have a problem. If you can stop but are spending a huge amount of energy in managing not to have a drink, you have a problem.

You may not like the simplicity and definitive part of these assessments. You may want to argue with me, but I think of alcohol dependence as simply an extension of sugar sensitivity. If you are highly sensitive to sugars, you will be even more sensitive to alcohol.

If you find yourself trying to convince yourself (or me in your mind) that the few drinks before dinner can't possibly mean you have a problem, that is one more clue. People who do not have a problem with alcohol simply stop having it. They do not argue or cut deals or manage their use of it.

Staying Safe

If alcohol is part of your sugar addiction, it will be important for you to adapt your detox plan. Do an alcohol detox *before* you do your entire sugar detox. If you are having more than three drinks a day, seek professional support in going off alcohol. Do not

think you can do this alone. Find support in your community. Find another person who is in recovery from alcohol addiction and who understands what you are going through. If you cannot find a person who understands sugar addiction and alcohol dependence, come to the website at www.radiantrecovery.com.

Final Preparations

Picking a Time

Now you are ready to go for it. You have done your homework and know the drill. When you detox from sugar, you will go through something similar to a drug detox, but it will be less extreme. Because your sugar-sensitive body reacts to sugar as if it were a drug, you may have withdrawal symptoms. Your brain will be begging you to eat some sugar. You may get the shakes, feel nauseous and edgy, or have diarrhoea or headaches for a few days. That's normal – and it's why you need to plan your sugar detox for a time when you will not be under severe stress. But remember, if you have been doing the steps in the recovery programme for a while, these symptoms will be far less severe than if you simply were to go cold turkey on day one.

The actual sugar detox process usually takes five days, with the fourth day being the hardest. You will want to really *plan* the timing of your detox. Schedule it so that on the fourth day you have time to yourself. Give yourself space so you can be cranky or have the physical withdrawal symptoms without their affecting your big meeting at work or your daughter's wedding day.

Be strategic about this and you'll be successful. Chances are, you'll wake up on the fifth morning of your detox feeling great!

Knowing Your Style

Getting ready for your detox should include a review of your style of making change. Let's take a look at a few helpful questions.

When you have to do something, do you like to get all your ducks in a row, then work through each task one at a time? Or do you like to jump in and start doing it all at once? Now ask yourself the same question about your sugar detox. Are you going to ease into it or are you going to just *do* it? Are you going to cut down slowly or cut out all sugar at once?

Do this step in whatever style you like to do other things in your life. Over the years, most of my clients have used a combination of approaches. They cut down on white things and sugars first, then pick a time to go cold turkey and eliminate whatever sugars are left in their diets. This seems to work best for most people, but again, *do what's right for you*. If the detox style fits your natural rhythm, it is more likely to work smoothly and successfully.

No Sugars!

Pick your day. This is the start of no sugars. Read labels, be vigilant. Choose the degree of attentiveness you will have in your own detox.

When you are doing a detox, however, being strict with yourself seems to work better at the beginning. While the actual biochemical detox will take five days or so, the emotional detachment may take a few months. I find that it is easier to decide not to have any sugars than to constantly slip around trying to figure out how much is right. But if you feel that being totally strict will not work for you, listen to yourself and create your own way. The most important instruction here is to feel comfortable with what you can do. This is *your* healing plan for *your* body.

There's one thing you do want to be aware of, though. Denial is a powerful operating factor in addiction. Sometimes, in the name of being kind to oneself, sugar-sensitive people will be slow or sloppy about actually getting off sugars. So pay close attention to your process. Ask yourself your motivation in designing your plan. Are you going slowly because it's healthy or

because you don't want to let go of your best friend? Be honest. The results you will get are well worth the work you will do on this one.

Tips from the Field: Take as Much Time as You Need

Remember to keep in mind that this programme is a PROCESS . . . a JOURNEY. Take it slow and be gentle with yourself along the way. I'm preaching to myself here, too, believe me. I love cappuccinos. They are a major hit of caffeine and sugar! I used to have a cappuccino every day. I'm now down to one per week, and this is major progress for me. I have to look at how far I've come, and not allow myself to dwell on how far I have to go.

I think when I am ready to completely give up cappuccinos, it will not be a traumatic event. Even now, they are losing their hold on me. I can drive by a coffee shop without stopping. I don't even gaze longingly in the windows. I can visualize life without cappuccinos. I know it's coming!

– L.

I never believed I could get off sugar. But understanding that the feelings were withdrawal helped a lot. I made it through three days and was ready to quit. The fourth day was horrible. I felt like I wanted to bite my boss's head off. I went home early and just kept eating those three meals with protein. Mr Spud helped, too. On the fifth day, I woke up and felt clear and peaceful. I couldn't believe it! It keeps getting better. Is this magic or what?

– K.

What to Eat

Let's take a look at how you can support your detox even more. What you eat in this phase makes a big difference in how

successful you will be. By now you are eating plenty of protein three times a day and have got yourself pretty much shifted from white things to brown things. You are being diligent about Mr Spud every night and are taking your vitamins every day. In many cases, this shift will have already eliminated a fair amount of the sugar in your diet.

Before you take the plunge and drop more things out of your food plan, let's add something. Make sure that you are getting regular browns in each meal. Having a sufficient amount of complex carbohydrates will substantially decrease the discomfort of your detox. Have whole grain bread, brown rice, potatoes with skins, beans, oats, nuts, whole wheat pasta, and the like.

Eating more veggies, especially dense ones like broccoli and cauliflower (I know, I know, it seems really weird to talk about cauliflower when you are trying to pay attention to sugar), will help the transition. Butternut squash with nutmeg and cheese can ease a whole lot of sugar sadness.

So now you have a solid food plan, are emotionally stable and are doing the vitamins, the spud and the veggies. You are ready. Let's do it!

Your Actual Detox

After all this preparation, your actual detox will go pretty smoothly. After many years of hearing how people go through this process, I am amazed at how direct and simple it is. In many ways it is kind of anticlimactic. Sugar detox has the biggest negative charge when you try to do it as Step 1. Then it makes you off the wall, nasty, not at all pleasant to be around. Then you could only go three days before giving in and eating sugar again.

But when you do your detox after all the work on the first five steps, it will seem natural, logical and not at all difficult. And best of all, you will have a huge sense of satisfaction. You will be

doing what you have tried to do a thousand times before. But this time it will work!

The Big Day!

Pick your no-sugar day carefully. Choose a time when you will have five days without a major event. You have cleaned your cupboards. You have warned your family. Be especially vigilant about your food during this time, take your vitamins and make sure to have Mr Spud nightly. Keep busy. If you are cranky or edgy, go for a walk. Go to the gym. Swim, lift weights and sit in the hot tub. Go to a museum; take your kids to the zoo. Don't go to a movie; you will want popcorn and a chocolate bar. The entire movie environment is designed to get you to eat. Stay away from dangerous places for the time being.

Stay busy so you don't get bored and want to eat as a way to cope. Get connected to your support network. Write in your diary. Sing, dance, laugh, make love . . . even if you are crabby. These things help raise your beta-endorphin levels.

Here are a few other ideas from people in the Community Forum:

- *I take a bubble bath, maybe even by candlelight.*
- *I just sit outside when I am not up to really doing anything. I might take a book or something, but mostly I just soak in the out-of-doors, the light, the breeze, the sights.*
- *I like to listen to a comforting CD.*
- *I feel a lot better just by bringing fresh flowers into my home.*
- *I curl up and watch the old Jimmy Stewart movie* It's a Wonderful Life.
- *My cure for crabbiness is to put lavender essential oil on my pillow and duvet, and take an afternoon nap.*

Most important, don't spook yourself. Doing a sugar detox does *not* have to be a big thing. It is only that way if you do it off

the bat without a safety net. But you are ready, you are informed and you have been practising. Think of this as simply one more step on your path. I know you can do it!

Tips from the Field: One Meal at a Time

The best advice I ever got about this programme is this: Just keep making the best meal choice you can – one meal at a time.

– M.

Life After Detox

Your sugar detox is not the end of the addiction story; it is the beginning of a new way of living. You will start to adjust to a sugar-free life. You may be very excited and diligent for months. At some point, sugar will call you. Doughnuts will hop into your mouth unexpectedly, someone will bring a box of your favourite chocolates or biscuits; you will forget your resolve and have some sugar. Because your brain has now adapted to life without sugar, the first taste and response to the sugar will be wonderful. You will feel euphoric, mellow and very comforted. Your addictive brain will tell you that just a little bit is all right. Your addictive brain is very seductive and *loves* the feelings that come with sugar. It will try to make you forget the old days of addiction and seduce you into thinking that you are healed and can now have some sugar in moderation.

During the time you were sugar free, your beta-endorphin receptors have upregulated. You now have more of them. The more rigorous you have been, the more sites you have grown. When you have sugar, you activate all the new ones. When they empty out, they will scream big-time. They will object more than they did before. Your craving will wake up and insist,

demand and cry out for more sweet stuff. Your addictive brain
will tell you that you can manage it. It will say that just a little will
be okay. More than likely, you will slip into a wobbly place.

The wobbly place is a critical juncture for you. If you are attentive and remember the seductive nature of your addictive
brain, you will forgive yourself the little slip and go back to your
regular recovery plan. Three meals with protein, brown foods
and Mr Spud. You will be kind to the screaming beta-endorphin
sites, eat an apple with cheese and give away the biscuits.

And if by chance your wobble becomes a full-blown relapse,
you will be kind to yourself and remember that all of us have
been there. Healing from addiction means coming back from
relapse. You don't have to feel guilty or beat yourself up; just
come home to the programme and start again. Think of it as a
learning experience and come home to recovery.

Holding true to a life of recovery over the long haul is a
process. You don't get there straight off. You get better and better after each slip or relapse. You learn to get more support, you
get stronger in your commitment, you become more attached
to feeling good. And somewhere down the line, your love of recovery is so strong that nothing will get in the way of it. Chocolate won't be worth it. Biscuits will make you smile. You will feel
filled up rather than deprived. And you won't trade the feelings
for anything.

9

Staying with the Programme over Time: Step 7

Working your programme over time takes some practice. There are a set of skills that will help you get through the transition to an easy sugar-free life. Let's take a look at some of them that will help you with Step 7: create a new life.

Socializing Without Sugars

So many social gatherings – from holiday dinners to birthday parties or summer picnics – revolve around food, usually foods that are not the best for you: grilled hot dogs and hamburgers on fluffy white buns, mashed potatoes and biscuits, strawberry shortcake, ice cream. But you can stick with your plan even at special events. Let me suggest a new way of planning for these times and creating alternatives for special occasions.

Christmas is the granddaddy of all sugar holidays. If you celebrate Christmas or just work in an office and are a sugar addict, you will struggle with wanting to eat sweets around the holidays. But there are creative solutions. You might take heart and

inspiration from Gretel, who brainstormed on the forum about how she reframed her usual associations with Christmas. This is her list:

- Christmas is *The Nutcracker Suite* with sugar plum fairies.
- Christmas is Hansel and Gretel and gingerbread houses.
- Christmas is roasting chestnuts (or marshmallows) on an open fire.
- Christmas is eggnog.
- Christmas is leaving milk and biscuits for Santa.
- Christmas is stockings filled with sweets, fruit and nuts.
- Christmas is Christmas biscuits.
- Christmas is baking cakes, mince pies and breads to share.
- Christmas is carolling and stopping for hot chocolate afterwards.
- Christmas is open houses with food and drink I don't have control over.
- Christmas is office parties I don't plan.

Then she asked herself what Christmas *might* mean if she took all the Christmas foods out of the equation and looked at the bigger picture. She decided to include her spiritual self. Here's what she discovered:

- Christmas is the birth of a child.
- Christmas is giving.
- Christmas is celebration.
- Christmas is beautiful music.
- Christmas is twinkling lights on a starlit night.
- Christmas is snow glistening in the sunlight.
- Christmas is Santa coming down the chimney.
- Christmas is puppies and kittens.
- Christmas is surprises.
- Christmas is love.

- Christmas is family.
- Christmas is friends.

Gretel reframed her old associations of food with love. Socializing without sugar is not that difficult if you can shift your energy to the *meaning* of the holiday or special occasion rather than the food.

If sweets are given to you at the office or at your place of work, give them to your non-sugar-sensitive friends. You can reframe any holiday in this same way. Simply focus on non-food things as an expression of your love. Enlist your friends and families in this process. They may be dismayed that you are no longer baking their favourite holiday goodies, but if they participate in creating alternatives, they will be willing to support your recovery.

How to Say No to Your Family and Friends

Saying no to family and friends who encourage, nudge or even push you to move away from your food plan is very hard. These friendly saboteurs often go right to the heart of your own ambivalence. You may have friends who insist you have a piece of birthday cake or go to a Thai restaurant with them, or come over for a bite of the coffee cake they just baked.

How can you set your boundaries with these people? How can you say no gracefully? There are two tasks for you in dealing with these people. One is learning how to refuse gracefully; the other is understanding how your own ambivalence may affect the outcomes.

The Art of Graceful (or Humourous) Refusal

On the Community Forum, we came up with great list of ideas for coping with holiday meals. Laura's tips combine practical advice with humour and are especially helpful when you're trying to avoid alcohol and dessert! They truly offer wonderful options for saying no in a new way.

1. Matter-of-factly request a mineral water when the host asks what you would like. Throw a slice of lime in it. That way, it will look like what everyone else is drinking and they'll leave you alone.

2. If there's no mineral water, throw your lemon or lime slice in a glass of ordinary water with ice.

3. Throw your lemon or lime slice at anybody who enquires about your strange eating habits.

4. Deftly turn the conversation so you direct it back to the person who is inquiring about your 'diet'. 'How come you don't eat sugar?' they ask. 'I have found I feel better,' you reply. 'What about you? Are there any foods that you don't eat because you feel better without them?' (People love to talk about themselves!)

5. Disappear when dessert is served. Go to the bathroom for an especially long visit. Drop by the TV room and instantly get interested in whatever show the kids are watching. Suddenly develop the need to go out to your car and get that evening wrap because you are cold. Studiously start removing those tiny, natty little balls from your polyester evening gown.

6. When dessert is served, say, 'Thanks, but the main course was so delightful I filled up on it. But I would love a cup of tea.' (Hosts love to please their guests and will run to get whatever the guest asks for. So keep them busy and help them do their job as hosts.)

7. Be honest. Of course, you will become the centre of attention and people will instantly feel guilty about the dessert they are about to put into their mouth and hate you for it! Expect glares and wicked looks behind your back. Shrug them off.

8. Tell your partner/friend/spouse that you need help at the party. Instruct him or her that when dessert comes, it is their job to stick to you like glue and divert the conversation away from you – even if they have to do the macarena without music or recite the Ten Commandments.

9. Choose to eat dessert and feel miserable. Then let everybody know how you feel by having a blood sugar/beta-endorphin crash right in the middle of the living room. They'll never serve you dessert again. They'll never serve you again, period. But who needed them as friends anyway?

10. You could forewarn the hostess that you have some discomfort in this area. Could you bring a dessert that is allowable to you but bring enough for everybody? Could the hostess say she made it so attention is off you? You can then smirk when the guests eat the dessert and gag because it is so, well, sugar-free.

11. Don't go to the party.

12. At 8:00 P.M. announce that you have to get back to the facility; nightly check-in is mandatory by 8:30, as sugar addicts in your programme need to be locked up for the night.

13. Go to the party virtually. Get the latest 'See You See Me' computer programme and appear on screen at appropriate moments. Tell them it's a new work project the boss asked you to do. Virtually eat dessert with them.

14. Wear a paper bag on your head. That is sure to get more attention than a little ol' diet thing.

15. Bring enough copies of this book so when somebody asks you to elaborate, you can put a book in her hand and walk away. Tell her the discussion group on brain chemistry will begin after dinner.

16. Wear a sign that says, 'I do Kathleen's plan; wanna do it with me?'

17. As everyone else eats dessert, smoothly pull a baked potato out of your evening bag and ask someone to pass the salt and pepper, please.

18. Start boring them with personal stories of the difference between a beta-endorphin crash, a serotonin drop and low-blood-sugar shakes. ('You know, last Wednesday when I had that beta-endorphin crash, I thought I was going to take my boss's head off, I was so irritable, but in retrospect it was probably low serotonin because I didn't have the impulse control necessary to stop, so I kept yelling . . . Though it could have been low blood sugar because I missed breakfast and had a mediocre lunch and got all light-headed and jittery.') When their eyes glaze over, you have created a safe space for yourself at the party. They will avoid you, of course, but the attention is off you.

19. Pre-print cocktail napkins with the sugar/carbohydrate content of everything being served that night (you'll need to coordinate with the

hostess on this one). Then trip lightly from guest to guest, informing them what they're doing to their pancreas, using the napkin as a visual aid.

20. Invite Oprah. No one will even notice you're there.

You can add to or adapt this list to fit your own style and your own needs. Many in our community copied Laura's list and carried it with them to millennium parties.

Tips from the Field: You Can Go Home Again

My parents seem to feel personally rejected when I don't eat their food. My dad and I had a silly argument during a recent visit about real potatoes vs fake potatoes. When I do succeed with my parents, it's because of two things: first, I bring my own food supplies to their house and park them right in the kitchen for all to see. Early in the day, I may ask my mum what she is planning for dinner. I ooh and aaahh over things, saying something like, 'Mmmm, sounds great! How about if I steam some broccoli to go along with that?' She is always glad for the help, and what mother could resist their kid eating vegetables? It's when I let myself get emotionally wrapped up in their need to parent me that I get into trouble.

– M.

How Your Ambivalence Can Affect Your No

But let's take a look at how your own feelings towards sugar recovery can affect saying no. The 'helpful' person urging you to have her coffee cake might be ignoring your 'No, thank you' because she can sense you aren't fully committed to your programme. A critical key to successfully saying no is getting your own feelings sorted out. Once you are absolutely convinced that

your recovery is more important to you than sweets, your friends and family will get the message clearly. This may take many months or even more. One of the markers for your own progress is the respect you command from those around you about the food. The more serious about it you become, the more they will honour your commitment.

Staying Out of Trouble

It's not only family and friends that can get us in trouble. Sometimes we do it to ourselves. That's why the best way to stay *out* of trouble is to know what people and places will get you *into* trouble. Let's look at slippery places first. They will be different depending on where you found your old comfort foods. Trouble spots can be bakeries, ice cream parlours or coffee shops, but they can also be Italian restaurants or Jewish delis with lavish dessert cases. In fact, any place that has an old emotional cue (when you go there you always have their pie, or you used to go there with your dad and get ice cream) can be a trouble spot for you.

When you are just starting to stay off sugars, be vigilant and don't go into those shops or restaurants at all. Three or four months down the road, when your brain and body quieten down, you'll be able to go in those places without fear of immediately falling off the programme.

Why? Your brain chemistry will change and those places won't trigger you any more. Your brain will respond to the visual and smell cues differently. When something (like sweet food) is emotionally charged, you see it everywhere. By the same token, when things are not charged, you don't see them. For example, if you are primed (and thus craving sugar) and you go into Starbucks, all you will see are the biscuits and pastries in the glass case. But if you are solid with your programme, you will simply order a decaf latte and won't even *see* the stuff in the case.

Do you know what your trouble spots are? Ask yourself this:

'What are the places that I drift to under stress?' Make a note of them below.

Where do I go? (Be specific)	When and why do I go there?	What do I eat?

Getting Support

Getting a lot of support is key to your success with this programme. Whether you have one sympathetic friend or family member, a buddy to do the programme with, a large local support group or the huge resources of online support on our Community Forum, you will find that support makes all the difference in sticking to your plan over time.

Getting Friends and Family to Help

Your new way of eating may have got you support from friends and family in the beginning, but you need support for the long

term. This is best provided either by others who are on the programme or by people who are not sugar addicts themselves. Here's an example. I went out to lunch recently with someone who is doing the programme. Her partner came with us. We were at a restaurant that had really good bread. When the waiter came with a big basket of warm breads (you can be sure no browns were included) and a pair of tongs for serving it, the woman on the programme said thanks, but she didn't want any. Her partner – who is *not* a sugar addict – also turned down the bread, not because she didn't want any, but as a gesture of support. I was very touched.

You can create your own little support group of people who are interested in what you are doing and who aren't in denial about their own sugar sensitivity. Ask your friends to exchange 'safe' recipes. See if someone would like to do the programme with you. Invite your group to one of the elegant dinners listed in Chapter 7. Have a potato taste-testing using white, yellow, purple and all the other varieties of potatoes now available.

Email one another, make phone calls, connect every day. This is important and will make a huge difference.

Online Support

You can find lots more support if you have access to the Internet. If you don't own a computer, you can try hooking in via your television set, using a friend's computer or seeing if your local library offers Internet access.

You can reach my website at www.radiantrecovery.com. There you will find an overview of the programme along with answers to frequently asked questions, helpful hints, products to support your programme and other great resources like our news-letter, the Community Forum, a listing of support groups and our special-interest online support groups. There is no charge for any of these services.

> ### Tips from the Field: Using Online Support
>
> This support is priceless. For me, it's the glue that holds the whole thing together.
>
> *– L.*

Critical throughout this whole process is a commitment to getting support. You cannot heal addiction in isolation. Community moves you from self-sabotage into progress. It keeps you honest, encourages you and delights in your success. Build your community and find what you want.

What to Do When You're Cranky

Even though you have a good support system, there will be times when you are cranky. 'Cranky' is the code word that I use to describe the feeling of 'wanting to kill!' The first step in dealing with cranky is to notice it when it comes up. The clues are that you will be edgy and irritable, feeling like everything and everyone are against you.

When you notice this, go back to your food diary. Have you eaten something sweet, something that primed your beta-endorphin system and brought up cravings that are setting off your crankiness? Have you been eating enough? You may not be eating enough food at your meals or you may be skipping meals. Or your meals may be light on the protein. Also look to see if you are getting enough complex carbohydrates. Sometimes people just do protein and vegetables, and they get really cranky. Protein and veggies aren't enough. You have to eat some browns every day: whole grain bread, brown rice, beans or any whole grain products. (If you are a One-Pot/One-Meal

type, this means that every pot you cook will need to include browns.) And don't forget your evening spud.

The Way Out of Cranky

The solution to cranky is very simple. Get back to the basics. Eat breakfast with protein. Eat three meals a day with protein. And be sure you are getting enough brown things. What's enough? Well, it's different things for different people.

If you are just getting off sugar, your meals will consist of protein, browns and vegetables. The ratio of browns to greens will probably be two browns to one green. As you continue with the plan, the ratio will shift to about one to one. If you decide to use the plan to lose weight, you would shift to one brown to two greens. These shifts seem to occur spontaneously. When I wrote *Potatoes Not Prozac*, I didn't discuss this, but I have noticed that this is what people on the programme usually do spontaneously.

You May Be More Sensitive to Sugar Now

When you first go off sugar, your brain and your receptors are going to be much more edgy and volatile. So if you have a little bit of sugar, you are going to feel it a whole lot more than you will after you've been on the programme a while and everything quietens down.

Here's the time frame we are talking about. For the first four months off sugar, you may feel euphoric and really excited about doing the programme. You have got through your detox, which was uncomfortable but manageable, and overall you feel quite steady. From about four to seven or eight months, your brain chemistry quietens down and your receptors aren't so reactive, but they are now like newborns. They are very receptive and vulnerable to sugar. During this period, people may also have more food allergies. Their systems seem to be more reactive and volatile, even though they have changed their food dramatically. After eight or nine months, the entire system

seems to quieten down and fall into a regular routine, and you'll be less vulnerable to slipping. If you slip a little, you won't slide down the entire mountainside. On a practical level, what that means is that if you do go to a party, it won't matter what they are serving. If you have to eat white things or even sweet things, it will be okay. You won't be severely triggered and you won't fall apart.

Tips from the Field: The Blessings of Time

Now that I have been on the programme for fifteen months, I am much less sensitive to sugar than I was at three to nine months. It is like my body is now more grounded and absorbs the shock better. This doesn't tempt me to go back on my substances, but it does make for a smoother ride. My chemistry is not so volatile. It is more stable, so shocks don't shatter me; they just rock me a little and I can get back on track more easily.

– D.

Tips from the Field: The Bottom Line

If you remember nothing else, remember this: *Eating sugar makes you want more sugar.* Period. Early on in the process, I couldn't understand when people told me that 'a little bit is harder than none'. But it's true.

– L.

What About Relapse?

We talked in Chapter 6 about slipping and full relapse. Slipping is when you slip off the plan for a meal or two. Relapse is when

your slip stretches into days or weeks or months. Relapse rarely descends on you from out of the blue. It is usually preceded by a number of slips and some clearly recognizable symptoms. The warning signs of relapse are:

Emotional fragility	Inability to concentrate
Fatigue	Irritability
Feeling on edge	Low tolerance for stress
Feeling inadequate	Thinking that goes round
General edginess	and round

Don't Expect Perfection

There is no such thing as perfection. Every one of us makes mistakes from time to time – and sometimes we make them frequently. We are not striving for perfection. We are seeking commitment and progress. Work to know what and why you are eating what you do. You may well choose a date to commit to going off sugars and into detox, but there is no magic date for being fixed in recovery from sugar addiction. The Sugar Addict's Total Recovery Programme is not a short course in change. Rather than simply giving up sugars, you are working on a life plan.

If you set yourself to believe that you will be totally abstinent for the rest of your life, you are setting yourself up for failure. Doing this programme doesn't work that way. It is a *process* of becoming more aware, more attentive and more committed as you go. It is cumulative. That means it builds on itself over time. And it builds on the problem solving you do as you go.

As you learn to handle new situations, as you learn to recover from a slip, you will be smarter and savvier each time. Food will no longer be your enemy, but your support. Your body will be a trustworthy guide and you will be having fun with your life.

Tips from the Field: Making Better Choices

When I am tempted to eat sugar, I always picture a balance scale. On one side is how I feel now and how I hope to change, and on the other side is the piece of dessert or whatever choice I am facing at the moment. Then I ask myself: is it worth giving up my contentment and emotional stability for this particular choice? For me, looking at it in that stark way really makes it clear exactly what I'm contemplating.

– L.

If You Fall Off Your Food Plan

When you feel your worst and can't cope with anything, just go back to eating breakfast every day with protein. As you start feeling better, expand to three meals a day with protein. And so on. Don't spend a lot of time or energy beating yourself up. Just pick up the programme and get going again.

How to Get Back to Your Plan

How do you get back on the plan when you haven't just slipped, but have seriously relapsed? The answer is: take a special day and pay attention. Eat three meals with protein at regular intervals and record your food and feelings in your diary.

One client I see gets a fresh start by treating herself to three meals out. She has a fancy omelette with fresh fruit and wholemeal toast for breakfast, a Greek salad or Caesar salad with grilled chicken for lunch (she brings her own salad dressing to avoid covert sugars) and fish or beef as the main course for dinner. She says it's worth the expense to get herself back on her food plan without feeling deprived!

If you have been off the programme for some time, you have some choices about how to get back on it. Some people like to

start back in slowly, working their way up through the steps. Others jump back into a sugar detox. It's your own call.

Take Chris, for example. She had been doing the programme for eighteen months when she really got into trouble. She ended up being off the programme for three months. She was not able to control her eating and she was losing her grip. She was scared she might go back to being the way she was before she started dealing with her sugar addiction.

I recommended that she give herself three weeks to get fully back on the programme. The first step was for her to reconnect to the Web community. Chris agreed. She knew she couldn't do it by herself. So she started posting and answering messages on the Community Forum. The next action I asked her to take was to move the chocolate she ate to mealtime.

After she had achieved this, I encouraged her to use bananas rather than chocolate, even if she had to eat three bananas a day. In this way, we created a banana 'bridge' that would ease the pain of her detox. This is not something I would recommend to someone doing their first detox, but I recommended it with Chris because we wanted her to stop being primed by the emotional cues from the chocolate. She could cope with the sweetness of the banana. The bananas were sort of medicinal. (There's no way you can think of chocolate as medicinal!) They probably had almost the same amount of sugar in them, too, since Chris wasn't eating huge amounts of chocolate.

After a week, she found she didn't need the banana and got fully back on track. So she didn't end up needing the whole three weeks, but by permitting her to take that long if she needed to, I took away the emotional pressure.

Creating Other Kinds of Comfort

When you were regularly eating sweet food and foods made with refined flour in order to comfort yourself, you probably thought

the only thing that could comfort you was sugar. But that was just your sugar-addicted body speaking. Now that you have shifted from white things, which are often high in sugar, to brown things, you may notice your mind opening to the possibility of other forms of comfort. This is a sign that sugar is losing its grip on you.

The comfort that sugar and white flour give you when you are feeling down is really our old friend the beta-endorphin spike, which makes you feel great for a moment, then sends you into beta-endorphin withdrawal – and creates huge cravings for more sugar.

Things That Will Trigger a Beta-Endorphin Spike

The danger of a beta-endorphin spike is that it *increases* your risk of slipping or relapsing. If you don't eat, if you skip a meal, you will get a beta-endorphin spike, which will prime your system and set you up for big cravings. If you have a wildly enthusiastic exercise session, the same thing can happen. One woman on the programme told me that the day she started her Christmas shopping, she bought a lot of gifts, and that made her feel so good, she couldn't stop buying. Another example of beta-endorphin release.

Other things that can trigger a too-big beta-endorphin release are:

- Going into a casino and hearing coins jingle in metal cups
- Making love a lot all at once
- Going on a vision quest (coming down after a big high can make people have cravings)
- Staying up all night and cramming for an exam
- Having a baby

Do you get the idea? Going to extremes in a short period of time is going to flood your system with too much beta-endorphin. So watch out for activities of high intensity and short duration.

How to Get a Nice Slow Rise in Your Beta-Endorphin

When you use comfort foods and activities that produce a *slow* rise in beta-endorphin, you will feel better and keep feeling better. No rush, no withdrawal symptoms, no cravings.

The list of activities that have been scientifically documented to raise your beta-endorphin slowly includes meditation, yoga, exercise, prayer, music, eating food that tastes good (other than sweet or white-flour-based foods), making love, laughing, listening to Mozart and other classical music, and listening to inspirational talks. It's my guess that the complete list includes much more, even though these other things have not been tested in the laboratory or reported in the science literature. They include dancing, gardening, puppy kisses, kitty snuggles, children and grandchildren sleeping or running or laughing, bubble baths, candles, even going to the movies with a dear friend.

Our community has named these activities BE raisers, meaning beta-endorphin raisers. Make your own list. You may be surprised at the number of BE raisers you can find.

Tips from the Field: Lifting Your Spirits

Here are some of the things I do when I'm feeling really depressed:

- **Go to the park with a book (even if just for ten minutes) – it's good because it gets me out of the house.**
- **Go to the library and stay there long enough to read three magazines.**
- **Cook a pot of soup (all that chopping is very therapeutic!).**
- **Do a jigsaw puzzle.**
- **Go look in a pet shop (providing it's not near a doughnut shop!).**

– C.

Here are some beta-endorphin raisers that work for me:

- **Go watch a football game in the local park – whichever teams are playing, kids or adults. (You don't have to know any of the players or even know what time the game started.)**
- **Clean off one surface in the house – maybe a table, a section of cabinet. Getting it to look its best, perking it up, brightens the whole room and me.**
- **If it's winter, build a fire, put on soft music and curl up.**
- **Eat out on my balcony or have my morning quiet time there.**
- **Meet a friend out for coffee or a meal, with the motivation of having them really enjoy it (like they have been under stress lately).**
- **Go to a public event – any event – and participate as a spectator.**

– D.

Here are a few things I do to nurture myself in non-food ways:

- **Write poetry.**
- **Listen to *The Cowboy Junkies* or other favourite CDs.**
- **Meditate.**
- **Do deep-breathing exercises.**
- **Lift weights and stretch.**

– S.

Seems like whenever I need comfort or am stressed, I start heading for sweets or food! But I do have a few non-food things I've done that work for me.

- **Take a leisurely hot bath.**
- **Float in a pool, all by myself.**
- **Hug my bird.**
- **Call a dear friend from whom I haven't heard for a while.**
- **Put lavender essential oil on my pillow and duvet, and take an afternoon nap.**

– L.

Here are some things that work for me. Maybe they will work for you.

- **Go back to reading *Potatoes Not Prozac*. Start at the beginning.**
- **Take a walk.**
- **Exercise.**
- **Watch a comedy-romance movie with a good friend you can snuggle up with.**
- **Go window shopping.**
- **Read a romance (or any other book of your choice).**
- **Go dancing!**
- **Review your diary just to see how far you've come along since the beginning and remember how it felt to be powerless over food.**
- **Go roller-skating just for the fun of it!**
- **Play board games with your friends and/or family.**
- **Go online and chat with someone on the Community Forum.**
- **Send an email to a close friend whom you haven't sent mail to in a while.**

Finally, remember to smile when you look at yourself in the mirror! You are your own best friend. *No one* can take better care of you than you. You know what is good and not so good for you. Choose what's best for you because *you deserve it*!

– L.

As you start to identify your personal beta-endorphin raisers, you are going to start connecting to the idea that life can be more than food. Growing up, many of us learned to get our comfort, safety and security from what we ate. As adults, we don't realize that it isn't the food so much as the feeling associated with the food that makes us feel so good. The feeling is

about beta-endorphin. Feeling safe, confident and loved. Feeling connected. This is beta-endorphin.

Learning that we can have these feelings from a thousand things other than food is a wonderful insight. The quality of the beta-endorphin rise from puppy kisses is not as dramatic as that from an ice cream sundae, but it sure has a bigger upside to it. And the best part of beta-endorphin-raising activities is you can do a lot of them at once. Get in the tub, light a candle, make a cup of tea, get your cat on the windowsill, put on some wonderful music and get your spouse or partner to rub your back. For a beta-endorphin boost, these things may well equal that of a hot fudge sundae – and you won't be hungover the next day.

10

Special Situations

H ave you noticed that life rarely goes according to plan? This isn't necessarily a bad thing – many of the surprises we run into can be wonderful ones – but it can throw our programme off if we aren't expecting them. In this chapter, I'll give you some help in planning for the unexpected and in adapting the programme to your special needs if you are diabetic, pregnant or a vegetarian, or you take antidepressants.

Making Contingency Plans

Most sugar addicts who have not started to heal do not plan much. We tend to be impulsive and call it spontaneity. This actually means we rarely think ahead. One of the real markers for your recovery is to begin to think about your food needs *before* you get into trouble.

That's why you must always have a contingency plan – no matter what your cooking style. If you are going to a potluck

dinner, for example, make sure the dish you are bringing is something you can eat. That way, if every other dish is loaded with sugar or white things, you will at least get some dinner. (You'll also need to make sure everyone else doesn't finish off your dish before you get some!)

Other contingency plans are to keep your own protein snacks in the car or make sure you have a little bag of almonds in your bag so if you get stranded somewhere, you have something to tide you over. (For other suggestions, go back and take a look at the sections in Chapter 6 on foods to carry with you, what to do if you are over the cliff, and what to do if you miss lunch.) The key is to *think ahead* about the situations in which you might have difficulty getting the food you need and *plan* for them! Let's take a look at some of these special situations that call for a little planning.

Going Out to Eat

When you are eating out, you can eat in almost any restaurant, but you will need to follow a few ground rules in order to enjoy yourself and care for your sugar-sensitive body at the same time.

First, if possible, familiarize yourself with the menu of the restaurant before you go in. Make sure there are foods you can eat. Ask the waiter not to bring the bread basket to your table. And don't peek at the dessert list when you are looking over the menu.

Focus on finding the most enjoyable food you can have. Ask the waiter to have the chef adapt an entrée to suit your needs. For example, you could ask for a baked potato instead of pasta. You could ask for a sandwich with wholemeal bread – or without bread! I have had cooks come up with the most delightful options in response to my requests.

Tips from the Field: Restaurants to the Rescue

When I am in danger of going off the plan, I drop everything and get myself to a restaurant. I am an expert now on which restaurants around here meet my needs. I don't hesitate to take something from home to combine with what I know they have. Sometimes I take my tuna and dump it on their beautiful salad. Sometimes I slip a piece or two of whole grain bread in a plastic bag so I can have bread with their meal or make my own sandwich with their fillings.

– D.

I love eating out on this plan. My favourite things to order for lunch are a chicken Caesar salad, a Cobb salad, or a chef salad. For days when I'm in a rush, I take a couple of whole wheat tortillas down to the Mexican food stand and ask them to make chicken burritos without rice on them. If I run out of whole wheat tortillas, I just order the same burrito, open it up, and eat the insides.

– M.

Dining Out for Business or Pleasure

When you go out for a meal, first of all, enjoy yourself – especially if you are someone's guest! Scan the menu and decide what your main dish – your protein – will be. Steer clear of pasta dishes (unless you ask for the pasta sauce to be put on a baked potato instead of pasta) and dishes without substantial protein. Then decide about the accompaniments. Most restaurants will offer salads and side orders of veggies you can eat. If not, ask them to *cook* you a side order of steamed or sautéed veggies. Many will be glad to do so.

Asking for What You Want at a Restaurant

Even if something you want is not on the menu, you can ask them to make it for you. I do this all the time. I look at the

menu to see what ingredients are there. For example, they may be serving chicken with cherry wine sauce. Now, I know that this sauce won't work for me, but I also know that they have chicken in the kitchen. Or there may be a great pesto sauce being served on the meat-and-pasta dish. So I bravely say, 'Would you be willing to ask the chef [or cook] if I might have some chicken with that pesto sauce?' I have never had anyone refuse me. If the chef is huffy about your choice, you can always simply ask to have the chicken grilled.

Other ideas? You can order a double serving of vegetables. You can ask for any sandwich on the menu and end the request with 'without the bread' and a smile. Or you can ask them to put any of their protein things on any of their salads – such as adding prawns to a Caesar salad. Simply tell them you will be happy to pay for it, smile, and assume they will accommodate your request.

Really Good Places to Eat Out

Eating out can be just as much fun on the programme as it was before; you just need to know where to go. My favourites are fish or seafood restaurants, steakhouses and grills.

People on our Community Forum have even found a lot of possibilities in fast food restaurants. Here are some things they recommend:

- Hamburgers or cheeseburgers with lettuce, tomato and onion, but without the roll. (Throw it out. If you just leave it in the bag on your table, you'll probably pick at it.)
- Salad bars or side salads (be careful about the covert sugars in their dressings; try taking your own homemade salad dressing – it'll be tastier, too).
- Chicken or beef tacos on corn tortillas at Mexican fast food restaurants. Other foods that will work are pinto

(black) beans with cheese, fajitas on a corn tortilla, and a taco salad (dump it out of its white flour shell and throw it out or it will call to you all through dinner).

- Roast chicken without the skin at Kentucky Fried Chicken. (They also have good steamed corn-on-the-cob.)
- Baked potato with chilli, cheese and/or salad bar stuff on top of it. You can also tear up pieces of a hamburger and put that on top if there's no other protein available.
- Grilled chicken salads (at McDonald's). Order two if you're concerned about not getting enough protein.
- Chicken strip salad with an extra grilled chicken breast and potato skins.
- Chicken nuggets, though they are admittedly boring without the dipping sauce, plus they are breaded with white flour. But if you are desperate for protein, most fast food places have them.
- Fried chicken and green beans.
- Salads and sandwiches.

Foreign Food

Some foreign food is great for people on the programme. And some is not. Here's how to tell the difference.

Asian

Chinese restaurants tend to put sugar in everything. It's my experience that they may do so even if you ask them not to. If you taste Chinese food that's truly cooked without sugar, you will know immediately. It tastes completely different. My advice is to either stop going into Chinese restaurants or really learn which dishes are least likely to have sugar in them. If you have a special place that you want to keep on your list, develop a relationship with the staff. If you are a known quantity to the staff, they are more likely to honour your request for no sugar.

Thai food is also loaded with sugar. It's rare to find a Thai place that can serve you a dish without sugar, though you can always ask for steamed vegetables without sauce. Some people have had luck with that.

Japanese food also has sugar in it, though way less than Chinese or Thai food. Even the sticky rice used to make sushi has sweetener in it. Now, I still eat sushi on occasion because I love it. Sushi once in a while works for me. I know that the morning after I have it, I may crave all sorts of things. And I just laugh at myself and remember that it is the sushi being seductive and I don't have to do anything in response to the cravings. But remember, I have been doing the programme for eleven years. If you are just starting off, you may want to be more rigorous and not flirt with triggering yourself.

Indian

In general, Indian food is not a problem for people on the programme. In particular, Indian restaurants are wonderful with vegetables. What's more, curry evokes a positive beta-endorphin response because it is hot. You can feel relaxed and mellow and not be triggered.

Italian

Sometimes people on the programme avoid Italian restaurants because of the pasta and bread, but the truth is, Italian restaurants can be great places to eat because they also have grilled fish and vegetables, wonderful salads and antipasto. The key is to know what your choices are before you go in and to ask them not to bring the bread to the table. Try reading the menu before you are falling off the cliff. And take care about the bread. That warm, crusty bread calls to me big-time. I want to be sloshing it in the olive oil and garlic. But I ask them not to bring it. Its call is too intense.

Mexican

Mexican is a good alternative, though it is not long on vegetables outside chopped tomatoes and beans. Be sure to ask for corn tortillas (blue is even better) instead of white-flour tortillas, and skip the rice. Eat the beans – they are a tasty, slow brown. Also, chilli is comforting – it's warm in your tummy, and if it's spicy hot, it too evokes another positive beta-endorphin response.

Further Plans for Special Occasions

Special occasions call for special skills in dealing with them. Whether you are faced with trying to stay on your plan during holidays, birthdays, plane trips or long car rides, remember: You can do it! Here are some tactics you can use.

Holidays

Head off your holiday crisis before it happens. Here's the bottom line:

Emergency Preparation = A Successful Celebration

Holidays and other family celebrations are times of high stress, and your body may get thrown for a loop as much by the stress (even good things can be stressful!) as by an excess of sugar and white things. This means that the best defence is a good offence: plan ahead and be careful to eat right and to note in your diary every mouthful and every feeling as you approach periods of high stress (if you know about it ahead). This will help your body be well prepared to handle the foods and moods of the holidays.

Another tactic is to find out ahead of time what will be served so that you know what foods you will and won't eat when you get there. If there's not enough to fit your plan, ask if you can

bring your favourite salad or side dish. If that won't work for your hostess, at least she will be forewarned about your passing up her dishes that contain sugar and white stuff.

Two other helpful hints are to eat something before you go so you are not famished if dinner is late, and to plan an after-dinner walk with people. That will raise your beta-endorphin level so you are feeling happy and solid when you sit back down at the table and watch other people eating sugary desserts. You could also bring a dessert that you know you can eat (see the recipes in Chapter 11).

Another idea is to go to a restaurant for your holiday meal where you can get exactly what you want and you aren't offending your hostess by not eating her pasta dish or homemade eight-layer lemon cake.

Or you could also skip the big meal altogether and create an alternative celebration. Christmas, for example, could be about doing service (helping cook dinner at a soup kitchen for homeless people) instead of eating a fancy meal together. Many families have found renewed gratitude and joy in celebrating the holidays this way.

Go back to the opening of Chapter 9 and take a look at the brainstorming list that Gretel did about Christmas. How might you apply that tactic to other holidays and special events? Remember *food* is not love, *love* is love. We often use food to express our love, but there are other ways to express love as well. Here's a good example.

Every Valentine's Day, the chocolate ads shout, 'Show her you love her!' and accompany their command by a photo of a huge heart-shaped box of chocolates. But think of all the other ways someone could express his or her devotion and celebrate a true holiday of the heart:

- Spend extra time with the one you love.
- Write her a love letter.

- Read love poems out loud to him.
- Go for a walk together and hold hands.
- Give his dog a bath.
- Wash, wax and vacuum her car.
- Buy her flowers or lingerie.
- Cook her a meal that fits the plan.
- Bring him breakfast in bed every Sunday for a month.
- Make a collage of all the images that remind you of him.
- Prepare her a scented bubble bath with candles and background music, and then keep her company while she takes it. Scrub her back if she wants and wrap her in a thick soft towel afterwards.

There are lots of ways someone can show his or her love for you without sending your blood sugar sky-high.

Birthdays

For me, five minutes in the mouth isn't worth it any more. With that in mind, here's a story about food, birthdays and love.

My birthday was coming. A dear and supportive friend offered to make a special birthday cake that would fit my food plan, using whole grains, a little treacle and very little sweetness. Chewy, moist and spicy was what we were aiming for.

My friend, who doesn't actually cook very much, came to my house for the big cake-making day. She unpacked the ingredients she had purchased and lined them up on the counter with great ceremony. Then confusion set in. Every few minutes she appeared in the study, where I was working. 'Why do I have to simmer the ginger?' 'Do I really need to sift the oat flour?' 'Is bicarbonate of soda the same as baking powder?'

Eventually she had concocted a gooey brown mass and was ready to pour it into the cake pan. This generated another visit

to the study. 'Kathleen, it says to put it in six miniature dariole moulds. What are dariole moulds?' By this time I was laughing so hard, I could hardly stand, let alone find a dariole mould of any sort. But my neighbour, the baker, came to the rescue and found something she thought would do. We cooked the cake and sprung it from the pan.

Frankly, it looked a little strange, like something that had died or been in the refrigerator too long. My son said it resembled a mosquito disk. I wondered how we would manage to eat it.

Everyone else at my birthday party slathered ice cream over their portion of the mosquito disk. I used apple sauce. The cake was pretty strange; actually it was awful, but the whole experience was so funny, I didn't really care that I didn't have real cake.

Tips from the Field: Friends Are Better Than Cake

It was a tradition at work to have a cake for the birthday person, as many jobs do. One birthday, everyone knew I was trying really hard to lose weight, so that year they made me a delicious fruit salad, with lots and lots of cut-up fresh fruit. They had 'extras' to put with it, like whole grain crackers, yogurt and cheeses. I truly did not miss the cake at all – nor did anyone else! There was not a crumb left after the party, unlike the times when we had to try to pawn off a half a cake on someone at the end of the day. I have always remembered this, because I actually *preferred* it to a birthday cake (and believe me, it takes a lot to make me choose fruit over cake), it was so delicious and refreshing. Most of all, it showed how much my friends cared about me and took my food plan seriously. Friends like that are priceless.

– L.

It's been many years since I have had a rich chocolate cake with white icing on my birthday, but like I said, five minutes in the mouth isn't worth it any more.

Don't let anyone tell you, 'You won't miss it after a while'. Of course you will. It's like losing a dear friend. But over time, things shift. Your attachment will move from the sugar (the cake) to the love (the people). The joy will be in the party, the celebration, family and friends. The taste of cake won't be your standard of love. There was more love in that 'mosquito disk' than any cake I have ever had.

Tips from the Field:
To Eat or Not to Eat . . . Birthday Cake

Whichever choice you make, it's a learning experience. Hurray if you choose not to eat the cake, but don't beat yourself up if you do choose to eat it. If you choose to eat it, think about all the times you ate cake without having the choice. Just the idea that you could ponder, take the time to make a decision – why, that's pretty amazing in itself. Remember all the times the cake plate was empty before we even had a chance to taste it – let alone decide whether or not to eat it? Now, before you so much as see or smell that cake, you are already ahead of the game!

– P.

Travelling

Business travel, more than business meals, poses a problem for me. The only solution is to have a plan. When my first book was published, I went on an extensive book tour. I had asked my publicist to make sure that the local person escorting me to and from the airport, book signings and media interviews knew that eating a healthy lunch was critical to me.

Unfortunately, my very first book signing took place at lunchtime. My escort brought me a can of tuna fish and a can opener. It wasn't quite what I had hoped for. But I learned my lesson quickly. *Do not trust that anyone other than you will understand that meals on the road are very important.*

When I saw the tuna can, I should have sent my escort across the street to get me a cup of lentil soup, some whole grain toast and a piece of fruit. I didn't, and by 3:00 P.M., when we were driving to my next appointment, I was falling off the cliff. I might have slipped if I had gone into a coffee shop at that point and seen all those goodies looking me in the eye. Don't let yourself get into a blood sugar crisis.

Identify the windows of time during which it is critical that you eat. Ask about the restaurants in the place you'll be. Always get protein at your meals. And make sure you get enough to eat. If you are hungry and you get tired, you'll lose it on your trip. Stay in hotels with room service, because they will always make you a baked potato. The server who brings it won't think you are strange, only that you know what you want.

If you get into trouble, find a fast food place. Know ahead of time which ones offer foods that will work for you. (Refer to the specific suggestions earlier in this chapter.) Maybe even keep a

---

Tips from the Field: Travelling Light

If you're travelling, it helps to take a small cool bag. I found one that is soft-sided and collapses when I'm not using it, so I can actually put it in a suitcase if it's empty. If you are flying, you can pack it away and go to a grocery store to fill it up with food and ice when you get to your destination.

– K.

list of fast foods that fit your plan in your purse so you don't have to wrack your memory when you're hungry and stressed.

And don't forget to write in your diary. Without it, I guarantee you won't be able to think straight or know what you have eaten when. Finally, cut yourself some slack. Travelling is stressful at best, and a lot of it is out of your control. Just do your best.

Surviving Long Plane Trips

Plane trips are a challenge! You can try ordering the special meals, but the best thing is to just bring your own food. Make a sandwich ahead of time and include cut-up veggies and some dressing to use as a dip. Pack a salad, too, and bring some salad dressing in a little plastic bottle. Bring fruit, too, or whatever you think of as a treat. Maybe cheese and whole grain crackers. And bring *plenty* of food. Use plastic bags or old yogurt containers to pack your foods so you can toss them out when you reach your destination.

If you are on the return leg of a journey where you've been staying in a hotel, eat a solid meal before you leave and get the hotel restaurant to make you a whole grain sandwich – or whatever works for you – so you can take it on the plane with you.

Plan for the fact that you will get stuck in an airport that has minimal food options. I keep a container of George's Shake (see page 57) with me whenever I travel. It has saved my blood sugar a number of times.

Eating in the Car

For the occasional meal in your car, you can use the suggestions in Chapter 6 on getting food in convenience stores and buying foods to carry with you. This advice also applies to holidays that involve a considerable amount of travel by car, but in this case there are lots of other things you can do.

- Start your day with a George's Shake plus some breakfast food such as eggs, bacon or sausage. You can pack the powder and a container in which to mix it, and order the milk and/or orange juice at the restaurant where you are stopping. Or carry the milk with you. If you are staying somewhere without a refrigerator, you can keep a pint of milk on ice overnight in an ice bucket in your room. It will melt, but the milk will still be okay in the morning.

- Don't rely solely on restaurants. Travel with a stash of emergency foods such as whole grain crackers, peanut butter, almonds, apples and cheese.

- Many supermarkets have good deli sections now, and often you can get half a chicken and some cooked vegetables for a decent price (and save tipping).

- Keep your eyes open for roadside fruit and vegetable stands. These aren't so common as they were, but if you see one, you might stop for a stretch and pick up a fresh treat or two. Make sure to eat protein with your fruit – nuts or cheese or plain yogurt – if it is a snack.

- Don't forget Mr Spud. You can get baked potatoes many places. Order a takeaway baked potato or wrap up part of the potato that came with your dinner in a napkin to eat later as your evening spud. You can sometimes get fries, potato salad and even mashed potatoes with skins on. Just look around and be flexible.

- Make sure you plan ahead and bring whatever kitchen stuff you need: sharp knife, plastic bags, paper towels, baby wipes (for cleanup), cutlery (or plastic), plastic cups, salt and pepper. Think about it and make up a little box of supplies.

- Remember when you are travelling that getting even a little dehydrated can lead to cravings. If you don't drink your water (or if you miss your evening potato or skimp on protein), I can almost guarantee you will go for the fizzy drinks or sweets when you pull in for a pit stop.

Also, stretching, fresh air, a change of position, a change of activities and beta-endorphin raisers (ranging from a quick walk to watching the clouds drift by as you sit in a field dotted with wildflowers) will all help your chemistry stay up and stable.

Other Special Situations

Many people ask me what to do if they have a 'special circumstance'.

You Take Antidepressants

If you are taking antidepressants, this programme is an ideal addition to your medication. Many people find that 'doing the food' enhances the effectiveness of their medication. Talk with your doctor. Give him or her this book. Plan to spend at least six months being steady with your food before you even consider going off your medication. If and when you are ready to do so, talk with your doctor to plan a slow and reflective taper that fits your lifestyle.

You're a Vegetarian

A very active group of vegetarians is doing this programme. It is absolutely possible to have a successful plan and retain your commitment to your vegetarian programme. Here are suggestions from some who are already on the plan.

Try some of the high-protein prepared foods you will find in the natural food stores. These include things like:

- Baked tofu, which comes in vacuum-sealed packets and quite a few different flavours (examples are Thai, smoked, teriyaki, barbecue)
- Tofu spreads or pâtés
- Seitan, which is wheat gluten and extremely high in protein

- Other imitation-meat items that you can find in the refrigerator or freezer sections, such as sausages, bacon and tofu hot dogs

Use tofu and tempe and beans as your protein source. Tofu is really flexible. You can mash it and make burgers. You can cube it and sauté it with garlic and soy sauce. You can scramble it with an egg for breakfast. You can food-process it and add it to pancake or muffin batters. Check your local bookshop for cookbooks geared to tofu.

Tempe is the more textured by-product of tofu making. It has chunks of soyabean in it and a firm texture. Tempe can be sliced into strips and sautéed with soy sauce and garlic, or you can marinate it in anything (for example, barbecue sauce) and bake it. These bars of flavoured baked tempe are firm enough to be used in sandwiches.

Get a good bean cookbook and learn to make different dishes. Bean spreads will probably be very useful to you – you can eat them on bread or crackers, or scooped up with pieces of green or red pepper (a favourite for me). The easiest bean spread/dip in the world is to take a can of drained black beans and put it in the food processor with a couple of tablespoons of your favourite salsa and maybe some extra chilli pepper flakes and garlic. If it isn't creamy enough, add a teaspoon or so of olive oil and blend again.

I think variety can be an issue, and if you do some of these plant-food alternatives, eggs and cheese will look less boring to you. The most important part will be to get creative and stay committed to maintaining the level of protein that will work for you.

You're Pregnant

If you are sugar sensitive and pregnant, this plan can truly enhance how both you and the baby feel during your pregnancy. There are a few simple precautions to remember. Do *not* do a

fast detox. You may be impulsive and want to clear out all that sugar quick so you can get on with the programme. But your baby should not do a quick detox under any circumstances! Do *not* go cold turkey. Ease into it. Substitute fruits for your typical sweet foods. Shift slowly.

You may also need to eat more frequently than the three meals a day I recommend. Plan to have a mid-morning and mid-afternoon snack with both protein and complex carbs. If you are getting nauseated, it often means that your blood sugar level has dropped. Your growing baby comes first and your body will give it your glucose first, leaving you going over the cliff. Do not let yourself get into an over-the-cliff state. Eat enough and eat frequently enough so that your blood sugar stays steady for both you and your baby.

You Have Diabetes

While this programme was not originally designed for people with diabetes, it seems to have a very positive effect. Most of the diabetics we are working with have Type 2 diabetes, which means not only are their glucose levels high but the insulin doesn't work properly for them. Because simple carbs are converted very quickly to glucose, they can cause your glucose levels to rise very high. The brown and green (and yellow and red) carbs you will eat on the programme will be far less likely to spike your sugar levels than the simple white carbs you may be most drawn to.

The combination of the protein at every meal and the slow carbs can make a huge difference for you. If you are working at controlling sugar levels with diet only, you need to be even more on top of what you eat than someone who is taking medication does. This programme will give you guidelines and support for creating a plan that fits your needs. Not only will you tailor your plan to your style, but you can also factor in your own individual diabetes concerns. This is not a one-size-fits-all plan. It is your plan for your body.

Many diabetics are reporting their blood sugar levels going down and stabilizing as they do the programme. If you are diabetic, however, it is better *not* to use a regular potato for your evening carb snack. Choose complex carbs that have a lower glycemic index, such as sweet potatoes, wholemeal bread or whole grain crackers. Visit my website for more information geared specifically to your needs.

Tips from the Field: From Someone Who's Been There

So you've been diagnosed with diabetes and you're a little bummed. I was too, but now I look at it as a blessing in disguise. My life did change, but for the better. I see richer, deeper colours now. Being a diabetic on this programme is no different than being anyone else on it, except I pay attention to my sugar levels as well. That's the beauty of the programme.

I eat three meals a day. Each meal contains protein and a complex carbohydrate. I eat a snack at night. I choose what is best for my blood levels.

I feel good now. I *feel* now. I'm not numbing myself with too much sugar and too much food. My blood sugar isn't so high that I'm constantly sleeping. It's in the normal range the majority of the time.

Just because you've been diagnosed with diabetes doesn't mean it's the end of your life. With this programme, it's just the beginning of life.

– S.

In Closing

As we tie things up, remember that the most special situation to consider always is your sugar-sensitive body. All this work will have enormous gains for you. As you 'do the food', you are

going to reconnect with your birthright. You will remember creativity, humour, clarity, intuition and power that you have long since disconnected from. For a while, you may struggle with the concept that 'doing the food' – something so simple and so not sexy – could be so powerful. But you will keep coming back to it. And the more you do, the stronger you will get and the more powerful your recovery will be.

Before we move on to the recipes, I want to share with you a very inspiring letter I received. It sums up what we are seeking:

After eight months of living/breathing/eating the programme, I am happy to report a very radiant recovery. Last week a friend I hadn't seen in a year ended her long rave about how great I looked with 'I wouldn't have recognized you if I'd seen you on the street'. While it's wonderful to know that I look so much better, what is truly remarkable is how I feel and how I function now.

- *Gone are the aches and pains. In their place, I feel a fluid motion and an increasing strength as I've come to actually look forward to exercising.*
- *Gone are the brain fogs and indecision. In their place is a renewed vitality, a sense that I can accomplish what needs to be done.*
- *Gone are the restless, sleepless nights. In their place is deep, comforting sleep – and only six hours instead of eight or nine.*

Freedom. Great word. I'm free from the addiction that took away my pleasure in life, that life, which caused me to obsess and hate myself. I'm free from an addiction that skewed my view of the world and my place in it.

So I look at sugar and I put it in my left hand. And I put life as I know it now in my right hand and I ask my higher self to choose. Freedom, radiance versus a chocolate éclair and a lifelong addiction to sugar?

I did the sugar when I saw no other alternative, no other way to comfort myself. I did the sugar because I didn't know what else to do. Now I have a choice. And I've made that choice. I am on the other side and I like it here! At long last, life is good.

May your own recovery from sugar sensitivity bring you this same freedom and joy!

11

Recipes from Fellow Travellers

These recipes have come from members of our Community Forum, people like you who are sugar sensitive and who are looking for simple solutions. The comments on the recipes have come from your neighbours and friends.

You don't have to be a 'Cooking' type to enjoy these recipes. Some are so simple that even the most cooking-phobic of you will be willing to give them a try. Many have been designed to provide the simple nutrition-filled meals loved by 'Functional/ Factual' and 'I Don't Want to Change' types. 'One-Pot' and 'Salad' types will also find treasures in here.

After you try them out, let us know what you think at www. radiantrecovery.com.

Breakfast

Oat Apple Pancakes

I love these pancakes. They make a great Sunday-morning breakfast – tasty, filling, and wholesome.

125 g porridge oats (not instant)
500 ml milk or buttermilk
3 eggs
2 tablespoons safflower oil
100 g wholemeal flour
1 teaspoon baking powder
1 teaspoon cinnamon
150 g chopped apple

Soak the oats in the milk or buttermilk for 5 minutes. In a separate bowl, beat together the eggs and oil. In another bowl mix the flour, baking powder and cinnamon. Add the dry ingredients to the egg mixture, then stir in the oat mixture and the apple. Lightly grease a griddle or frying pan and heat until a few drops of cold water sprinkled on the pan dance. Drop a ladleful of the pancake batter on to the griddle. Cook, then turn to cook on the other side. If you want a topping, try apple sauce or one of the toppings suggested for Cottage Cheese–Cinnamon Pancakes, below.

Cottage Cheese–Cinnamon Pancakes

A great topping for these pancakes is to cook some frozen blueberries or blackberries in a saucepan with a little water until they get syrupy. Or use one banana and some strawberries frothed and mixed together thoroughly with a simple hand mixer. Some people also like to put soured cream or plain yogurt on top.

75 g rolled oats

170 g low-fat cottage cheese

2 egg whites

2 teaspoons vanilla extract

½ teaspoon cinnamon

milk

fresh or frozen fruit

Chop the oats in a blender or food processor; add the cottage cheese and blend until the mixture is smooth. Beat the egg whites until fluffy. Add to the oat and cheese mixture. Add the vanilla and cinnamon. If the batter seems thick, thin it by adding a little milk. After blending, stir in pieces of fresh or frozen fruit. Cook on a nonstick frying pan or lightly greased griddle over a medium heat, dropping the batter on to the griddle using 2 tablespoons batter per pancake. Turn when the edges are lightly browned.

Yogurt Ricotta Delight

This is a quick, simple and creamy breakfast for one. It is a mainstay for many of us.

100 ml nonfat plain yogurt

85 g nonfat ricotta

75 g fruit (strawberries, raspberries, blueberries, bananas, fresh or frozen but unsweetened)

7–8 unsalted almonds (raw or roasted)

Mix together the yogurt and ricotta until creamy. Blend in the fruit and enjoy! Add almonds for extra protein. Try adding a little vanilla, cinnamon or nutmeg according to your preference.

Microwave Nut Butter Porridge

This one sticks with you all morning. This has been tested in our community and has been called 'a must for the sugar-sensitive breakfast hater'. It is equally yummy made with almond butter, cashew butter or tahini (sesame butter). If you like this breakfast for one, you can keep ready-sealed bags of premeasured oats and peanut butter in the fridge so you can just grab one in the morning.

20 g uncooked rolled oats

100 ml cup milk

1 tablespoon nut butter, sugar-free and preferably organic*

Combine the ingredients and microwave on high for 1 minute 20 seconds. This comes out fairly thick and a little sticky, so if that's not your style, add some banana slices, apple chunks or raspberries before microwaving to smooth out the consistency.

*I recommend using organic peanut butter because there is some concern about the degree of pesticide concentrations in ordinary peanut butter. You can find organic peanut butter at natural foods stores.

Easy Egg and Oat One-Pan Breakfast

Here is a breakfast recipe (for one) that is quick and tastes great! Some people like it with plain yogurt on top. This is another one of those we all play with to add, subtract and change to suit our taste.

2 eggs

175 ml milk or yogurt

85 g porridge oats

1 small apple, diced

Nutmeg and cinnamon to taste

Preheat the oven to 180° C, gas 4. Beat the eggs well. Stir in the milk. Add the oats, apple, nutmeg and cinnamon. Pour into a buttered (or sprayed) flan tin and bake for 30 to 40 minutes or until set.

Let stand for 5 to 10 minutes.

Oat Muffins

Thanks go to Allison for this recipe.

150g wholemeal flour
4 teaspoons baking powder
½ teaspoon salt
100 ml milk or soya milk
1 egg, well beaten
1 banana or 1 jar banana baby food
1 heaped tablespoon organic peanut butter
85 g cooked porridge

Preheat the oven to 200° C, gas 6. Grease a 12-muffin tin.

Combine the flour, baking powder and salt. In a separate bowl, stir the milk, egg, banana and peanut butter into the porridge. Now stir the dry ingredients into the porridge mixture. Spoon into muffin cups and bake for 20 minutes or until brown.

George's Shake

Here's the basic recipe for George's Shake and a couple of variations that people from the community have sent in.

500 ml milk, soya milk or oat milk
100 ml fruit juice
2 tablespoons protein powder (choose a sugar-free one)
2 tablespoons porridge oats (not instant)

Put all the ingredients in a blender and blend on high for about a minute. If you do it for less time, you will be crunching oats at the bottom of your shake. If you prefer not to use milk in your shake, use water and a little juice. What makes this shake work as a great breakfast choice is that it combines nutritious foods with plenty of protein.

These two variations use the premixed version of George's Shake (available to order via the website at www.radiantrecovery.com).

The frozen berries in this version make the shake really cold and thick.

20 g George's Shake mix
250 ml milk
½ banana
Some frozen unsweetened berries

Combine all the ingredients in a blender until smooth.

Here's a nondairy version. It has lots of protein, fibre, phytochemicals, essential fats and flavour. This texture will be much thicker. Add more soya milk to taste.

20 g George's Shake
250 ml soya milk
75 g frozen unsweetened blueberries or blackberries
100 ml water (or a little less if you like your shake thicker)
4 macadamia nuts

Combine all the ingredients in a blender until smooth.

Lunch

Crustless Quiche

A slice of this quiche makes a great lunch – or breakfast. Have it with a salad and a slice of whole grain toast. You can add meat to it if you need more protein.

115 g grated cheese (use your favourite)
115 g chopped onion
85 g broccoli

6 eggs

75 ml milk

Preheat the oven to 180° C, gas 4.

Spray a glass flan dish with a little olive oil spray. Add the cheese and veggies. Beat together the eggs and milk until frothy, then pour over the cheese and veggies. Bake for 35 to 40 minutes.

After the quiche has cooked and cooled, cut into 6 slices.

Potato-Crusted Quiche, With or Without Meat

The first version of this quiche calls for meat. A vegetarian version follows. This dish is delicious cold and reheats well in the micro-wave. The recipe comes from Shani.

CRUST

450–550g potatoes sliced into 6-mm thick rounds

FILLING

1 tablespoon olive oil

350 g chopped onion

350 g chopped green or red peppers (or a mixture of both)

1 teaspoon Jamaican blend spices (or any spice you like)

225–350g pork sausage or ham

115 g grated cheese (mozzarella, Cheddar or a blend of mozzarella and
    Parmesan)

EGG MIXTURE

8 to 10 eggs (depending on how much room your fillings take up and how
    big your baking dish is). If you make the meat-free version below, use
    more eggs.

½ teaspoon ground black pepper

Preheat the oven to 180° C, gas 4. Spray a 23 × 33-cm glass baking dish (a ceramic or metal dish will lengthen the cooking time, and may be more apt to stick) with vegetable oil.

Steam the potato rounds until just tender, 6 to 10 minutes. Transfer to a rack and allow to cool (or rinse with cold water if pressed for time). Line the prepared baking dish with enough potato rounds to cover, overlapping slightly.

Warm the olive oil in frying pan over a medium heat. Add the onion, peppers and spices and sauté for 5 minutes or so. Add the sausage and sauté until the meat is just cooked through. Remove from the heat and drain off any excess oil. Mix in the cheese. Spoon the mixture evenly over the potatoes.

Whisk together the eggs and pepper in a large bowl or blender. Pour the egg mixture over the filling. Top with a little more cheese, if desired. Bake the quiche until set in the centre, about 35 to 40 minutes. Allow to cool for 20 minutes, then slice. Serve warm or at room temperature.

Here's the vegetarian version. Feel free to try any combination of veggies you like. Use the same crust and egg mixture and follow the same procedure for assembly as above.

FILLING

1 tablespoon olive oil (or spray)

225 g chopped onion

225 g chopped courgettes

115 g chopped mushrooms

1 teaspoon thyme

115 g crumbled feta cheese (plain or the tomato-basil feta)

Tofu Scramble

This nicely spicy dish comes from Zoe. You can mix the spices up in bulk beforehand and keep them handy for a super-quick meal.

1–2 tablespoons vegetable oil

225 g tofu

50 ml water

Cooked vegetables, such as sliced onions, peppers, courgettes, broccoli
  and/or yellow squash (optional)

SPICE MIXTURE

1 teaspoon turmeric

1 teaspoon cumin

1 teaspoon curry powder

4 teaspoons onion powder

4 tablespoons nutritional yeast

4 teaspoons dried chives

4 teaspoons dried parsley

1 teaspoon sea salt

Heat the oil in a large frying pan. Mash and cook the tofu, stirring, for 2 to 3 minutes. Add the water and 2 to 4 tablespoons of
the spice mixture. Stir and cook for 2 to 3 minutes.

Add the cooked vegetables (optional) before serving.

Feta-Walnut Spread for Veggies or Sandwiches

*This is a great spread to take to a party. If you like strong cheeses,
it's to die for. This spread is good on crackers or pitta, or stuffed into
celery. Also very nice with sliced ripe tomatoes on the side, or ripe
cherry tomatoes. The recipe comes from Aliza Grayer Earnshaw.*

225 g feta cheese

85 g shelled walnuts

175–250 ml plain nonfat yogurt

1–2 cloves garlic (to taste), peeled and crushed

Freshly ground pepper (to taste)

2 pinches marjoram

Break up the feta into a food processor. Process until finely
crumbed, then put into a bowl. Now process the walnuts until
finely crumbed, and add to the cheese. Be careful with the

walnuts – if you process them for too long, they will become a paste. If you like added texture, reserve a few nuts and chop by hand, then add to the finer walnut and cheese crumbs. Mix all the crumbs together with a wooden spoon until well blended.

In a separate bowl, combine 175 ml of the yogurt, the crushed garlic, the coarsely ground black pepper and the marjoram. Now add the feta-walnut mix. Add more yogurt if you want the mix to be more like a dip than a spread. Once you have the consistency you desire, add just a little more yogurt – about a heaped tablespoon. The mixture will thicken in the refrigerator, as the chopped walnuts absorb liquid from the yogurt.

Feta Frittata

This is a great way to get a good serving of veggies and protein together. It is surprisingly quick, and tastes great cold tucked inside a buttered pitta, for lunch. It also reheats nicely. This recipe comes from Aliza Grayer Earnshaw.

Note: You can substitute spinach for the greens, but you will then need more than 350 g, as it shrinks more. It also requires less cooking time than Swiss chard or kale.

115–150 g tofu

A few shakes of soy sauce (I prefer shoyu – it's milder)

4 eggs

2–4 tablespoons water

About 350 g greens such as kale, Swiss chard or mustard greens,
	or a combination

Olive oil

1 large clove of garlic (or several small cloves)

Chilli pepper flakes or black pepper to taste

55–85 g crumbled feta

Preheat the oven to 200° C, gas 6.

Drain the tofu and mash it with a fork in a bowl or on a plate. Shake some soy sauce on it, so the tofu is dark in places, but don't saturate it. If you use shoyu, you can use more of it; if using conventional soy sauce, use less – it's very salty.

In a separate bowl, beat the eggs with the water. Chop the greens. Heat a 25-cm cast-iron frying pan and pour in enough olive oil to coat the bottom and sides of the pan. Swirl it around once the pan is hot.

Chop (or crush) the garlic and add it to the oil. Then add the chopped greens, cover the pan, and reduce the heat to medium-low. After a few minutes, uncover the pan and stir the greens down, adding a dash or two of chilli or black pepper to taste.

Now add the tofu and stir everything together. Lower the heat, and spread the mixture evenly over the bottom of the pan. Arrange the crumbled feta evenly over the top. Slowly pour in the beaten eggs, being careful not to disturb the crumbled feta.

Turn off the heat and put the frying pan into the preheated oven. Bake until set, about 10 to 18 minutes. It's okay for the frittata to brown on top.

Turkey Burgers

Turkey patties are pale and, to some people, unappealing in taste and appearance. Fixing them using this recipe from Terri solves that problem, and they taste really good. Even people who don't like mustard have liked these. Try eating the burgers in a wholemeal pitta with onions, topped by a cucumber/yogurt mixture.

50–75 ml low-sodium tamari sauce
2–3 tablespoons grain mustard

550 g minced turkey, formed into 5 patties (or 5 frozen minced turkey patties, thawed overnight in the refrigerator)

In a 25–30-cm frying pan over medium-low heat, mix together the tamari sauce and mustard. Place the turkey patties into the sauce. Turn the patties to coat both sides, then cook without a lid over medium heat until done.

Variations: You can press finely chopped onions into the patties before putting them in the pan and/or melt grated cheese on top just before they're done.

Asian Salad

This recipe, from Zoe, is a great way to get your veggies. Feel free to experiment with the ingredients!

SALAD

½ head pak choy, thinly sliced

4 spring onions, sliced

115 g bean sprouts

3 carrots, grated

115 g broccoli florets

DRESSING

50 ml rice vinegar

50 ml soy sauce

50 ml orange juice

2 teaspoons sesame oil

Pinch cayenne

Salt if desired

Combine all the vegetables in a bowl. Mix together the dressing ingredients, pour over the vegetables, and toss.

T 'n' T Salad

This easy salad from Terri is attractive – and very satisfying on a warm day. Serves two.

1 can water-packed lightmeat tuna steak
Approx. 170 g cottage cheese
½ to 1 tablespoon mayonnaise
Dill to taste (optional)
1 whole tomato per person
Salt and pepper

Drain the liquid from the tuna. Place in a bowl and flake apart with a fork. Mix in enough cottage cheese to at least double your volume (do this to your taste preference). Add the mayo and a sprinkling of dill to taste. Mix thoroughly. Set aside.

Wash a whole tomato and then slice off the stem end. Set aside. Scoop out the tomato's seeds and pulp, leaving the shell intact. Mix the seeds and pulp into the tuna and cottage cheese; season with salt and pepper to taste.

Fill the tomato shells with the mixture, mounding it up above the top of the shell, then place the stem-end slice of the tomato back on top like a jaunty cap. Serve with whole grain crackers.

Simple Tofu Salad

This recipe allows you to experiment on your own with ingredients and amounts.

Tofu
Mayonnaise
Mustard
Chopped gherkins
Salt and pepper to taste

Mash up the tofu with mayo and mustard, add gherkins, salt and pepper. That's it! You can also add chopped celery or what else appeals to you. Be creative!

Chilli Layered Casserole

This recipe from Laurie W. is way easy and it makes a lot. It also tastes great the next day.

1 packet of fresh corn tortillas (*not* tortilla chips)
3 to 4 cans of turkey or chicken chilli without sugar
450 g grated cheese (your choice of cheese, such as Cheddar)

Preheat the oven to 180° C, gas 4.

Tear up the tortillas into small bite-sized triangles. Put a layer of these tortilla triangles across the bottom of a 23 × 35-cm baking tin. Spoon a layer of chicken or turkey chilli over the tortillas. On top of the chilli, sprinkle grated cheese, as much or as little as you like.

Repeat the layers of tortilla, chilli and cheese once more – or even twice if your tin has room. Bake for 30 minutes or until the cheese gets bubbly. Allow to cool for 15 minutes before cutting and serving.

Beef Chilli

Here's a rich and satisfying chilli from Jeanie that her family raves about. She tops it with chopped onions and grated cheese and serves with homemade cornbread.

450 g minced beef
1 onion, chopped
1 to 3 cloves garlic (according to your taste), finely chopped
Red, yellow and/or green peppers (or green chillies), chopped (optional)

1 400-g can chopped tomatoes

1 400-g can tomato sauce

3 or more tablespoons of chilli powder, to taste

2 teaspoons cumin

2 or 3 900 g cans of pinto beans – or whatever kind of beans you like

Brown the minced beef in a frying pan, then add the onion, garlic and peppers. Sauté until the vegetables are soft. Add the tomatoes, tomato sauce, chilli powder and cumin, and simmer for 30 minutes to 1 hour. Add the pinto beans and simmer for 20 minutes or so to allow the flavours to mix.

Dinner

Roast Sticky Chicken

This recipe from Marie is a great way to roast a large chicken. It is reminiscent of those rotisserie-style chickens that are so popular now, and it is surprisingly easy to make. The meat comes out very moist and flavoursome, so leftovers taste as good freshly cooked. Once you try it, you will never roast chicken any other way. Note: You need to season the chicken overnight, and the cooking time is 5 hours.

1 large roasting chicken, as big as you can find

4 teaspoons salt

2 teaspoons paprika

1 teaspoon cayenne pepper

1 teaspoon onion powder

1 teaspoon thyme

1 teaspoon white pepper

½ teaspoon garlic powder

½ teaspoon black pepper

225 g chopped onion

In a small bowl, thoroughly combine all the spices. Remove the

giblets from the chicken, rinse out the cavity well, and pat dry with paper towels. Rub the entire spice mixture into the chicken, both inside and out, making sure it is evenly distributed and down deep into the skin. Put the chicken in a plastic bag, seal and refrigerate overnight.

When ready to roast the chicken, preheat the oven to 120° C, gas ½. Stuff the cavity with the chopped onion and set in a shallow roasting tin. Roast uncovered for 5 hours (yes, 120° C, gas ½ for 5 hours).

After the first hour, baste the chicken occasionally (every half hour or so) with the pan juices. The pan juices will start to caramelize on the bottom of the tin and the chicken will turn golden brown.

Allow the chicken to rest for about 10 minutes before carving.

Chicken Roasted with Garlic

Here's another great spice combo from Marie for roast chicken. Note: You can put a whole peeled onion and 3 to 5 peeled cloves of garlic in the cavity instead of using onion and garlic powder in the spice mix.

1 large roasting chicken
Olive oil
1 teaspoon garlic powder
1 teaspoon onion powder
1 teaspoon salt
½ teaspoon ground pepper
1 teaspoon paprika
1 teaspoon either fresh or dry basil
Dash of cayenne or chilli powder

Remove the giblets from the chicken, rinse out the cavity well, and pat dry with paper towels. Rub the chicken with some olive oil to prevent dryness.

Mix together the spices in a bowl and rub this mixture on the chicken. At this point, you can either let the chicken marinate in the spices for a few hours or go ahead and roast it.

Roast the chicken at 150° C, gas 2 for one hour, then lower the temperature to 100° C, gas ¼ and cook for another hour.

You can make some dressing with garlic and stuff the bird.

Kathleen's Roast Chicken with Vegetables

This is how I like to do my chicken. It makes the veggies especially delicious.

1 roasting chicken (1.8 – 2.4 kg)
6 garlic cloves, peeled
8 carrots, peeled and quartered
4 potatoes, peeled and cut in quarters

Preheat the oven to 220° C, gas 7.

Rinse the chicken and pull the skin away from breast. Insert the garlic between the skin and breast. Re-cover with skin.

Fill a roasting tin half full with water.

Place the chicken upright on a chicken roasting stand (you can get these at specialty cook shops or mail order from Lakeland). Put the carrots and potatoes in the tin.

Roast for 45 minutes. Reduce the heat to 150° C, gas 2 and continue to roast for a further 20 to 30 minutes, depending on the size of the bird. Add more water to the tin as needed.

When done, remove the chicken and veggies. Make gravy from the juice in the pan. (If you don't know how to do this, look in any basic cookbook.)

Beef Stew

This is a great basic beef stew recipe, which comes from Barbara. You can dress it up if you want by adding lots more garlic and pa-

*prika, plus frozen sweetcorn and frozen peas. Note: If you cook this
in a Crock-Pot, all you need to do is coat the beef with the flour, put
it in the Crock-Pot, then add all the other ingredients on top. Cook
for 4 to 5 hours on high or 8 to 10 hours on low.*

If you don't have a Crock-Pot, see the instructions below.

900 g beef, cubed or cut in chunks
1 to 2 tablespoons wholemeal flour
2 tablespoons olive oil
3 potatoes with skins, cubed
4 carrots, cut in quarters
2 onions, sliced
3 sticks celery, cut in chunks
1 teaspoon salt
1 teaspoon pepper
2 or more cloves garlic
1 teaspoon paprika
1 400-g can chopped tomatoes (optional)
Liquid as needed (V8 juice, more chopped tomatoes or tomato sauce)

Coat the meat in the flour and brown it in the olive oil. Then
add all the other ingredients, plus enough liquid to cover.
Cook, covered, on a low heat for 1 to 2 hours. Optional: To
spice this up, add lots of garlic and some more paprika.

Kathleen's Meatloaf

*This was my first meatloaf recipe thirty years ago, and I am still
quite fond of it.*

MEATLOAF
225 g minced beef
225 g minced pork
85 g porridge oats (not instant)
2 eggs

2 tablespoons toasted onion flakes

100 ml bolognaise sauce (I use one that has no sugar)

TOPPING

100 ml bolognaise sauce

100 ml water

Preheat the oven to 180° C, gas 4.

Grease a 450-g loaf tin with olive oil. Combine the meatloaf ingredients and pack into the tin. Pour over the topping.

Bake for 45 minutes to an hour, depending on how you like your meatloaf. (I like mine crispy, so I let it cook longer, until it gets a little dark around the edges.)

Jeanie's Meatloaf

Here is a very moist and juicy meatloaf recipe from Jeanie. She recommends serving it with a big pile of mashed potatoes with the skins on and lots of fresh veggies.

225 g of the leanest minced beef you can get

20 g wholemeal breadcrumbs

2 eggs

100 ml tomato sauce

½ green pepper, chopped

115 g mushrooms, chopped

1 or 2 medium carrots, chopped

1 medium onion, chopped

¼ to ½ teaspoon thyme

¼ to ½ teaspoon marjoram

½ teaspoon basil

Salt and pepper to taste

Preheat the oven to 190° C, gas 5.

Mix all the ingredients together and pack into a loaf tin (13cm × 24cm). Bake for about an hour.

Chicken Meatloaf

If you've never tried minced chicken, here's your chance. (It's de-lightful in burgers, too.) This recipe is from Allison.

Taco seasoning to taste (use one of the brands that has no sweeteners)

75 ml mayonnaise (use sugar-free mayo if you are concerned that regular
    mayo will trigger you)

550 g chicken

1 400 g can black beans, drained

1 onion, grated

100 ml salsa, or to taste

Preheat the oven to 180° C, gas 4.

Mix the taco seasoning into the mayonnaise. Combine all the ingredients in a bowl. Pack into a loaf tin (13cm × 24cm) and bake for 1 hour.

Soya Meatloaf

This vegetarian recipe is courtesy of Betty and her husband. It is also good cold or warmed the next day in sandwiches.

1 packet soya meat crumbles, thawed (found in freezer section)

2–3 eggs

85 g of whole grain crackers or rolled oats

Onions, chopped (we like lots of onions, but adjust amount to your taste)

Salt and pepper to taste

Preheat the oven to 180° C, gas 4.

Dump everything into a bowl and mix (using your hands works best). If the mixture feels a little dry, add a tablespoon of water or olive oil. Form into a loaf or just press into a loaf tin (13cm × 24cm) and cover with foil. Bake for 30 to 45 minutes, or until the centre is hot. (Remember, this isn't meat you are trying to cook; soya crumbles come cooked.)

Italian Frittata

This is delicious, and you can add extra protein (and moistness) to it by adding cottage cheese to the egg mixture. The recipe comes from Zoe.

2 tablespoons olive oil
115 g fresh mushrooms, sliced
140 g courgettes, sliced
½ red pepper, sliced
½ green pepper, sliced
1 spring onion, chopped
1 garlic clove, finely chopped or crushed
6 eggs
3 tablespoons freshly grated Parmesan cheese
Freshly ground pepper to taste
Dash dried basil
Dash dried oregano
3 tablespoons water

Heat the olive oil in a large frying pan. Add the mushrooms, courgettes, peppers, spring onion and garlic. Cook, stirring occasionally, until the vegetables are tender, about 5 minutes.

While the vegetables are cooking, combine the eggs in a bowl with 1 tablespoon of the Parmesan. Add the remaining seasonings and water. Pour the mixture over the cooked vegetables. Loosely cover and cook over a medium heat until the eggs are set, 6 to 8 minutes. Sprinkle with the remaining Parmesan and a dash of paprika.

Salmon Patties

This recipe is from Robin, who recommends freezing some for quick meals. She says they are great with a baked potato and fresh or frozen green beans.

1 small (200-g) can skinless, boneless salmon

1 egg

55 g red onion, finely copped

1 teaspoon finely copped parsley

1 teaspoon finely chopped rosemary

1 piece wholemeal or spelt bread, crumbled

Mix all the ingredients together. Form into three good-size patties. (They won't hold together too well at first, but they will get firmer as they cook.) Fry them in a lightly oiled pan.

Baked Chicken and Lentils

Allison, who created this recipe, says there is a wonderful broth at the bottom of the casserole when it is done. You can either eat the broth with the dish or use it for something else.

4 medium carrots, thinly sliced

225 g onion, chopped

1 400-g can chicken broth

2 bay leaves

1 teaspoon salt

½ teaspoon poultry seasoning

⅛ teaspoon pepper

170 g dry lentils

1.15–1.35 kg chicken pieces (breasts, thighs, drumsticks and/or wings)

Preheat the oven to 180° C, gas 4.

Mix everything but the chicken together in a 3-litre casserole with a lid and bake, covered, for 15 minutes.

Brown the chicken in a lightly oiled frying pan. Place on top of the lentil mixture and bake for 1 hour, or until both the lentils and chicken are done.

Sweetcorn and Bean Hash

This satisfying dish from Allison has some neat texture contrasts.
The celery and sweetcorn are crispy, the beans are soft and creamy,
and the TVP soya granules are sort of chewy.

250 ml beef (or vegetable) stock

225 g TVP (textured vegetable protein) soya granules (available in health
   food stores)

1 onion, chopped

2 sticks celery, sliced

1 clove garlic, finely chopped

1 tablespoon olive oil

1 400-g can black beans, drained

1 400-g can pinto beans, drained

1 400-g can sweetcorn or 1 packet frozen sweetcorn

Salsa to taste

Chilli powder to taste

Any other seasonings you fancy

Bring the stock to the boil and mix in the soya granules. Cover
and set aside.

Sauté the onion, celery and garlic in oil until the onion starts
to brown. Add the beans and sweetcorn and stir. Then add seasonings to taste. You'll need to experiment, but that's part of
the fun!

Now stir in the soya granules and stock. Heat, stirring constantly, until heated through and the flavours have mixed
together.

Bread, Soup and Side Dishes

Spelt and Flaxseed Bread

Cheryl says this bread is a wonderful beta-endorphin raiser! Spelt flour is good for people with wheat allergies or intolerance. It is a very old grain in the same family (Triticum) as wheat. It is also lovely to work with, and its flavour is exquisite. For more information on spelt, do a search on the Web.

1 tablespoon dried yeast

400 ml warm water

2 tablespoons vegetable oil

450 g spelt flour plus 25–55 g, reserved

2 teaspoons dry milk powder

2 teaspoons salt (optional)

55 g whole flaxseeds

Dissolve the yeast in the warm water. Add the honey and oil and mix well. Allow to sit until foamy. Mix together half the spelt flour, the milk powder and salt. Now add the yeast liquid to the dry ingredients. Stir well (some people like to use their hands). Add the flaxseeds. Mix well. Add remaining spelt flour and knead until the mixture forms a ball.

Use some of the reserved flour to dust a bread or cutting board and lightly knead the dough until smooth and elastic. Shape and place in an oiled loaf tin. Allow to rise until doubled in size.

Bake at 180° C, gas 4 for 45 to 50 minutes, or until done.

Allow to cool in the tin on a rack for 10 minutes. Remove the loaf from the tin and allow to cool completely.

Great Potato Soup

Here is a great soup recipe from Cheryl. She sometimes uses it as her nighttime 'spud'.

2 tablespoons olive oil

55 g onion, chopped

2 cloves garlic, finely chopped

½ teaspoon whole cumin seeds

1 tablespoon wholemeal flour

300 ml milk

1 large baking potato, cubed and boiled (do not peel)

250 ml cup water

1 tablespoon mustard

Salt and pepper to taste

Heat 1 tablespoon of the olive oil in nonstick frying pan.

Add the onion and cook until soft.

Add the garlic and cumin seeds, cook until slightly browned (not too long, as they will become bitter). Remove to a saucepan.

Add the second tablespoon of olive oil to the frying pan and heat. Add the tablespoon of flour to make a roux.

After browning, add 50 ml milk to make a white sauce, and cook over a medium heat for 10 minutes until thick and bubbly. Add to the onion mixture in the saucepan, along with the potato, the rest of the milk and the water.

Bring to a gentle boil and add the mustard. Stir to blend. Add salt and pepper and cook for 15 minutes.

Roast Potatoes

These potatoes are one of my favourites.

1 kg white or russet potatoes
1 teaspoon garlic powder
2 tablespoons toasted onion powder
1 teaspoon basil, freshly chopped
A little salt and pepper
1 tablespoon olive oil

Preheat the oven to 180° C, gas 4.

Slice the potatoes lengthways into strips. Mix all the remaining ingredients in a plastic bag. Shake the mixture and add the potatoes to coat.

Place on a baking sheet that has been covered with foil. Bake skin sides down for approximately 30 minutes.

Roasted Lemon Potatoes

Here is another potato option from Marie. These are great!

5 medium potatoes
Juice from 1 large lemon
1½ tablespoons dried oregano
4t ablespoons olive oil
100 ml water
Black pepper to taste

Preheat the oven to 180° C, gas 4.

Cut the potatoes into small to medium chunks. Put in a 33 × 23-cm baking tin sprayed with cooking oil.

Mix all the other ingredients together and pour over the potatoes. Mix together well.

Bake until done, approximately 1–1½ hours, stirring every 15 minutes.

Spicy Oven-Fried Potatoes

Marie keeps us from getting bored with our potatoes.

6–8 medium potatoes, cubed
3 tablespoons olive oil
½ teaspoon salt
3 tablespoons Parmesan freshly grated
2 teaspoons garlic powder
1 teaspoon paprika
¼ teaspoon cayenne pepper
Black pepper to taste

Put the potatoes into a large bowl. Pour the olive oil over the potatoes and stir to coat.

Mix all the other ingredients together and pour over the potatoes. Stir well.

Place the potatoes in a 33 × 23-cm baking tin sprayed with cooking oil. Roast in the oven for 1–1½ hours or until tender and brown, stirring occasionally.

Stir-Fried Lemon Asparagus

This is a great dish for when company comes. It was sent in by Tammy.

900 g asparagus
2 tablespoons sesame oil
2 cloves garlic, finely chopped
1 200-g can water chestnuts, drained
1 chicken or vegetarian bouillon cube (preferably without MSG)
3 tablespoons fresh lemon juice
2 teaspoons grated lemon rind
3 teaspoons soy sauce
Salt and freshly ground black pepper to taste

Wash and dry the asparagus and break off the tough part of the stems. Cut diagonally into 5-cm pieces.

Heat the oil in a nonstick frying pan or wok over a medium-high heat. Stir-fry the garlic for 1 minute. Add asparagus and water chestnuts. Stir-fry for about 3 minutes. Add the crumbled bouillon cube, lemon juice, lemon rind and soy sauce.

Cook for a further minute or so until the asparagus is tender but still crisp and all the ingredients are heated through.

Season with salt and pepper to taste. Serve immediately.

Larry's Famous Green Beans

This recipe comes from Aliza Grayer Earnshaw.

900 g fresh green beans

7 Italian plum tomatoes

2–4 tablespoons extra-virgin olive oil

1 large or several small cloves garlic

Salt and black and red pepper

1 teaspoon dried marjoram

½ teaspoon dried basil

1 onion, thinly sliced into rounds (optional)

Juice of 2 small lemons

Wash, top and tail beans, and break into halves or thirds. Trim the stem point from the tomatoes, then either chop the tomatoes in a food processor or chop finely by hand.

Heat the olive oil in deep frying pan or casserole. Crush or finely chop the garlic and sauté in the oil until just brown. Add the salt, pepper and chopped tomatoes. Allow to simmer for a few minutes, then add the herbs and green beans. Add the onions, if using. Stir everything together, cover, and simmer, stirring a few times so the beans don't stick to the bottom, until the beans are nicely soft, but not falling apart. They should still have shape and texture. When the beans are tender, add the

lemon juice, stir, and check for seasoning. You can add more salt, pepper or lemon juice to taste.

Serve warm or cold.

Note: Instead of marjoram and basil, you can use fresh basil only (lots) or tarragon and basil.

Kathleen's Apple Carrots

This is one of my favourites.

8 carrots
Olive oil for sautéing
100 ml cup apple juice
100 ml cup water

Peel and slice the carrots. Sauté in olive oil until browned. Add the apple juice and water. Bring to a simmer and cook until soft.

Scalloped Cabbage

This is one of Cheryl's delicious recipes. Even if you are not a big fan of cabbage, I recommend trying it at least once.

1 head of cabbage, sliced into thin strips
1 300-g can cream of mushroom soup
85 g whole grain cracker crumbs*
25 g butter
3 tablespoons milk

Preheat the oven to 180° C, gas 4.

Boil the cabbage until tender. Drain and put in a 1.5-litre casserole. Stir in the remaining ingredients. Cover and bake for 35 to 45 minutes.

*Make cracker crumbs by breaking up crackers into small chunks and placing between two sheets of greaseproof paper. Roll with a rolling pin to crunch the bits down to crumb size.

Fried Aubergine with Yogurt-Garlic Dressing

This recipe comes from Susan S., who writes: 'One of the joys of having a Turkish husband is learning 101 ways to cook aubergine – it is practically the national vegetable of Turkey. Aubergines are wonderful in texture and can make a very convincing substitute for meat. This is my favourite aubergine recipe – and my simplest.'

1 medium aubergine
Olive oil for sautéing, as little as possible

DRESSING
250 ml plain yogurt
finely chopped or crushed garlic to taste
Salt to taste

Preheat the oven to 180° C, gas 4. Slice the aubergine into 2.5-cm-thick slices, either widthways or lengthways, whichever you prefer. Roast in the oven until slightly golden in colour and slightly tender. Then fry in olive oil.

Whip the yogurt until smooth and add the garlic and salt. Top the aubergines with the dressing.

Oven-Fried Sweet Potatoes

This is a recipe for one, suggested by Cheryl. Try this as your before-bed potato. If you want to make these as part of a meal, allow one potato per person.

1 sweet potato
Vegetable oil
Salt and pepper to taste
Onion powder to taste
Garlic powder to taste

Wash and peel the potato, then cut it into french fry–size pieces. Put a little oil on a baking sheet or in the tray of your

combination microwave oven, and dump the fries on it. Turn them to coat all the sides with oil. Then sprinkle with salt, pepper, onion powder and a little garlic powder. (Or substitute nutmeg for the onion and garlic powders.)

If you are using a conventional oven, bake at 230° C, gas 8 for 15 minutes, turning once so the bottoms don't burn.

If you are using a toaster oven, bake at 220° C for 20 minutes, turn them (the bottoms get nicely brown), then turn off the oven and let them sit for another 10 minutes.

Sweet Potato Puff

This recipe from Jeannie D. has received rave reviews everywhere, but remember, because of the eggs, you can't use this dish for your nightly spud. Also, you will need to experiment with the amount of nutmeg, as it tends to be quite overpowering if you use too much.

3 or 4 medium sweet potatoes
1 teaspoon baking powder
Dash of cinnamon or more, to taste
Dash of nutmeg or more, to taste
3 eggs
15 g butter

Puncture the sweet potatoes with a fork, then bake in an oven preheated to 180° C, gas 4 for an hour, or until fork-tender. Take them out and immediately peel them. (You will find that when they are still hot, the skin virtually falls off.) Chop roughly and put in a food processor with the baking powder, cinnamon, nutmeg, eggs and butter. Process right away (so the heat from the potatoes doesn't get a chance to cook the eggs) until the mixture is as smooth as baby food.

Place the mixture in an ovenproof dish sprayed with cooking oil and return to the oven for about 30 minutes. The puff will be

soufflé-like. Watch it to make sure the edges do not get overly brown. When you spoon into it, it will collapse (like it's supposed to!).

Sweet Potato Pie

Cheryl makes a sweet potato pie by adding the sweet potato puff recipe to a wholemeal piecrust.

Fried Brown Rice with Onions, Almonds and Cumin

This recipe from Cheryl makes enough for one serving. Multiply it if you are cooking for others. It's best eaten immediately, as the lovely crunchy browned almonds go soft after a short while.

15 g butter
¼ onion, chopped
Small amount slivered almonds
115 g *cooked* brown basmati rice
½–1 teaspoon ground cumin (to taste)

Melt the butter in a nonstick frying pan. Add the onion and nuts and cook until the onion is translucent and the nuts are browned. Add the precooked (or leftover) rice and cumin, and cook until warmed through.

Salad Dressings

Basic Vinaigrette

Here's one to experiment with. It is good for marinating cooked veggies, and I put it on my potato.

4 tablespoons cold-pressed extra-virgin olive oil

2 tablespoons balsamic vinegar

1 teaspoon toasted garlic flakes

1 teaspoon grated fresh ginger

1 teaspoon dried orange peel

Combine all the ingredients and shake. It tastes even better the next day.

Simple Salad Dressing

My favourite salad dressing.

4 tablespoons fresh lemon juice (1 large or 1½ small lemons)

175 ml olive oil (or sometimes I mix vegtable and olive)

1–2 tablespoons tamari soy sauce

2 large cloves garlic, crushed

Freshly ground black pepper to taste

Shake all the ingredients in a bottle.

Treats and Desserts

Squash Pie with Peanut Butter Glaze

Allison sent in this wonderful dessert recipe.

1 acorn squash

115 g tofu

115 g organic peanut butter

Juice from ½ orange

Cinnamon

Nutmeg

Ground ginger

Wholemeal pie shell, purchased or homemade

TOPPING

15 g butter
15 g peanut butter
Grated rind from the same ½ orange

Cut the squash in half, remove the seeds, and bake on a greased baking sheet in an oven preheated to 180° C, gas 4, skin up, until it's soft. Scoop the flesh out of skins into a bowl. Add the tofu, peanut butter and orange juice. Mix with an electric beater until well blended. Add cinnamon, nutmeg and ground ginger to taste. Fill the pie shell with the mixture and bake at 180° C, gas 4 for 30 minutes.

When pie is nearly cool, heat the topping ingredients in small saucepan, stirring constantly to prevent burning. Pour over the pie. Refrigerate and serve cold.

Carrot Cake

This recipe comes from Allison.

225 g carrots, grated
2 eggs
100 ml oil
1 jar banana baby food
115 g whole grain flour (wheat, oat, rice, etc.)
1 teaspoon bicarbonate of soda
1 teaspoon cinnamon
½ teaspoon salt

ICING

225g cream cheese
¼ teaspoon lemon extract
1½ teaspoons vanilla extract

Preheat the oven to 180° C, gas 4.

Combine the carrots, eggs, oil and baby food in a large bowl. In a smaller bowl, mix together the flour, bicarbonate of soda, cinnamon and salt. Then stir these dry ingredients into the carrot-egg mixture. Pour into a greased 20-cm square tin. Bake for 30 minutes, or until a skewer or cocktail stick comes out clean.

While the cake is cooling, combine the ingredients for the icing and adjust the seasonings to taste. Ice when the cake has cooled.

Pumpkin Tofu Cheesecake

Another creation from our dessert queen, Allison.

CRUST

125 g whole grain cracker crumbs

85 g butter, melted

FILLING

350 g silken tofu

115 g canned pumpkin

1 jar banana baby food

1 teaspoon cinnamon

½ teaspoon ground cloves

115 g cream cheese

1 teaspoon vanilla extract

Make crust first. Combine cracker crumbs and butter and press into pie plate. Pre-bake crust at 350° F. for 10 minutes, or until lightly browned. Set aside.

In a blender, combine filling ingredients, blend well, then pour into crust. Bake for 1 hour at 325° F., or until knife comes out fairly clean and middle is not liquid. Cool overnight before serving.

Pumpkin Cake with
Cashew Butter Frosting

Here's an interesting dessert variation that Allison came up with.

200 g whole grain flour (try a mix of oat and brown rice flour)

3 teaspoons baking powder

¾ teaspoon salt

1 tablespoon cinnamon

1 tablespoon nutmeg

1 teaspoon allspice

1 teaspoon ginger

2 eggs, beaten

100 ml oil

115 g canned pumpkin

75 ml water

1 jar banana baby food

FROSTING

Cashew butter

Preheat the oven to 180° C, gas 4.

Stir together the flour, baking powder, salt and spices. In a separate bowl, mix together the eggs and oil. In another large bowl, combine the pumpkin, water and baby food. Add the egg mixture to the pumpkin mixture. Then add the dry ingredients and stir until well mixed. Pour into a greased 20-cm-square tin and bake for 30 minutes, or until a skewer or a cocktail stick comes out clean.

Cool, then spread with cashew butter and enjoy.

Ricotta Fruit 'Pudding'

This is a lovely dessert for one. Feel free to substitute other dried or fresh fruit for the dried apricots. Allison sent in this one.

3 dried apricots

3 almonds

45 g ricotta cheese

Couple of drops of vanilla, almond, or orange extract (optional)

⅛ teaspoon (or less) cinnamon or a dash of grated lemon rind (both are
    optional)

Chop the apricots and almonds into small pieces and mix into the ricotta cheese along with (optional) the vanilla extract (or whatever other flavour you may have chosen). Microwave on high for one minute. Top with cinnamon or lemon rind.

Bibliography

Abrahamson, E.M., and A.W. Pezet. *Body, Mind and Sugar.* New York: Holt, 1951.

Anderson, I.M., et al. 'Dieting reduces plasma tryptophan and alters brain 5-HT function in women.' *Psychol Med* 20(4): 785–791, 1990.

Arem, R. *The Thyroid Solution.* New York: Ballantine, 1999.

Barnard, R.J., et al. 'Effects of a high-fat, sucrose diet on serum insulin and related atherosclerotic risk factors in rats.' *Atherosclerosis* 100(2): 229–236, 1993.

Beattie, M. *Codependent No More.* Center City, MN: Hazelton, 1992.

Bertoli, A., et al. 'Differences in insulin receptors between men and menstruating women and influence of sex hormones on insulin binding during the menstrual cycle.' *J Clin Endocrinol Metab* 50(2) 246–250, 1980.

Besson, A., et al. 'Effects of morphine, naloxone and their interaction in the learned-helplessness paradigm in rats.' *Psychopharmacology* (Berlin) 123(1): 71–78, 1996.

Black, B.L., et al. 'Differential effects of fat and sucrose on body composition in A/J and C57BL/6 mice.' *Metabolism* 47(11): 1354–1359, 1998.

Blass, E.M. 'Interactions between contact and chemosensory mechanisms in pain modulation in 10-day-old rats.' *Behav Neurosci* 111(1): 147–54, 1997.

Blass, E., E. Fitzgerald, and P. Kehoe. 'Interactions between sucrose, pain and isolation distress.' *Pharmacol Biochem Behav* 26: 483–489, 1987.

Blass, E.M., and A. Shah. 'Pain-reducing properties of sucrose in human newborns.' *Chem Senses* 20(1): 29–35, 1995.

Blass, E.M., and D.J. Shide. 'Opioid mediation of odour preferences induced by sugar and fat in 6-day-old rats.' *Physiol Behav* 50: 961–966, 1991.

Bowen, D.J., and N.E. Grunberg. 'Variations in food preference and consumption across the menstrual cycle.' *Physiol Behav* 47: 287–291, 1990.

Brewerton, T.D., et al. 'Comparison of eating disorder patients with and without compulsive exercising.' *Int J Eat Disord* 17(4): 413–416, 1995.

Brown, G. 'CSF serotonin metabolite (5-HIAA) studies in depression, impulsivity, and violence.' *J Clin Psychiatry* 51(4; suppl.): 31–41, 1990.

Brown, R. *An Introduction to Neuroendocrinology.* Cambridge: Cambridge University Press, 1994.

Brunani, A., et al. 'Influence of insulin on beta-endorphin plasma levels in obese and normal weight subjects.' *Int J Obes Relat Metab Disord* 20(8): 710–714, 1996.

Bujatti, M., and P. Riederer. 'Serotonin, noradrenaline, dopamine metabolites in trancendental meditation-technique.' *J Neural Transm* 39: 257–267, 1976.

Christie, M.J., and G.B. Chesher. 'Physical dependence on physiologically released endogenous opiates.' *Life Sci* 30(14): 1173–1177, 1982.

Cleary, J., et al. 'Naloxone effects on sucrose-motivated behaviour.' *Psychopharmacology* 176: 110–114, 1996.

Cronin, A., et al. 'Opioid inhibition of rapid eye movement sleep by a specific mu receptor agonist.' *Br J Anaesth* 74(2): 188–192, 1995.

Czirr, S.A., and L.D. Reid. 'Demonstrating morphine's potentiating effects on sucrose intake.' *Brain Res Bull* 17: 639–642, 1986.

Dalvit-McPhillips, S.P. 'The effect of the human menstrual cycle on nutrient intake.' *Physiol Behav* 31: 209–212, 1983.

de Waele, J.P., K. Kiianmaa, and C. Gianoulakis. 'Distribution of the mu and delta opioid binding sites in the brain of the alcohol-preferring AA and alcohol-avoiding ANA lines of rats.' *J Pharmacol Exp Ther* 275(1): 518–527, 1995.

de Waele, J.P., et al. 'The alcohol-preferring C57BL/6 mice present an enhanced sensitivity of the hypothalamic beta-endorphin system to ethanol than the alcohol-avoiding DBA/2 mice.' *J Pharmacol Exp Ther* 261(2): 788–794, 1992.

DesMaisons, K. *Biochemical Restoration as an Intervention for Multiple Offense Drunk Drivers.* Diss. The Union Institute. Ann Arbor: UMI, 1996. 9704758. www.libumi.com/dxweb/results

———. *Potatoes Not Prozac.* New York: Simon & Schuster, 1998.

Dienstfrey, H. *Where The Mind Meets the Body.* New York: HarperCollins, 1991.

Drewnowski, A. 'Why do we like fat?' *J Am Diet Assoc* 97(7; Suppl.): S58–62, 1997.

Drewnowski, A., and C.L. Rock. 'The influence of genetic taste markers on food acceptance.' *Am J Clin Nutr* 62(3): 506–511, 1995.

Drewnowski, A., and R.C. Greenwood. 'Cream and sugar: Human preferences for high-fat foods.' *Physiol Behav* 30: 629–633, 1983.

Drewnowski, A., C.L. Kurth, and J.E. Rahaim. 'Taste preferences in human obesity: Environmental and familial factors.' *Am J Clin Nutr* 54(4): 635–641, 1991.

Drewnowski, A., et al. 'Diet quality and dietary diversity in France: Implications for the French paradox.' *J Am Diet Assoc* 96(7): 663–669, 1996.

———. 'Naloxone, an opiate blocker, reduces the consumption of sweet high-fat foods in obese and lean female binge eaters.' *Am J Clin Nutr* 61(6): 1206–1212, 1995.

Drewnowski, A., and J. Holden-Wiltse. 'Taste responses and preferences

for sweet high-fat foods: evidence for opioid involvement.' *Physiol Behav* 51(2): 371–379, 1992.

―――. 'Changes in mood after carbohydrate consumption.' *Am J Clin Nutr* 46: 703, 1987.

Dufty, W. *Sugar Blues.* New York: Warner, 1975.

Eades, M.R., and M.D. Eades. *Protein Power.* New York: Bantam, 1996.

Eipper, B.A., and R.E. Mains. 'The role of ascorbate in the biosynthesis of neuroendocrine peptides.' *Am J Clin Nutr* 54: 1153S–1156S, 1991.

Fantino, M., J. Hosotte, and M. Apfelbaum. 'An opioid antagonist, naltrexone, reduces preference for sucrose in humans.' *Am J Physiol* 251(R): 91–96, 1986.

Fernstrom, J.D., and D.V. Faller. 'Neutral amino acids in the brain: Changes in response to food ingestion.' *J Neurochem* 30: 1531–1538, 1978.

Fernstrom, J.D., and R.J. Wurtman. 'Brain serotonin content: Physiological regulation by plasma neutral amino acids.' *Science* 178 (Oct. 27): 414–416, 1972.

―――. 'Brain serotonin: Increase following ingestion of carbohydrate diet.' *Science* 174 (Dec. 3): 1023–1025, 1971.

Fernstrom, J.D., F. Larin, and R. Wurtman. 'Correlations between brain tryptophan and plasma neutral amino acid levels following food consumption in rats.' *Life Sci* 13: 517–524, 1973.

Fernstrom, J.D., Ph.D. 'Acute and chronic effects of protein and carbohydrate ingestion on brain tryptophan levels and serotonin synthesis.' *Nutr Rev* 1986 May; 44suppl: 25–36.

―――. 'Dietary amino acids and brain function.' *J Am Diet Assoc* 94: 71–77, 1994.

Fernstrom, M.H., and J.D. Fernstrom. 'Large changes in serum free tryptophan levels do not alter brain tryptophan levels: studies in streptozotocin-diabetic rats.' *Life Sci* 52(11): 907–916, 1993.

―――. 'Brain tryptophan concentrations and serotonin synthesis remain responsive to food consumption after the ingestion of sequential meals.' *Am J Clin Nutr* 61: 312–319, 1995.

Forsander, O.A. 'Is carbohydrate metabolism genetically related to alcohol drinking?' *Alcohol Alcohol* 1: 357–359, 1987.

Fredericks, C. *Carlton Fredericks' New Low Blood Sugar and You.* New York: Putnam, 1987.

Free, V., and P. Sanders. 'The use of ascorbic acid and mineral supplements in the detoxification of narcotic addicts.' *Journal of Orthomolecular Psychiatry* 7(4): 264–270, 1978.

Froehlich, J.C., et al. 'Importance of delta opioid receptors in maintaining high alcohol drinking.' *Psychopharmacology* 103: 467–472, 1991.

Frye, C.A., and G.L. Demolar. 'Menstrual cycle and sex differences influence salt preference.' *Physiol Behav* 55(1): 193–197, 1994.

Genazzani, A.R., et al. 'Central deficiency of beta-endorphin in alcohol addicts.' *J Clin Endocrinol Metab* 55(3): 583–586, 1982.

Gentry, R.T., and V.P. Dole. 'Why does a sucrose choice reduce the consumption of alcohol in C57BL/6J mice?' *Life Sci* 40: 2191–2194, 1987.

Giannini, A., et al. 'Symptoms of premenstrual syndrome as a beta-endorphin: two subtypes.' *Programme Neuropsychopharmacol Biol Psychiatry* 18(2): 321–327, 1994.

Gianoulakis, C., and J.P. de Waele. 'Genetics of alcoholism: Role of the endogenous opioid system.' *Metab Brain Dis* 9(2): 105–131, 1994.

Gianoulakis, C., et al. 'Endorphins in individuals with high and low risk for the development of alcoholism', in *Opioids, Bulimia, and Alcohol Abuse and Alcoholism*, L.D. Reid, ed. New York: Springer-Verlag, 1990, 229–247.

Gianoulakis, C., B. Krishnan, and J. Thavundayil. 'Enhanced sensitivity of pituitary beta-endorphin to ethanol in subjects at high risk of alcoholism.' *Arch Gen Psychiatry* 52(3): 250–257, 1996.

Gianoulakis, C., et al. 'Different pituitary beta-endorphin and adrenal cortisol response to ethanol in individuals with high and low risk for future development of alcoholism.' *Life Sci* (England), 45(12): 1097–1109, 1989.

Goas, J.A. 'Endocrine factors underlying the ethanol preference of rodents.' *Pharmacol Biochem Behav* 10(4): 557–560, 1979.

Goldman, J.A., et al. 'Behavioural effects of sucrose on preschool children.' *J Abnorm Child Psychol* 14(4): 565–577, 1986.

Gosnell, B.A., et al. 'Centrally administered mu- and delta-opioid agonists increase operant responding for saccharin.' *Pharmacol Biochem Behav* 45(4): 979–982, 1993.

Gosnell, B.A., and D.D. Krahn. 'The relationship between saccharin and alcohol intake in rats.' *Alcohol* 9: 203–206, 1992.

Grau, J.W., R.L. Hyson, and S.F. Maier. 'Long-term stress-induced analgesia and activation of the opiate system.' *Science* 213(18): 1409–1410, 1981.

Greden, J. 'Anxiety or caffeinism: A diagnostic dilemma.' *Am J Psychiatry* 131(10): 1089–1092, 1974.

Hall, F.S., et al. 'Effects of isolation-rearing on voluntary consumption of ethanol, sucrose and saccharin solutions in fawn hooded and Wistar rats.' *Psychopharmacology* (Berlin) 139(3): 210–216, 1998.

———. 'The effects of isolation-rearing on sucrose consumption in rats.' *Physiol Behav* 62(2): 291–297, 1997

Harte, J.L., et al. 'The effects of running and meditation on beta-endorphin, corticotropin-releasing hormone and cortisol in plasma, and on mood.' *Biol Psychol* 40(3): 251–265, 1995.

Heitkamp, H.C., et al. 'Beta-endorphin and adrenocorticotrophin after incremental exercise and marathon running – female responses.' *Eur J Appl Physiol* 72(5–6): 417–424, 1996.

Heller, R., and R. Heller. *The Carbohydrate Addict's Diet.* New York: Dutton, 1991.

Hetherington, M., and J. MacDiarmid. 'Chocolate addiction: a preliminary study of its description and its relationship to problem eating.' *Appetite* 21: 233–246, 1993.

Holt, S., et al. 'A satiety index of common foods.' *Eur J Clin Nutr* 49: 675–690, 1995.

Hong, S.M., et al. 'Self-esteem: the effects of life-satisfaction, sex, and age.' *Psychol Rep* 72(1): 95–101, 1993.

Ipp, E., R. Dobbs, and R.H. Unger. 'Morphine and beta-endorphin influence the secretion of the endocrine pancreas.' *Nature* 276: 190–191, 1978.

Israel, K.D., et al. 'Serum uric acid, inorganic phosphorus, and glutamic-oxalacetic transaminase and blood pressure in carbohydrate-

sensitive adults consuming three different levels of sucrose.'
Ann Nutr Metab 27: 425–435, 1983.

Jenkins, D.J.A., et al. 'Slowly digested carbohydrate food improves
impaired carbohydrate tolerance in patients with cirrhosis.'
Clinical Sciences 66: 649–657, 1984.

Jias, L.M., and G. Ellison. 'Chronic nicotine induces a specific appetite
for sucrose in rats.' *Pharmacol Biochem Behav* 35(2): 489–491, 1990.

Kampov-Polevoy, A.B., et al. 'Association between preference for
sweets and excessive alcohol intake: a review of animal and
human studies.' *Alcohol* 34(3): 386–395, 1999.

———. 'Suppression of ethanol intake in alcohol-preferring rats by
prior voluntary saccharin consumption.' *Pharmacol Biochem Behav*
52(1): 1–6, 1994.

———. 'Evidence of preference for a high-concentration sucrose solution in alcoholic men.' *Am J Psychiatry* 154(2): 269–270, 1997.

Kanarek, R.B., and N. Orthen-Gambill. 'Differential effects of sucrose, fructose and glucose on carbohydrate-induced obesity in
rats.' *J Nutr* 112: 1546–1554, 1982.

Kanarek, R.B. 'Does sucrose or aspartame cause hyperactivity in children?' *Nutr Rev* 52(5): 173–175, 1994.

Keim, N.L., et al. 'Effect of exercise and dietary restraint on energy intake of reduced-obese women.' *Appetite* 26(1): 55–70, 1996.

Kinsbourne, M. 'Sugar and the hyperactive child.' *N Engl J Med*
330(5): 355–356, 1994.

Kirkby, R.J., and J. Adams. 'Exercise dependence: the relationship between two measures.' *Percept Mot Skills* 82(2): 366, 1996.

Krahn, D.D., et al. 'Fat-preferring rats consume more alcohol than
carbohydrate-preferring rats.' *Alcohol* 8(4): 313–316, 1991.

Krauchi, K., et al. 'High intake of sweets late in the day predicts a
rapid and persistent response to light therapy in winter depression.' *Psychiatry Res* 46(2): 107–117, 1993.

Kuzmin, A., et al. 'Enhancement of morphine self-administration in
drug naive, inbred strains of mice by acute emotional stress.'
Eur Neuropsychopharmacol 6: 63–68, 1996.

Laeng, B., K. Berridge, and C. Butter. 'Pleasantness of sweet taste

during hunger and satiety: effects of gender and sweet tooth.' *Appetite* 21: 247–254, 1993.

Leibach, I., et al. 'Morphine tolerance in genetically selected rats induced by chronically elevated saccharine intake.' *Science* 221: 871–873, 1983.

Lloyd, H.M., et al. 'Acute effects on mood and cognitive performance of breakfasts differing in fat and carbohydrate content.' *Appetite* 27(2): 151–164, 1996.

Lowinson, J., P. Ruiz, and R. Millman, eds. *Substance Abuse: A Comprehensive Textbook,* 2nd ed. Baltimore: Williams & Wilkins, 1992.

Macdiarmid, J., and M. Hetherington. 'Mood modulation by food: an exploration of affect and cravings in "chocolate addicts". ' *Br J Clin Psychol* 34 (Pt1): 129–138, 1995.

Mann, P.E., G.W. Pasternak, and R.S. Bridges. 'Mu 1 opioid receptor involvement in maternal behaviour.' *Physiol Behav* 47(1): 133–138, 1990.

Mathews-Larson, J., and R.A. Parker. 'Alcoholism treatment with biochemical restoration as a major component.' *International J of Biosocial Res* 9(1): 92–106, 1987.

McDonald, R.B. 'Influence of dietary sucrose on biological aging.' *Am J Clin Nutr* 62(1 Suppl.): 284S–292S; discussion 292S–293S, 1995.

McGuire, W.J., et al. 'Enhancing self-esteem by directed-thinking tasks: cognitive and affective positivity asymmetries.' *J Pers Soc Psychol* 70(6): 1117–1125, 1996.

Morley, J.E., and A.S. Levine. 'Stress-induced eating is mediated through endogenous opiates.' *Science* 209(12): 1259–1260, 1980.

———. 'The role of the endogenous opiates as regulators of appetite.' *Am J Clin Nutr* 35: 757–761, 1982.

Moyer, A.E., and J. Rodin. 'Fructose and behaviour: does fructose influence food intake and macronutrient selection?' *Am J Clin Nutr* 58(5): 810S–814S, 1993.

Muller, B.J., and R.J. Martin. 'The effect of dietary fat on diet selection may involve central serotonin.' *Am J Physiol* 263(3 Pt 2): R559–R563, 1992.

Palmer, L.K. 'Effects of a walking programme on attributional style, depression, and self-esteem in women.' *Percept Mot Skills* 81(3 Pt 1): 891–898, 1995.

Panksepp, J., R. Meeker, and N.J. Bean. 'The neurochemical control of crying.' *Pharmacol Biochem Behav* 12: 437–443, 1979.

Parekh, P.I., et al. 'Reversal of diet-induced obesity and diabetes in C57BL/6J mice.' *Metabolism* 47(9): 1089–1096, 1998.

Paul, G.L., et al. 'Preexercise meal composition alters plasma large neutral amino acid responses during exercise and recovery.' *Am J Clin Nutr* 64(5): 778–786, 1996.

Pennington, J.A. *Food Values of Portions Commonly Used.* Philadelphia: J. B. Lippincott, 1994.

Pierce, E.F., et al. 'Beta-endorphin response to endurance exercise: relationship to exercise dependence.' *Percept Mot Skills* 77(3 Pt 1): 767–770, 1993.

Pike, R.B. *Nutrition: An Integrated Approach.* New York: Macmillan, 1984.

Quigley, M.E., and S.S.C. Yen. 'The role of endogenous opiates on LH secretion during the menstrual cycle.' *J Clin Endocrinol Metab* 51(1): 179–181, 1980.

Rakatansky, H. 'Chocolate: Pleasure or pain?' *Am J Psychiatry* 146(8): 1089, 1989.

Rappoport, L., et al. 'Gender and age differences in food cognition.' *Appetite* 20(1): 33–52, 1993.

Reid, L.D., and G.A. Hunter. 'Morphine and naloxone modulate intake of ethanol.' *Alcohol* 1(1): 33–37, 1984.

Reid, L.D., et al. 'Tests of opioid deficiency hypotheses of alcoholism.' *Alcohol* 8: 247–257, 1991.

Ripsin, C.M., et al. 'Oat products and lipid lowering: A meta-analysis.' *JAMA* 267(24): 3317–3325, 1992.

Sears, Barry. *The Zone.* New York: ReganBooks, 1995.

Shide, D.J., et al. 'Opioid mediation of odour preferences induced by sugar and fat in 6-day-old rats.' *Physiol Behav* 50(5): 961–966, 1991.

Simopoulos, A., and J. Robinon. *The Omega Plan.* New York: Harper-Collins, 1998.

Snyder, S. 'The opiate receptor and morphine-like peptides in the brain.' *Am J Psychiatry* 135(6): 645–652, 1978.

Somer, E. *Food & Mood.* New York: Holt, 1995.

Van der Kolk, B.A., M.S. Greenberg, S.P. Orr, and R.K. Pitman. 'Endogenous opioids, stress induced analgesia, and posttraumatic stress disorder.' *Psycho Pharmacol Bull* 25(3): 417–421, 1989.

Van der Kolk, B.A. *The Body Keeps Score: Memory and the Evolving Psychobiology of Posttraumatic Stress.* Boston: Massachusetts General Hospital, 1993.

Van Ree, J. 'Endorphins and experimental addiction.' *Alcohol* 13(1): 25, 1996.

Vanderschuren, L.J., et al. 'Mu- and kappa-opioid receptor-mediated opioid effects on social play in juvenile rats.' *Eur J Pharmacol* 276(3): 257–266, 1995.

Vliet, E. *Screaming to Be Heard.* New York: M. Evans, 1995.

Williams, R.J. 'Alcoholism as a nutritional problem.' *J Clin Nutr* 53: 32–36, 1952.

Willner, P., et al. ' "Depression" increases "craving" for sweet rewards in animal and human models of depression and craving.' *Psychopharmacology* (Berlin) 136(3): 272–283, 1998.

Wurtman, J.J., H.R. Lieberman, and B. Chew. 'Changes in mood after carbohydrate consumption among obese individuals.' *Am J Clin Nutr* 44: 772–778, 1986.

Wurtman, R.J., and J.J. Wurtman. 'Brain serotonin, carbohydrate-craving, obesity, and depression.' *Obes Res 3* (Suppl. 4): 477S–480S, 1995.

Wurtman, R.J. 'Ways that foods can affect the brain.' *Nutr Rev* (Supp.): 2–5, 1986.

Zorrilla, E.P., R.J. De Rubeis, and E. Redei. 'High self-esteem, hardiness and affective stability are associated with higher basal pituitary-adrenal hormone levels.' *Psychoneuroendocrinology* 20(6): 591–601, 1995.

Resources

Twelve-Step Programmes

Addiction can take many forms. Alcoholics Anonymous is an excellent resource to guide you. Most large towns have a central office of Alcoholics Anonymous. They can refer you to AA or other types of meetings more suited to your needs. They will know about:

CA (Cocaine Anonymous)
OA (Overeaters Anonymous)
Al-Anon (for families of alcoholics)
DA (Debtors Anonymous)
NA (Narcotics Anonymous)
ACOA (Adult Children of Alcoholics)
CODA (Codependents Anonymous)
SLAA (Sex and Love Addicts Anonymous)

Look in *Yellow Pages*, under Counselling & Advice, for the telephone number of your local AA branch.

George's Shake

George's Shake is a premade powder that provides a unique combination of protein, complex carbohydrates, vitamins, and minerals. It has no sugar, tastes wonderful, and can be an excellent support for your programme. Order it from our website at www.radiantrecovery.com.

Newsletter

We offer a free online newsletter through the website at www.radiant recovery.com.

Web Pages

Visit us at www.radiantrecovery.com. We are delighted to have your feedback and comments. Every email is answered personally. The Web page posts our scheduled appearances and lists seminars, talks and other opportunities to meet with us. The Web page can also connect you with a number of listservs that gather people interested in special topics. Here is a partial list.

radiant12step	For those wishing to integrate twelve-step with PNP
radiantathletes	For sugar-sensitive athletes
radiantaussies	For those doing the programme in Australia
radiantbigones	For people more than 45 kg overweight
radiantbingecontrol	For sugar-sensitive bingers
radiantbrits	For those doing the programme in the UK
radiantbulimia	For sugar-sensitive bulimics
radiantdepression	For sugar-sensitive people who are depressed
radiantdiabetes	For sugar-sensitive diabetics
radiantelders	For older sugar-sensitive participants
radiantguys	For guys who are sugar sensitive
radiantjournal	For those wanting to learn how to use the food diary
radiantkiwis	For those doing the programme in New Zealand

radiantparents	For parents of sugar-sensitive children
radiantpets	For sugar-sensitive people with pets
radiantpms	For the special needs of sugar-sensitive women
radiantpregnancy	For pregnant and breastfeeding women
radiantrecipes	For those wanting to share recipes
radiantrecovery	For those seeking recovery from alcohol, drug or other addiction
radiantvegetarians	For sugar-sensitive vegetarians
sarpbookstudy	For those interested in discussing *The Sugar Addict's Total Recovery Programme* in depth

Private Consultation

Private consultations can be scheduled by emailing radiantkd@mind spring.com. Information on consultation fees and process can be found at www.radiantrecovery.com.

Acknowledgments

This book came from the questions and demands of sugar-sensitive people all over the world. Your needs pushed me to go further with the story of sugar sensitivity and tackle the sugar-addiction demon. Thank you for your energy, courage and commitment. Your voices have made the book come alive with its connection to real-life stories. Thanks to all of you who cook so well and were willing to share your special recipes.

Special thanks to Margot Silk Forest for helping my vision get tucked into useful concrete specifics. I would never have done this without your help.

Thanks to Ned Leavitt for your diligence and commitment in finding a home for this wonderful story. I am deeply indebted to my editor at Ballantine, Leslie Meredith, who had the commitment to push my vision way beyond my dreams. You called the recovery voice, helped me to craft the language to give it power, and made the story come alive.

Index

About the Author

KATHLEEN DESMAISONS, PHD, revolutionized the field of chemical dependency treatment with her pioneering work in addictive nutrition. In her best-selling book, *Potatoes Not Prozac,* she coined the term 'sugar sensitivity' to describe a common biochemical tendency towards addiction, depression and obesity. Her dietary recommendations have offered simple solutions with profound results for people who have followed many 'diets' without long-lasting success.

A graduate of the Union Institute, Dr DesMaisons created her field of study, earning the first degree ever awarded in addictive nutrition. She currently lives in Albuquerque, New Mexico, where she serves as President/CEO of Radiant Recovery, maintains a private consulting practice and nurtures a thriving online community. Thousands of her readers regularly contribute to the exceptionally welcoming website (www.radiant recovery.com), together creating a safe and supportive circle for sugar addicts seeking recovery. Dr DesMaisons can be reached by email at kathleen@radiantrecovery.com.

POCKET
B O O K S

Potatoes Not Prozac
ARE YOU SUGAR SENSITIVE?
Kathleen DesMaisons

'This book could be the answer to your prayers'
HEALTHY EATING

Have you ever wondered why you can't say no to
fattening foods or alcohol? Why you overspend or
overwork, have mood swings or depression? The
answer is not that you're undisciplined. The
problem lies in your body chemistry. Millions of
people are sugar sensitive and their diet can
actually trigger feelings of exhaustion and low
self-esteem.

With compassion and insight DesMaisons guides
you through the process one choice at a time until,
as your body becomes balanced, you feel
empowered and in control. More than just a book
about food, this is a book about possibilities. You
can change your life with *Potatoes Not Prozac*.

PRICE £6.99
ISBN 0 671 77377 1

POCKET
B O O K S

This book and other health and nutrition titles are available from your bookshop or can be ordered direct from the publisher.

0 671 02954 1 **Natural Hormone Balance/Suzannah Olivier**	£6.99
0 671 77313 5 **Allergy Solutions/ Suzannah Olivier**	£6.99
0 671 02953 3 **Banish Bloating/Suzannah Olivier**	£6.99
0 671 02955 X **Maximising Energy/Suzannah Olivier**	£6.99
0 671 03781 1 **Eating for a Perfect Pregnancy /Suzannah Olivier**	£6.99
0 671 03782 X **The Detox Manual/Suzannah Olivier**	£6.99
0 671 77377 1 **Potatoes Not Prozac/Kathleen DesMaisons**	£6.99
0 671 03735 8 **Food Your Miracle Medicine/Jean Carper**	£8.99
0 671 03736 6 **The Food Pharmacy/Jean Carper**	£8.99

Please send cheque or postal order for the value of the book, free postage and packing within the UK; OVERSEAS including Republic of Ireland £1 per book.

OR: Please debit this amount from my
VISA/ACCESS/MASTERCARD..
CARD NO:...
EXPIRY DATE..
AMOUNT£...
NAME...
ADDRESS...
....
SIGNATURE..

Send orders to SIMON & SCHUSTER CASH SALES
PO Box 29, Douglas Isle of Man, IM99 1BQ
Tel: 01624 836000, Fax: 01624 670923
www.bookpost.co.uk
Please allow 14 days for delivery. Prices and availability subject to change without notice

Printed in the United States
117214LV00003B/328/A